REASONABLE
DOUBTS

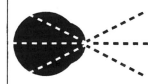

This Large Print Book carries the
Seal of Approval of N.A.V.H.

REASONABLE DOUBTS

The O.J. Simpson Case
and the
Criminal Justice System

ALAN M. DERSHOWITZ

Thorndike Press • Thorndike, Maine

110527

Published in 1996 by arrangement with Simon & Schuster, Inc.

Thorndike Large Print ® Basic Series.

The tree indicium is a trademark of Thorndike Press.

The text of this Large Print edition is unabridged.
Other aspects of the book may vary from the original edition.

Set in 16 pt. Century Schoolbook by Minnie B. Raven.

Printed in the United States on permanent paper.

Library of Congress Cataloging in Publication Data

Dershowitz, Alan M.
  Reasonable doubts : The O.J. Simpson case and the criminal
justice system / Alan M. Dershowitz.
    p.   cm.
  ISBN 0-7862-0785-X (lg. print : hc)
  1.Simpson, O.J., 1947–   — Trials, litigation, etc.
  2.Trials (Murder) — California — Los Angeles.
  3.Criminal justice, Administration of — California —
Los Angeles. I. Title.
  [KF224.S485D47   1996b]
  345.73′02523′0979494—dc20
  [347.30525230979494]   96-16211

This book is lovingly dedicated to my brother, Nathan, who was my secret legal weapon in the Simpson case as he has been in many other cases — and to Marilyn, Adam, and Rana, who are his secret weapons.

Contents

Introduction

The world seemed to stand still for a moment in time. Everyone would remember where they were when the verdict was announced in the case of *The People of the State of California v. Orenthal James Simpson*. They were either watching television or listening to radio. As one prominent media executive put it: "You have to look back to when Kennedy was shot to find another media event that virtually everyone saw during the day."[1] But the reading of the Simpson verdict was different from the Kennedy assassination, the Japanese attack on Pearl Harbor or the death of Franklin D. Roosevelt. Those were unexpected events which came out of the blue like bolts of lightning on a clear summer day. The announcement of the Simpson verdict had been carefully scheduled by Judge Lance Ito, who presided over the trial. Although the bell from the jury room signaling that a verdict had been reached after only four hours of collective deliberation sounded just before

3:00 P.M. Pacific time on October 2, 1995, Judge Ito decided to withhold announcement of the verdict until 10:00 A.M. the following day, so that the lawyers, the media, and the police could prepare for the unknown outcome of the most closely followed criminal case in history. On that day a worldwide audience estimated at more than 100 million would stop what they were doing to see or hear for themselves whether the Los Angeles jury of nine blacks (eight of whom were women), two whites, and one Hispanic had rendered justice.

Hours before the verdict was to be announced, President Bill Clinton was briefed on nationwide security measures in the event of possible rioting. The Los Angeles Police Department was on full alert. As the witching hour approached, long distance telephone calls dropped by 58 percent. There was a surge in electrical consumption as millions of Americans turned on television sets. Water usage decreased as fewer people used the bathroom between 10 and 10:15 A.M. Pacific time. Trading volume plummeted 41 percent on the New York Stock Exchange. A meeting between the secretary of state and the director of the C.I.A. was put off for several minutes. The President left the Oval Office to join staffers watching television. Another presidential hopeful, scheduled at 10:00 A.M. Eastern time to announce whether he would seek the nomination, postponed the announcement until after the verdict. Arrangements were made to pass notes to the justices of the Supreme Court sitting on the bench, telling them the verdict. Exercise stopped in gyms around the country. Work ceased in factories, in post offices, and in the surgical suites of hospitals. It was the most unproductive half hour in United States business history, costing an estimated $480 million in lost output.[2] Even in Israel, where the Yom Kippur holiday had already begun and where television was dark in commemoration of this holiest of days, thousands of Jews tuned into Jordanian television to watch the verdict.

Never before in history had so many people waited in anticipation to learn what twelve of their "peers" had decided in secret the day before. No one, aside from those twelve ordinary people, knew what their verdict sheet contained — not the judge, not the defendant, not the lawyers, not the police, not the President of the United States. *Time* magazine described it as "the single most suspenseful moment in television history."[3]

Nearly everyone had an opinion of how the case should or would be decided. During the night and morning before the verdict was announced, the media were overloaded with "informed speculation" about the likely outcome. Tea leaves were read, crystal balls gazed into, and tarot cards turned over. Trial lawyers, with long experience in "reading" juries, offered their interpretations of the brevity of the deliberations, the unwillingness of jurors to look the defendant in the eye, and the significance of the one portion of the trial transcript they asked to have reviewed.

At 1:00 P.M. Eastern time — 10:00 A.M. Pacific time — my office at Harvard Law School was bursting at the seams with students, journalists, TV cameras, and assorted friends and colleagues. When the word had come late the previous afternoon that there was a verdict, I was invited by the defense team to fly to Los Angeles to be in the courtroom when it was read. But it was the day before Yom Kippur and I wanted to remain in Cambridge to attend the Kol Nidre service with my family. I also thought I would have to begin preparing for an appeal.

Indeed, from the moment I learned that the jurors had reached their verdict, I began to outline the likely issues for the appeal.

As an appellate lawyer, I am programmed to be a pessimist. My job is to prepare for the worst, to provide a parachute in the event of a conviction. That is why O.J. Simpson always referred to me as his "God forbid" lawyer — "God forbid there should be a conviction, you've got to get it reversed on appeal." My own mind, therefore, is always on the likelihood of conviction — a likelihood that comes to pass in approximately 75 percent to 80 percent of contested criminal cases. I was prepared for that possibility as I watched Judge Ito call the hushed courtroom to order at precisely 10:00 A.M. A few quick formalities, and then came the critical words, uttered in the halting voice of a court clerk, which almost succeeded in blunting the drama of the moment. But there was no mistaking the jury's verdict: not guilty.

There was silence in my office. No one cheered. No one laughed. I turned to the television set on my desk, reached out my hand, and touched the screen. No one in the office understood the gesture, because they had not accompanied me on my numerous visits to O.J. Simpson in prison. When we met, he was always on the opposite side of a thick glass partition. We would extend a hand and "touch" through the glass — the prison handshake, as criminal lawyers and their clients know it. At the moment of the verdict, I shook hands with O.J. Simpson through the television set.

It was not a moment for celebration. There were two victims, brutally murdered. There were children who would never again be comforted by their mother; parents, sisters, and friends who would never again hug their loved ones. There was a man who had spent sixteen months in jail accused of a crime of which a jury had just ruled he was not legally guilty, but of which most Americans thought he was factually guilty. It was a moment for introspection and quiet professional satisfaction among the members of my team of student assistants.

The muted reaction to the verdict in my office was not typical of reactions around the country, which ranged from anger and outrage to jubilation. At predominantly black Howard University Law School "students crossed their fingers, held

14

hands, and when the clerk read the verdicts, the room erupted with a chorus of cheers. Many cried and hugged." At a battered women's shelter, women also cried and hugged — but not for joy. "It hurt my gut," one said. "I just had to leave." At Benjamin's Deli in a Jewish neighborhood of Milwaukee, "a dull groan" rolled through the restaurant as the verdict was read. At Clancy's Pub in Omaha, "people in the bar gasped." At the University of Nebraska, a white student shook his head, saying, "It's a payback for Rodney King." At a sports bar in Atlanta, rage was expressed. "As far as I'm concerned Cochran and Shapiro are accessories to murder!" one man shouted. Some booed. Others stood in stunned silence. A black woman on a District of Columbia street corner shouted, "We won!" Another thanked Jesus. A white man yelled, "Jesus!" but not in praise.

Many whites, convinced of Simpson's guilt, complained that the criminal justice system had failed them.[4] But angry whites did not riot as blacks had rioted following the initial acquittal of the police officers who beat Rodney King. Writer Ben Stein predicted that "the whites will riot the way we whites do: leave the cities,

15

go to Idaho or Oregon or Arizona, vote for Gingrich . . . and punish the blacks by closing their day-care programs and cutting off their Medicaid."[5] Some whites also "rioted" by sending me racist hate letters. Dr. John S. Blankfort, an orthodontist from San Francisco, wrote the following on his prescription pad: "Congratulations — a murdering butcher is on the street. [I]f the 'nigger' is so innocent, then he should have no problem speaking — may you catch cancer." Another letter read: "The homicidal 'nigger' (an epithet I've shunned all my life, but shall use from now on, having witnessed black America's reaction to the verdict) did it, and you know it!"

The content of these letters, and the hundreds like them I received, were not necessarily typical of the white reaction to the jury's unpopular verdict. But the passions reflected in them and in the immediate response to the verdict were representative of the very personal manner in which many people had viewed the case. It was a verdict that was not only *heard* throughout the world but was also *felt* throughout the world, especially in every corner of the United States. As one woman who had followed the case closely told me, "The acquittal was like a swift kick to my stomach. I felt nauseated, pained, frightened — even violated, when I heard the words 'not guilty.' "

Why this extraordinary *personal* reaction by so many to whom Nicole Brown, Ronald Goldman, and O.J. Simpson were complete strangers? Why the fascination with *this* murder in an age when, tragically, murders are all too commonplace? Why did this busy nation stand transfixed in front of millions of television sets during a working day to watch twelve people deliver their collective opinion on an issue about which most Americans had already made up their minds? Why has the Simpson case become for so many the preeminent symbol of what is wrong with the American criminal justice system — and, indeed, with America? Or as one commentator put it, "For many Americans, the O.J. Simpson trial has become the criminal justice system's Vietnam — an event of sickening revelation."[6] Why?

At a superficial level, the answers come easily. O.J. Simpson is the most famous American ever to stand trial for murder. His trial took place at a time of instant communications in a place that is the media capital of the world. Anyone with access to a television set could watch as the drama unfolded. Then the audience could read about what they had seen and hear experts analyze what had occurred and predict what would happen the next day. The Simpson case was the first and most pyrotechnic multiple car crash on the information superhighway, and the cars were all Mercedeses, Bentleys, and Rolls-Royces. There was wealth and celebrity, "the beautiful people," an interracial marriage, a vicious double murder, a charismatic defendant, the high drama of a car chase and a criminal trial — all the ingredients of a fictional whodunit, and they were true.

This surface analysis may explain the obvious fascination with the case and even with the verdict itself. But it does not begin to explain why so many serious people who would not be caught dead reading the tabloids or watching *Hard Copy* were caught up in the Simpson trial and its aftermath. The trial was not merely entertainment for a voyeuristic world obsessed with celebrity and a fall from grace. It became a morality play for Americans concerned about race, gender, violence, equality, and a wide range of other issues that have permeated the last decade of this millennium. The Simpson case — like the Sacco-Vanzetti, Scopes, Lindbergh, Rosenberg, Ruby, Manson, von Bülow, and other paradigmatic cases before it — touched upon the eternal themes of passion and revenge, but also on the pressing contemporary questions of equality and the perceived ineffectiveness of our criminal justice system.

I have written this book primarily for the majority of thoughtful observers who sincerely and understandably believe that O.J. Simpson killed Nicole Brown and Ronald Goldman and that the jury's verdict of "not guilty" was therefore a miscarriage of justice. I will try to explain why even jurors who thought that Simpson "did it" as a matter of fact could reasonably have found him not guilty as a matter of law — and of justice. It is not the purpose of *this* book to try to persuade readers that they are wrong if they think O.J. Simpson was guilty. Rather, it is my intention to explain how, under our system of criminal justice, the Simpson jury could properly have reached a verdict so at odds with the conclusion reached by millions of intelligent and decent people who watched what they believed was the same trial.

I agreed to join the O.J. Simpson defense team, in large part, because I knew that this case — for better or worse — would be an education for America, and indeed the world, about the realities of our criminal justice system. As a teacher of law, I wanted to be part of that process. But I now realize that many observers have derived the wrong lessons from this case, largely because of the way much of the press, radio, and television treated it — as daily entertainment. Most Americans relied, understandably, on secondary accounts of the trial, filtered through the prism of reporters and analysts. Even those who watched the trial's live coverage saw only what went on in the courtroom itself, and not in the field, where the investigation took place, or in the lawyers' offices, where many of the most crucial decisions were made.

It is the purpose of this book, therefore, to explore the larger issues raised by the course of the investigation, the conduct of the trial, the verdict, and the racially divided reaction to it. I will address criticisms of the jury system and the adversary process. And I hope to bring a broader perspective to the debate about the case and to explain the system that produced such a controversial verdict. I will describe the prosecution's "mountain of evidence" against Simpson, and ask why it apparently crumbled in the eyes of the jury. I will analyze the role of "truth" in the adversary process, and I will pose troubling questions about the extent of police perjury in the Simpson case and others, as well as questions about the role of race, gender, wealth, celebrity, and the media in the administration of justice.

I was an "insider" on the Simpson case from the very beginning, as a constitutional strategist and appellate expert for the defense. But as a law professor and a critic of our justice system, I am also an "outsider." And I hope to be able to bring that dual perspective to my observations about the case. My goal is not to convert those who believe that my client committed the crimes with which he was charged, but rather to help them understand why our system of criminal justice produced a verdict so at variance with their sincere beliefs. In the end, some who still insist that O.J. Simpson killed Nicole Brown and Ronald Goldman may conclude that the jury which acquitted him of those terrible crimes arrived at a correct and just verdict.

I

Was the Simpson Case Decided Even Before the Trial Began?

As soon as the morning newscaster announced that the bloody body of the woman found in Brentwood several hours earlier was that of Nicole Brown, the former wife of football great and Hollywood movie star O.J. Simpson, I told my wife, "O.J. probably did it. The former husband is generally the perp in a case like this." By "a case like this," I meant the murder of a woman whose ex-husband had been previously arrested and pleaded no contest to the charge of wife-beating — as the press was already reporting. The double murder on the steps of a walkway in the 800 block of South Bundy Drive in the exclusive Brentwood neighborhood of Los Angeles had all the earmarks of a crime of passion and revenge. Multiple "sharp force injuries," such as stab wounds, were the cause of the deaths.[1]

For the first week following the discovery of the bodies on June 13, 1994, I was an outside observer whose legal expertise was sought by the media. Like everyone else, I was riveted by the unfolding story. At the very beginning, few people wanted to believe that the universally beloved athlete, film star, and Hertz spokesman could have committed such vicious crimes. On the Larry King show of June 14, 1994, Los Angeles radio talk show host Michael Jackson summarized the feelings of Angelenos, black and white, when he said: "The callers are utterly sympathetic to O.J. and they are praying that he's not guilty."

But the Los Angeles Police Department and the Los Angeles County District Attorney's Office had a different view: They "knew" Simpson was guilty. They "knew" it because they had information the public did not yet have. And the district attorney's office was plainly worried about Simpson's almost universally favorable public image. As District Attorney Gil Garcetti told assembled reporters on June 18, the day after Simpson's arrest:

There is no doubt that O.J. Simpson — the persona, the hero of O.J. Simpson — is something that most people don't want to let go of. I mean this was a man. A beauty. A grace. A talent. He had succeeded. He had been through tough times and he had made it, made it big. And he was doing good things. Unfortunately, we now have a set of circumstances that changes that entirely.[2]

To counter the tremendous reservoir of goodwill enjoyed by Simpson, the police and the district attorney's office embarked on a well-orchestrated campaign to shatter his public image. During the days immediately after his arrest, they fed the public a steady diet of news leaks from unnamed "police sources," "detectives," and "sources familiar with the case." On June 19, the *Los Angeles Times* reported that unnamed "police sources" had informed them that "a trail of blood drops stretched across Simpson's cobblestone driveway"; that bloodstains at the crime scene matched Simpson's blood type; that bloodstains in a bathroom sink at Simpson's house matched Nicole Brown's blood type; and that a bloody glove found outside Simpson's house matched another glove found at the crime scene.[3]

Two days later, the *Los Angeles Times* reported that although "prosecutors would not comment on the results," "sources familiar with the case" were asserting that "preliminary DNA tests . . . conducted on . . . blood samples [taken from the crime scene and] from Simpson's driveway, as well as from clothes, shoes, and other items taken from his home . . . continue to link Simpson to the murders."[4] There were also reports that bloodstains on Simpson's Bronco were being examined, that unidentified "detectives" "suspect[ed]" that Simpson's failure to reconcile with his ex-wife "may have been the motive for the killing," that the limo driver who took Simpson to the airport had told detectives that Simpson wasn't home when he arrived at 10:45 P.M., and that "a sweaty and agitated Simpson got in the limo shortly after 11 P.M."[5]

On June 22, the 911 tape and the 1989 police report of the 1985 battery on Nicole Brown Simpson were provided to the press. A front-page story in the *Los Angeles Times* was headlined "911 Tape Tells of Stormy Simpson Relationship Inquiry." And the article began, "On tapes released Wednesday by the Los Angeles Police Department, O.J. Simpson's ex-wife is heard crying and pleading for help as a man identified as Simpson furiously screams obscenities in the background after breaking down her door."[6] ("Although the press had been seeking access to the tapes, the timing of the material's release — just in time for Wednesday's early evening newscasts — reeked of advance planning by the prosecution," commented the *Los Angeles Times*.[7])

Some of the other pieces of "evidence" leaked by "sources familiar with the case" in these early days would eventually prove to be unreliable, but they quickly became part of the rising mountain of incriminating facts pointing to Simpson's guilt. They included the following reports:

That the police had found a "bloody ski mask" in Simpson's house

That the police had found a "sharpened trenching tool" which they believed to be "the murder weapon"

That throughout his flight to Chicago, Simpson was seen with his hand inside a bag, suggesting that he may have been trying to hide cuts on his hand sustained during the murders

That "potentially damaging evidence" had been found in the golf bags Simpson had brought to Chicago that evening

That "a jogger passing through the neighborhood just before the time of the killings spotted a car that she said resembled Simpson's Bronco"

That a gas station attendant or patron had told the police that in the early morning hours of June 13 he had seen a man "resembling" Simpson in the wooded area just south of the O'Hare-Plaza Hotel where Simpson had briefly been staying while in Chicago

That police dogs in Chicago found sunglasses and a bag containing a pair of socks in that wooded area

That the "police believe[d] a military knife was used in the killings"[8]

On Sunday, June 19, 1994, Gil Garcetti had appeared on *This Week with David Brinkley* to assure the American public that his office had the right guy:

Well, it's not going to shock me if we see an O.J. Simpson, sometime down the road — and it could happen very soon, it could happen months from now — say, 'OK, I did it but I'm not responsible.' We've seen it in Menendez. It's going to be a likely defense here, I believe, once the evidence is reviewed by the lawyers.

And at a courthouse press conference on June 20, immediately after the arraignment, a confident Marcia Clark, the Los Angeles County assistant district attorney appointed to try the case, asserted that O.J. Simpson was charged with premeditated murder because the murders were "done with deliberation and premeditation." Clark went on to declare without hesitation, "Mr. Simpson is charged alone, because he is the sole murderer." At that same press conference, Garcetti commented that "We all saw the falling of an American hero."[9]

Nor did the defense remain silent. Simpson's first lawyer, Howard Weitzman, defended his client constantly in the days following the murders. He told the press that police officials had informed him that no bloody glove had been found in the

Simpson house, and that no official had informed him of any test results matching Simpson's blood type to samples taken from the crime scene. Responding to a reporter's question about Simpson's possible arrest, Weitzman said, "I hope that's not true, but as we know, they arrest innocent people on occasion."[10]

On June 14, I was scheduled to appear on *Larry King Live* to comment on the unfolding legal drama. In anticipation of my appearance, I phoned Weitzman, with whom I had worked on the John DeLorean case,* for a status report so that I could be as current and knowledgeable as possible. I was aware of the spate of rumors ranging from the discovery of a bloody glove and bloody ski mask in the Simpson house to an alleged "confession" by Simpson. Weitzman assured me that his client was absolutely innocent and that the reports of a confession were bogus. He also told me that no ski mask had been found and that no glove had been found "in the Simpson house." I did not know enough at that time to ask follow-up questions about

*DeLorean, a well-known automobile designer, had been charged with drug offenses and was acquitted on grounds of entrapment.

whether a hat of *any* kind had been found or whether a glove had been discovered *outside* the Simpson house.

Over the next few days, leaks about the case turned into hemorrhages; the media reported that Los Angeles Police Department detectives had concluded that Simpson would be charged with two counts of first-degree murder. Arrangements were made for Simpson to surrender to police on Friday, June 17, at 11 A.M. for his arraignment that afternoon.

When the appointed time arrived, however, Simpson was nowhere to be found. Garcetti announced that he was a "fugitive from justice." And there followed the dramatic announcement that he and his friend Al Cowlings were in a white Bronco, driving along the Los Angeles freeway, Simpson reportedly with a gun pressed to his head. Soon dozens of police cars had joined in pursuit. And the spectacle — which was watched by millions of TV viewers around the world — concluded with Simpson's return to his estate, where, after a phone call to his mother, he surrendered himself and was taken into custody.

The flight in the Bronco seemed further proof of Simpson's guilt, and I was certain that it would end in the suicide of a man who had killed his ex-wife. The narrative of love, jealousy, rage, murder, and suicide was Shakespearean and this modern-day Othello seemed to be moving inexorably toward the predictably tragic denouement. Instead, Simpson submitted to arrest and would, in all likelihood, be convicted of the murders and sentenced either to death — the district attorney had not yet decided whether to ask for capital punishment — or to life in prison.

The conventional wisdom at this point was that Simpson probably did it, but that he might still get off because he was a rich and popular celebrity. Race was not often mentioned in this connection. Indeed, some commentators were of the opinion that black jurors from South Central Los Angeles would have difficulty identifying with an affluent Brentwood celebrity who had been married to a white woman, lived in a white world, and could afford the best lawyers.[11] On the Charlie Rose show of June 20, the main focus was still on Simpson's celebrity and wealth and I was asked about how high-powered lawyers could affect the outcome of the case. I responded that "the quality of representation matters about ten percent in cases like this.

It's like the quality of the surgeon. Whether you have the cancer matters a lot more than the quality of the surgeon, [and] whether you've done it . . . matters much more than who your lawyer is. There's a myth that wealth and brilliant lawyers can really turn guilt into innocence. It happens very rarely."

Immediately after the Charlie Rose show taping, my older son, Elon, and I boarded a plane for Israel to attend a conference convened by President Ezer Weitzman. As soon as I checked in to the King David Hotel, Robert Shapiro — who had by then replaced Howard Weitzman as Simpson's lawyer — called and asked me to join the defense team along with F. Lee Bailey and Dean Gerald F. Uelmen. I told Shapiro, with whom I had previously worked on the Christian Brando appeal,* that I would have to think about it, since I had already made some comments about Simpson and the case. Unaware of my comments, he asked me to summarize them. I said that although I had emphasized the presumption of in-

*Marlon Brando's son shot his sister's lover — who was allegedly abusing his sister — and a plea bargain was eventually struck.

nocence, I was assuming that [ ] had probably committed the murd [ ] I had talked of a mental illness [ ] type of defense.

"You've been listening to Gar[ ] Shapiro responded. "That's what *he's* saying. It's not going to happen. [ ] swears he didn't do it, and that's what [ ] defense is going to be — innocence."

I told Shapiro that this was a refreshi[ ] change after the spate of "excuse" defens[ ] recently in the news, but I wonder[ ] whether my public speculations about the likely Simpson defense might make me less useful to the team.

"We really need you, Alan," Shapiro said. "They're going to put together the biggest and most powerful prosecution team ever assembled. Garcetti's career depends on winning this case. We need your brief-writing and constitutional expertise." I told Shapiro I still needed to think about it and would call him the next day.

During the evening, my son and I thought long and hard about whether I should join the Simpson defense team. I get hundreds of requests each week to become involved in cases and, necessarily, turn nearly all of them down, since I am a full-time professor with a heavy teach-

g load. I have several criteria for accept-
g a case. Among them are whether I can
se the case in my teaching, whether I
an make effective use of my students
whom I pay out of my own pocket),
whether it fits into my teaching schedule
(since I do not cancel classes), and
whether my academic skills will add a
special dimension to the defense. These
criteria alone would not pare down the
requests to a manageable number, so I
limit the cases further by several subjec-
tive factors: Is the case likely to raise
important issues of a general nature? And
is there something special about it which
gets my juices flowing? All of those criteria were met in the Simpson case, plus
one additional factor, which made this one
irresistible to me. I knew that the Simpson case would become the vehicle by
which a generation of Americans would
learn about the law. And as a professor of
law, I could not forgo such an important
educational opportunity.

The factors I do *not* consider in taking
a case are the following: my opinion —
usually uninformed, at least at the time
— of the defendant's guilt or innocence;
his popularity, unpopularity, or controversial nature; his wealth or poverty; and

34

his prospects of winning or losing. Because I am a professor with tenure, I believe I have a special responsibility to take on cases and causes that may require me to confront the powers that be — the government, the police, prosecutors, the media, the bar, even the university. The lifetime guarantee of tenure entails responsibilities to challenge the popular and defend the unpopular. And as I pondered my decision I could see that the tide of support was already turning away from Simpson and passions were running high. I had no idea whether he was guilty, innocent, or somewhere in between. Nor did I have any sense of his prospects for winning. What I did know was that this case was going to be an all-out war between a politically ambitious prosecutor determined to win at all costs, and a defense with the resources to fight on a level battlefield. I also knew that the Los Angeles Police Department — with whose reputation I was intimately familiar — was at the center of the investigation of this case and was responsible for the massive leaks to the press. My juices were certainly flowing and I decided to accept Shapiro's offer to join the defense team.

Over the next several days the phone

and fax lines between Israel and the United States were going nonstop. Since Los Angeles and Jerusalem are ten hours apart, there was little opportunity for sleep. My first assignment was to research whether any legal remedies were available to us in response to the massive pretrial publicity generated by the district attorney's office and the police. I asked my brother, Nathan, who practices law in New York City, to help me draft a memorandum in which we proposed filing "a motion to discharge the grand jury that was then hearing evidence against Simpson, on the ground that the deliberate prosecutorial and police leaks had improperly exposed the grand jurors to prejudicial information and misinformation." Our proposal was initially greeted with skepticism, because such a motion had never previously been granted under circumstances comparable to those in the Simpson case. But we persuaded the other lawyers to try, and the motion was filed.

I was acutely aware, as were the other members of the defense team, of the significance of the early phase of any criminal case. The way the media cover cases influences the way the public thinks about them. And because trials are now televised — or, even if not televised, covered extensively by television and the press — the public focuses on what goes on *in* the courtroom. They believe that cases are won or lost by the lawyers' arguments, by the testimony of witnesses, and by the judge's instructions, since these are what they see. These highly visible aspects of the case are, of course, important. But equally important, and in many cases far more important, is what is not visible to the TV camera or even accessible to the print journalist. The myth that cases are won and lost by the lawyers in the courtroom is perpetuated by those who cover trials, since they, too, want to emphasize the importance of what they are covering.

But I believe the outcome of the Simpson case was largely determined *outside* the courtroom in the first few weeks following the murders. That does not mean the defense could not have lost during the trial. Without the courtroom work of the trial team, defeat could have been snatched from the jaws of victory. But without the efforts orchestrated by Robert Shapiro well before the actual trial began, it is unlikely that any trial team could have won the Simpson case.

Among the first decisions Shapiro made

was to retain two of the world's leading forensic experts, Dr. Henry Lee and Dr. Michael Baden, who immediately flew out to Los Angeles and inspected and photographed the crime scene, the forensic evidence, the autopsy results, the crime lab, and everything else to which they were able to secure access. This material would enable the defense to scrutinize carefully what the police and prosecutors were doing during the earliest phase of their investigation — a strategy that would prove to be pivotal during the trial.

The defense decision to try to discharge the grand jury then hearing the case was another important pretrial strategy. We knew that if we won this motion, the prosecution's case would be presented before a judge at a preliminary hearing. And the differences between a grand jury hearing and a preliminary hearing are quite significant. There was no difference between the likely immediate outcome: We expected that "probable cause" to bring O.J. Simpson to trial was going to be found *either* by a grand jury *or* by a judge. As former chief judge Sol Wachtler of the New York Court of Appeals once put it: A good prosecutor could get a grand jury to "indict a ham sandwich!"[12] The standard for finding probable cause — either by a grand jury or by a judge — is quite low, and we anticipated that the prosecution would be able to meet it. So that was not a significant difference. The real difference was *in the processes* of a grand jury proceeding as distinguished from those of a preliminary hearing.

A grand jury hearing is conducted in secret. The defense does not get to cross-examine prosecution witnesses. The prosecution can put on a skeleton case, using hearsay and secondary source information. A preliminary hearing, in contrast, is open to the public — and, in this case, to television cameras. The defense has the right to cross-examine every prosecution witness. And because the case is presented in public, the prosecution will often try to put its best foot forward.

That created a dilemma for us. On the one hand, we knew from our forensic experts that the prosecution was not yet prepared to present a well-organized case. Its blood tests were incomplete, as were many of its other forensic evaluations. Several important witness interviews had not yet been conducted. A preliminary hearing, with its opportunity to cross-examine, would allow us to lock in the testimony of the prosecution's witnesses *before* it had the opportunity to coordinate its case. In this respect, time was on our side. By refusing to waive the statutory time limit for a preliminary hearing, we could force the prosecution to put its witnesses on the stand without the kind of preparation that avoids contradictions and other mistakes. This carried the prospect of a long-term advantage for the defense at the trial itself, which was still months away.

But there was a short-term downside: The preliminary hearing would be carried live on television, and it was the prosecution's show. The defense does not put on *its* case at a preliminary hearing, since its purpose is to determine whether the prosecutor's case is strong enough to go to trial. We feared that the televised preliminary hearing would be a public relations disaster for the defense. The world would see a parade of prosecution witnesses, with no defense witnesses to counteract them.

Why should lawyers care about public relations? Their job is to persuade judges and jurors, not the public or the pundits. But the jurors come from the same public that would be watching the preliminary hearing on television. And judges, too, are human beings, who are influenced by public opinion. We were worried, therefore, because we would be giving up a short-term public relations advantage in exchange for a longer-term legal advantage. But we decided to bite the bullet and go for the preliminary hearing by filing our motion to dismiss the grand jury.

In our motion we documented the numerous press leaks and prosecutorial pronouncements of Simpson's "guilt" and asked the court "to recuse the grand jury from further proceeding in this case." To our great surprise, on June 24, 1994, Superior Court Supervising Judge Cecil Mills agreed with our motion and ordered the grand jury to recuse itself — that is, remove itself — from the case, finding that "as an unanticipated result of the unique circumstances of this matter . . . some jurors have become aware of potentially prejudicial matters not officially presented to them by the District Attorney."[13] This was a judicial euphemism for accusing the prosecutor of having prejudiced the grand jury against the defendant by its many leaks and press conferences. It was an early victory for the defense and left the prosecution with the

41

choice of trying to proceed before a different grand jury — whose members might also have been exposed to prejudicial publicity — or to proceed by way of a preliminary hearing, the path eventually chosen by the district attorney's office. Perhaps more than any other legal action, it was a path that would have profound implications for the defense strategy, the trial, and the outcome of the case.

The initial effect of our victory was to allow the prosecution to put its case on in public. In fact, the prosecution put its case on *twice* before the defense ever called a single witness. And its case was based essentially on the following evidence, in order of importance:

1. The bloody glove found at Simpson's Rockingham estate. This glove, allegedly Simpson's size, in a style he had worn, and a match for one found at the crime scene, was said to contain fibers consistent with Goldman's shirt, Brown's and Goldman's hair, the Bronco, and limb hair from a black man. The blood was said to be a match for Goldman, Brown, and Simpson.

2. The bloodstained socks found on Simpson's bedroom floor, which the prosecution claimed contained blood that was

42

a DNA match for both Simpson and Brown.

3. The blood found on the back gate at the Bundy crime scene. Being off the ground and in a "clean" environment, this blood was claimed by the prosecution to be less degraded. It was found to be a DNA match for Simpson.

4. The blood found at various places in Simpson's Ford Bronco, on the driver's-side door, the floor, and the center console. The blood on the door was found to be a DNA match for Simpson; that on the console, a match for Simpson, Brown, and Goldman; and that on the floor, a match for Brown.

5. The drops of blood near the victims at the Bundy crime scene. The prosecution claimed that these drops matched Simpson's in DNA testing, and that one drop was tested and matched to Simpson with conventional serology testing.

6. The hair and clothing fibers found at the Bundy crime scene. Hair consistent with Simpson's was found in a knit cap at the scene, and on Goldman's shirt; other fibers on the cap were claimed to be consistent with carpet fibers in Simpson's Bronco; and blue-black fibers on Goldman's shirt were said to match fibers

found on the bloody glove at Rockingham and on the socks in Simpson's bedroom.

7. The bloody shoeprints at the crime scene, which were size 12 (Simpson's size) and had been left by Bruno Magli casual shoes that cost $160 at Bloomingdale's, where Simpson sometimes shopped.

8. The small amounts of blood matching Simpson's that were found in various locations at Rockingham — on the driveway and in the foyer; tests also revealed traces of blood in Simpson's bathroom sink and shower.

9. The history of spousal abuse, which included one physical assault and numerous incidents allegedly suggesting an attitude consistent with motive.

10. The time line, which, according to the prosecution, provided sufficient opportunity for Simpson to have committed the crimes and return home in time to meet the limousine driver.

It was a powerful case. Certainly, if all the evidence was accepted as authentic by the jury, it would lead them to convict Simpson. But we were hearing from our forensic team — which by this time included lawyers Barry Scheck and Peter Neufeld — that the prosecution's apparently solid mountain of evidence was not without its faults and crevices. Eventually, we learned that during the early hours of the investigation, police and prosecutors had made the following mistakes:

1. The police contaminated the crime scene by covering the bodies with a blanket from Nicole Brown's home, casting doubt on all the hair and fiber evidence they claimed to have recovered later.

2. The bodies of the victims were dragged around the crime scene before hair and fiber samples were taken from their clothing.

3. The police failed to notify the coroner's office in a timely fashion, as required by Los Angeles Police Department procedure.

4. The police failed to obtain a warrant to enter the Simpson estate, and instead came up with a story that seemed open to doubt.

5. The police misstated facts on the search warrant, causing the judge eventually to find that Detective Philip Vannatter was "at least reckless" in regard to the truth.[14]

6. The coroner's office had the autopsy performed by Dr. Irwin L. Golden, whom the prosecution eventually decided not to

45

call as a trial witness.

7. The LAPD sent to the crime scene a trainee, Andrea Mazzola, who collected blood samples along with Dennis Fung. Mazzola had never before had primary responsibility for collecting blood evidence from a crime scene.

8. Detective Vannatter carried around O.J. Simpson's blood in a vial in an unsealed envelope for three hours and went for a cup of coffee before booking it. Trial evidence would allow the defense to argue that 1.5 cc's of blood could not be accounted for by the prosecution.

9. The criminologists failed to find blood on the back gate and socks (if blood was, in fact, there) during the original investigation and only found it several weeks after Simpson's blood sample had been taken and carried around by Vannatter.

10. The criminalists did not count the blood samples when they collected them, did not count them when they were put in tubes for drying, and did not count them when they were taken out of the tubes. No documented booking of samples occurred until June 16.

The defense team began to develop a plan of attack directed at the most incriminating of the evidence — the bloody glove and socks, the blood on the back gate of the Rockingham estate, the blood in the Bronco, and the manner in which the evidence had been gathered and processed — but we did not want to disclose our battle plan until after the prosecution locked itself into its presentation at the preliminary hearing.

That hearing had a devastating impact. The vast majority of those who watched it concluded that Simpson was guilty and that the prosecution did, indeed, have a "mountain of evidence" against him. That the prosecution's case was really a mountain *range* — with a few high peaks, several smaller hills, and a large number of valleys — would not emerge until it was the defense's turn at the trial itself. But when that fact did emerge, it would confirm my view that the die was cast within the first few weeks after the discovery of those two bodies in Brentwood on June 13, 1994.

The Simpson case, like many others, was won and lost outside the courtroom, and beyond the view of the television cameras, before the trial even began. It was won by the early forensic work done by our experts, which cast grave doubts on the police investigation, and by the legal strategy that locked the prosecution into its initial mistakes at a public preliminary hearing.

II

Is the Criminal Trial a
Search for Truth?

The term "search for truth" was repeatedly invoked by both sides of the Simpson case. A review of the trial transcript reveals that this phrase was used more than seventy times. The prosecutors claimed that they were searching for truth and that the defense was deliberately obscuring it. Where it was in their interest to have the jury hear evidence that would hurt Simpson — such as the details of arguments between him and his former wife — the prosecutors argued that the search for truth required the *inclusion* of such evidence, despite its marginal relevance. On other occasions, they argued that the search for truth required the *exclusion* of evidence that demonstrated that one of their key witnesses, Los Angeles Police Detective Mark Fuhrman, had not told the truth at the trial. The defense also claimed the mantle of truth and accused the prosecution of placing barriers in its path. And throughout the trial, the pundits observed that neither side was really interested in truth, only in winning. They were right — and wrong.

In observing this controversy, I was reminded of the story of the old rabbi who, after listening to a husband complaining bitterly about his wife, replied, "You are right, my son." Then, after listening to a litany of similar complaints from the wife, he responded, "You are right, my daughter." The rabbi's young student then remarked, "But they can't both be right" — to which the rabbi replied, "You are right, my son." So too, in the context of a criminal case, the prosecution is right when it says it is searching for truth — a certain kind of truth. The defense is also searching for a certain kind of truth. Yet both are often seeking to obscure the truth for which their opponent is searching. In arguing to exclude evidence that Fuhrman had perjured himself when he denied using the "N" word, Marcia Clark said just that:

This is a search for the truth, but it's a search for the truth of who committed these murders, your Honor. Not who Mark Fuhrman is. That truth will be sought out in another forum. We have to search for this truth now, and I beg the court to keep us on track and to allow the jury to pursue that search for the truth based on evidence that is properly admissible in this case and relevant to that determination.[1]

The truth is that most criminal defendants are, in fact, guilty. Prosecutors, therefore, generally have the *ultimate* truth on their side. But since prosecution witnesses often lie about some facts, defense attorneys frequently have *intermediate* truth on their side. Not surprisingly, both sides emphasize the kind of truth that they have more of. To understand this multilayered process, and the complex role "truth" plays in it, it is important to know the difference between a criminal trial and other more single-minded searches for truth.

What is a criminal trial? And how does it differ from a historical or scientific inquiry? These are among the questions posed in a university-wide course I teach at Harvard, along with Professors Robert Nozick, a philosopher, and Stephen J. Gould, a paleontologist. The course, enti-

51

tled "Thinking About Thinking," explores how differently scientists, philosophers, historians, lawyers, and theologians think about and search for truth. The goal of the historian and scientist, at least in theory, is the uncovering or discovery of truth. The historian seeks to determine what actually happened in the recent or distant past by interviewing witnesses, examining documents, and piecing together fragmentary records. The paleontologist searches for even more distant truths by analyzing fossils, geological shifts, dust and DNA. Since what's past is prologue, for both the historian and the scientist, efforts are often made to extrapolate from what did occur to what will occur, and generalizations — historical or scientific rules — are proposed and tested.

Although there are ethical limits on historical and scientific inquiry, the ultimate test of a given result in these disciplines is its truth or falsity. Consider the following hypothetical situation. An evil scientist (or historian) beats or bribes some important truth out of a vulnerable source. That truth is then independently tested and confirmed. The evil scientist might be denied his Nobel Prize for ethical reasons, but the truth he discovered is no less the truth because of the improper means he employed to arrive at it. Scientists condemn "scientific fraud" precisely because it risks producing falsity rather than truth. But if a fraudulent experiment happened to produce a truth that could be replicated in a nonfraudulent experiment, that truth would ultimately become accepted.

Put another way, there are no "exclusionary rules" in history or science, as there are in law. Historical and scientific inquiry is supposed to be neutral as to truth that is uncovered. Historians should not favor a truth that is "politically," "patriotically," "sexually," or "religiously" correct. In practice, of course, some historians and scientists may very well skew their research to avoid certain truths — as Trofim Lysenko did in the interests of Stalinism, or as certain racial theorists did in the interests of Hitlerism. But in doing so, they would be acting as policy-makers rather than as historians or scientists.

The discovery of historical and scientific truths is not entrusted to a jury of laypeople selected randomly from the population on the basis of their ignorance of the underlying facts. The task of discovering such truths is entrusted largely to trained experts who have studied the subject for years and are intimately familiar with the relevant facts and theories.

Historical and scientific inquiries do not require that fact-finders necessarily be representative of the general population, in race, gender, religion, or anything else — as jurors must be. To be sure, a discipline that discriminates runs the risk of producing falsehood, since truth is not the domain of any particular group. But again, historical and scientific truths may be just as valid if arrived at by segregationists as if by integrationists. In history and science, truth achieved by unfair means is preferred to falsity achieved by fair means.

Nor are historical and scientific truths determined on the basis of adversarial contests in which advocates — with varying skills, resources, and styles — argue for different results. Although the quest for peer approval — tenure, prizes, book contracts, and so on — may become competitive, the historical or scientific method is not premised on the view that the search for truth is best conducted through adversarial conflict.[2]

Finally, all "truths" discovered by science or history are always subject to reconsideration based on new evidence. There are no prohibitions against "double jeopardy." Nor is there any deference to considerations of "finality"; nor are there statutes of limitations. In sum, the historical and scientific inquiry is basically a search for objective truth. Perhaps it is not always an untrammeled search for truth. Perhaps the ends of truth do not justify all ignoble means. But the goal is clear: objective truths as validated by accepted, verifiable, and, if possible, replicable historical and scientific tests.

The criminal trial is quite different in several important respects. Truth, although *one* important goal of the criminal trial, is not its *only* goal. If it were, judges would not instruct jurors to acquit a defendant whom they believe "probably" did it, as they are supposed to do in criminal cases. The requirement is that guilt must be proved "beyond a reasonable doubt." But that is inconsistent with the quest for objective truth, because it explicitly prefers one kind of truth to another. The preferred truth is that the defendant did *not* do it, and we demand that the jurors err on the side of that truth, even in cases where it is probable that he did do it.

Justice John Harlan said in the 1970 Supreme Court *Winship* decision that, "I view the requirement of proof beyond a reasonable doubt in a criminal case as bottomed on a fundamental value that it is far worse to convict an innocent man than to let a guilty man go free."[3] As one early-nineteenth-century scholar explained, "The maxim of the law . . . is that it is better that ninety-nine . . . offenders shall escape than that one innocent man be condemned."[4] More typically, the ratio is put at ten to one.

In a criminal trial, we are generally dealing with a decision that must be made under conditions of uncertainty. We will never know with absolute certainty whether Sacco and Vanzetti killed the paymaster and guard at the shoe factory, whether Bruno Hauptmann kidnapped and murdered the Lindbergh baby, or whether Jeffrey MacDonald bludgeoned his wife and children to death. In each of these controversial cases, the legal system was certain enough to convict — and in two of them, to execute. But doubts persist, even decades later.

Those who believe that O.J. Simpson did murder Nicole Brown and Ronald Goldman must acknowledge that they cannot know that "truth" with absolute certainty. They were not there when the crimes occurred or when the evidence was collected and tested. They must rely on the work and word of people they do not know. The jurors in the Simpson case were not asked to vote on whether they believed "he did it." They were asked *whether the prosecution's evidence proved beyond a reasonable doubt that he did it.* Juror number three, a sixty-one-year-old white woman named Anise Aschenbach, indicated that she believed that Simpson was probably guilty "but the law wouldn't allow a guilty verdict."[5] Had the Simpson trial been purely a search for truth, this juror would have been instructed to vote for conviction, since in her view that was more likely the "truth" than that he didn't do it. But she was instructed to arrive at a "false" verdict, namely that although in her view he probably committed the crimes, yet as a matter of law he did not.

This anomaly has led some reformers to propose the adoption of the old Scottish verdict "not proven" instead of the Anglo-American verdict of "not guilty." Even the words "not guilty" do not quite convey the sense of "innocent," although acquitted defendants are always quick to claim that they have been found "innocent." Some commentators have suggested that alternative verdicts — "guilty," "innocent," and "not proven" — be available so that when jurors believe that the defendant did not do it, they can reward him with an affirmative declaration of innocence rather than merely a negative conclusion that his guilt has not been satisfactorily proved.

At one level, we understand — and most agree with — the requirement of proving criminal guilt by a more demanding standard than that required for other decisions in which the risk of error is equivalent on both sides. Yet at another level, we rebel at the notion that a different "truth" may be found in different kinds of proceedings. Imagine the public reaction, for example, if Simpson were to be found liable by a jury in the civil case now pending against him by the heirs of the murder victims for the very same acts of which he was acquitted by the jury at his criminal trial. Would that mean "he did it" for purposes of the civil suit, but "he didn't do it" for purposes of the criminal prosecution? Most Americans would surely believe that it only went to prove that "the law is a ass," as Mr. Bumble put it in Dickens's *Oliver Twist*. But such a result, were it to occur, would rather show that the law is a relatively subtle instrument capable of making refined distinctions between the standards of proof required to deprive a person of his liberty, on the one hand, and to deprive him of money, on the other. As Justice Harlan further commented in his *Winship* opinion:

> If, for example, the standard of proof for a criminal trial were a preponderance of the evidence rather than proof beyond a reasonable doubt, there would be a smaller risk of factual errors that result in freeing guilty persons, but a far greater risk of factual errors that result in convicting the innocent.[6]

The burden of proof in a criminal case is "beyond a reasonable doubt," while the burden of proof in a civil case is "by a mere preponderance of the evidence." Simply put, this means that it takes more and better proof to convict a criminal defendant of a crime than to hold a civil defendant liable for monetary damages. How much more and how much better are not subject to precise quantification. We know what proof by a preponderance is supposed to mean: Even in a close case, the side that is more persuasive wins. In civil cases, truth is supposed to prevail, without the law's thumb on either side of the scales of justice.

We don't, however, have a very good idea of what "proof beyond a reasonable doubt" means in criminal cases. We know that the law's thumb is on the side of the defendant in a criminal case, but the courts are reluctant to tell us how heavy that thumb is supposed to be. My law students debate the following hypothetical case: A fatal accident is caused by a blue bus in a town where 90 percent of the blue buses are owned by the A Company and 10 percent by the B Company. That is all the evidence presented at the criminal trial of the A Company. Is this 90 percent "likelihood" that an A bus caused the accident enough to prove that fact "beyond a reasonable doubt"? Are we willing to convict a company — or an individual — in the face of a 10 percent likelihood of innocence?

Students often respond in the negative to this question, arguing that a clear statistical likelihood of innocence in the range of 10 percent is too high for a criminal conviction. I then ask these students if it would be enough for conviction — without the statistics — if an eyewitness were to testify for the prosecution that he was "sure" it was an A Company bus because he saw the A Company's logo. Most of these same students then say yes, it would be enough, because there was an eyewitness and eyewitnesses can be certain, whereas statistics are always probabilistic. I then ask them if their minds would change again if the defense introduced an acknowledged expert who testified that the kind of eyewitness testimony introduced by the prosecution is accurate in only 85 percent of cases. They still say yes, thus apparently preferring to convict with an 85 percent likelihood of truth rather than convict with a 90 percent likelihood. The debate goes on with numerous variations on these themes. And these are the very sort of difficult questions that the courts rarely address, because they do not have entirely satisfactory answers.

We do understand the reasons for permitting a lower standard of proof in civil than in criminal cases. In civil cases, the risk of error on each side is equal and we do not prefer one type of error over another. But in criminal cases, we prefer the type of error under which a possibly guilty defendant would go free to the type of error under which an innocent defendant would go to prison or be executed.

Nor are different standards of proof limited to legal cases. We apply varying standards in our daily lives. Consider, for example, a woman applying for a baby-sitting job who shows you a certificate proving that she was unanimously acquitted of child molesting. You would never hire her, because you are unwilling to take any chances with your child's baby-sitter.

In addition to the requirement of proof beyond a reasonable doubt in criminal cases, there are numerous other barriers to absolute truth that have been deliberately built in to the criminal process to serve other functions. Some of these barriers can be justified as perhaps contributing to the search for truth *in the long run,* while probably sacrificing truth in a particular case. The exclusion from evidence of a coerced confession may produce falsity in a case where the confession, although coerced, is nonetheless true and can be independently corroborated. Consider, for example, a case in which a defendant is coerced into admitting not only that he killed the missing victim but also where he buried the body. By excluding this true, coerced confession — and thus possibly freeing *this* guilty murderer — the law may be seeking to increase the long-term, truth-finding goals of the system, since many *other* coerced confessions may turn out to be false.

We could, of course, satisfy both long- and short-term truth goals by adopting a rule — which we have not adopted in this country — under which coerced confessions that can be *independently corroborated* will be admitted into evidence. Under such a rule, a coerced confession which produces merely a statement that "I did it" would not be admitted, but a coerced confession that leads to the victim's body covered with the defendant's fingerprints and DNA would be admitted. Or, perhaps as a fail-safe, only the body and the physical evidence would be admitted, but not the coerced confession itself, even though it has been proved to be true.

Instead, we have opted for an exclusionary rule under which the coerced confession *and all its fruits* are excluded, even if the fruits prove the truthfulness of the confession.[7] Such a broad exclusionary rule is not designed to serve only the goals of truth, either long- or short-term. It is also intended to serve an important set of values entirely unrelated to truth. Those include privacy (or, in the eighteenth-century language of the Fourth Amendment, "security"), freedom from unreasonable governmental intrusion, and the integrity of the mind and body. These values were regarded by those who introduced the "exclusionary rule" as being more important, at least on occasion, than truth. The exclusionary rule explicitly recognizes that the guilty will sometimes have to be freed in order to send a message to police and prosecutors that the noble end of seeking the truth does not justify ignoble means such as unreasonable searches or coerced confessions.

If the only goal of the adversary system were to find "the truth" in every case, then it would be relatively simple to achieve. Suspects could be tortured, their families threatened, homes randomly searched, and lie detector tests routinely administered. Indeed, in order to facilitate this search for truth, we could all be subjected to a regimen of random blood and urine tests, and every public building and workplace could be outfitted with surveillance cameras. If these methods — common in totalitarian countries — are objected to on the ground that torture and threats sometimes produce false accusations, that objection could be overcome by requiring that all confessions induced by torture or threats must be independently corroborated. We would still never tolerate such a single-minded search for truth, nor would our constitution, because we believe that the ends — even an end as noble as truth — do not justify every possible means. Our system of justice thus reflects a balance among often inconsistent goals, which include truth, privacy, fairness, finality, and equality.

Even "truth" is a far more complex goal than may appear at first blush. There are different kinds of truth at work in our adversary system. At the most basic level, there is the ultimate truth involved in the particular case: "Did he do it?" Then there is the truth produced by cases over time, which may be in sharp conflict. For example, the lawyer-client privilege — which shields certain confidential communications from being disclosed — may generate more truth over the long run by encouraging clients to be candid with their lawyers. But in any given case, this same privilege may thwart the ultimate truth — as in the rare case where a defendant confides in his lawyer that he did it. The same is true of other privileges, ranging from the privilege against self-incrimination to rape shield laws, which prevent an accused rapist from introducing the prior sexual history of his accuser.

Even in an individual case, there are different types — or layers — of truth. The defendant may have done it — ultimate truth! — but the police may have lied in securing the search warrant. Or the police may even have planted evidence against guilty defendants, as New York state troopers were recently convicted of doing, and as some jurors believed the police did in the Simpson case.

The Anglo-American criminal trial employs the adversary system to resolve disputes. This system, under which each side tries to win by all legal and ethical means, may be conducive to truth in the long run, but it does not always produce truth in a given case. Nor is it widely understood or accepted by the public.

One night, during the middle of the Simpson trial, my wife and I were attending a concert at Boston Symphony Hall. When it was over a woman ran down the center aisle. We thought she was headed toward the stage to get a close look at Midori, who was taking bows. But the woman stopped at our row and started shouting at me: "You don't deserve to listen to music. You don't care about justice. All you care about is winning." I responded, "You're half right. When I am representing a criminal defendant, I do care about winning — by all fair, lawful, and ethical means. That's how we try to achieve justice in this country — by each side seeking to win. It's called the adversary system."

I did not try to persuade my critic, since I have had little success persuading even my closest friends of the morality of the Vince Lombardi dictum as it applies to the role of defense counsel in criminal cases: "Winning isn't everything. It's the only thing."

There are several reasons why it is so difficult to explain this attitude to the public. First, hardly anybody ever admits publicly that winning is their goal. Even the most zealous defense lawyers proclaim they are involved in a search for truth. Such posturing is part of the quest for victory, since lawyers who candidly admit they are interested in the truth are more likely to win than lawyers who say they are out to win. Second, although defense attorneys are supposed to want to win — regardless of what they say in public — prosecutors are, at least in theory, supposed to want justice. Indeed, the motto of the U.S. Justice Department is "The Government wins when Justice is done."[8] That is the theory. In practice, however, each side wants to win as badly as the other. Does anyone really doubt that Marcia Clark wanted to win as much as Johnnie Cochran did? She told the jury during her closing argument that she had stopped being a defense attorney and became a prosecutor so that she could have the luxury of looking at herself in the mirror every morning and knowing that she always told juries the truth, and that she would only ask for a conviction where she could prove that the defendant was, in fact, guilty.[9] But notwithstanding these assertions, Clark and other prosecutors put Mark Fuhrman on the stand after having been informed that he was a racist, a liar, and a person capable of planting evidence even before they called him as a trial witness. An assistant district attorney, among others, warned the Simpson prosecutors about Fuhrman. The prosecutors also saw his psychological reports, in which he admitted his racist attitudes and actions. The only thing they didn't know was that Fuhrman — and they — would be caught by the tape-recorded interviews that Fuhrman gave an aspiring screenwriter, Laura Hart McKinny. If the tapes had not surfaced, the prosecutors would have attempted to destroy the credibility of the truthful good Samaritan witnesses who came forward to testify about Fuhrman's racism. Only the tapes stopped them from doing that.

Clark behaved similarly with regard to Detective Philip Vannatter. Any reasonable prosecutor should have been suspicious of Vannatter's testimony that when he went to the O.J. Simpson estate in the hours following the discovery of the double murder, he no more suspected Simpson of the killings than he did Robert Shapiro. That testimony had all the indicia of a cover story, and yet Clark allowed it to stand uncorrected.

In practice, the adversary system leads both sides to do everything in their power — as long as it is lawful and ethical — to win. Since most defendants are guilty, it follows that the defense will more often be in the position of advocating ultimate falsity than will the prosecution. But since the prosecution always puts on a case — often relying on police testimony — whereas the defense rarely puts on any affirmative case, it follows that the prosecution will more often be in the position of using false testimony in an effort to produce its ultimately true result.

Outrage at Simpson's acquittal is understandable in those who firmly believe that he did it. No one wants to see a guilty murderer go free, or an innocent defendant go to prison. But our system is judged not only by the accuracy of its results, but also by the *fairness of the process*. Indeed, the Supreme Court has said that our system must tolerate the occasional conviction, imprisonment, *and even execution* of a possibly innocent defendant because of considerations of finality, federalism, and deference to the jury. The United States Supreme Court recently recognized that "our judicial system, like the human beings who administer it, is fallible" and that innocent defendants have at times been wrongfully convicted. The Court concluded that some wrongful convictions and even executions of innocent defendants must be tolerated "because of the very disruptive effect that entertaining claims of actual innocence would have on the need for finality in capital cases, and the enormous burden that having to retry cases based on often stale evidence would place on the States."[10]

While reasonable people may, and do, disagree with that conclusion, it surely must follow from our willingness to tolerate some innocents being wrongly executed by our less than perfect system that we must be prepared to tolerate the occasional freeing of defendants who are perceived to be guilty. This is a Rubicon we, as a society, crossed long before the Simpson verdict — although one might not know it from the ferocity of the reaction to that verdict. As I mentioned earlier, the exclusionary rule is based on our willingness to free some guilty defendants in order to serve values often unrelated to truth. It is interesting to contrast the public reaction to the *jury's* acquittal with what would have happened if Simpson had gone free as a result of the *judge's* application of the exclusionary rule.

What would the public reaction have been if the trial judge had ruled that the original search of Simpson's estate had been unconstitutional and all its fruits had to be suppressed? Such a ruling might have wounded the prosecution's case — although perhaps not mortally. It would have excluded from evidence the bloody glove found behind Simpson's house, the socks found in his bedroom, the blood found in the driveway. It might also have tainted the warrants, which were based, at least in part, on the evidence observed during the initial search. These warrants produced a considerable amount of evidence which might also have had to be suppressed. Indeed, had the search of Simpson's estate been declared unconstitutional, virtually everything found in and around the estate might have been subject to exclusion.

That would still have left the other half of the prosecution's case — everything found at the crime scene — since no probable cause or warrant was required for searches and seizures at Nicole Brown's condominium. But the quantity of the prosecution's evidence against Simpson would have been considerably reduced if the evidence seized at the Simpson estate had been suppressed as the fruits of an unconstitutional search.

Had the trial judge suppressed all the Simpson estate evidence, there would have been a massive public outcry against the judge, the exclusionary rule, the Constitution, and the system. This outcry would have increased in intensity if this suppression had led — either directly or indirectly — to the acquittal of the defendant. "Guilty Murderer Is Freed Because of Legal Technicality," the headlines would have shouted. Conservatives would have demanded abolition of the exclusionary rule. But many liberals and civil libertarians who today rail against the jury verdict in the Simpson case would have defended the decision as the price we pay for preserving our constitutional rights.

This is all, of course, in the realm of the hypothetical, since it is unlikely that any judge — certainly any elected judge with higher aspirations — would have had the courage to find the search unconstitutional and thus endanger the prosecution's case. Recently, I had lunch with a former student who was seeking to be appointed to the California Superior Court. I asked her how she would answer the following question if it were put to her by the judicial nominating committee: "Would you have ruled the search unconstitutional if you believed the police were lying about why they went to Simpson's house, climbed the gate, and entered?" Without a moment's hesitation she responded: "No way. No judge would — are you kidding?"

I think my former student overstated the case in saying that *no* judge would have had the guts to find the police were lying in the Simpson case, but I believe that most judges would do what the two trial judges almost certainly did here: assume a variation of the position of the three monkeys, hearing no lies and seeing no lies. And judges speak the lie of pretending to believe witnesses who they must know are not telling the truth. What does it say about our system of justice that so many judges would pretend to believe policemen they know are lying, rather than follow the unpopular law excluding evidence obtained in violation of the Constitution? I am not alone in believing that the judges in the Simpson case could not really have believed what they said they believed. As Scott Turow argued in a perceptive op-ed piece the day after the verdict:

The detectives' explanation as to why they were at the house is hard to believe. . . . Four police detectives were

74

not needed to carry a message about Nicole Simpson's death. These officers undoubtedly knew what Justice Department statistics indicate: that half of the women murdered in the United States are killed by their husbands or boyfriends. Simple probabilities made Mr. Simpson a suspect. . . . Also, Mark Fuhrman had been called to the Simpson residence years earlier when Mr. Simpson was abusing his wife. . . .

The fact that the district attorney's office put these officers on the witness stand to tell this story and that the [judge] accepted it is scandalous. It is also routine. . . .

Turow then went on to blame the prosecutor and the judges:

To lambaste only Detectives Fuhrman and Vannatter misses the point. . . . It was the Los Angeles District Attorney's Office that put them on the stand. It was Judge Kennedy-Powell [the judge who presided at the preliminary hearing] who took their testimony at face value rather than stir controversy by suppressing the most damning evidence in the case of the century. And it was Judge Lance Ito who refused to reverse her decision. . . .[11]

Neither the prosecutors nor the judges were searching very hard for the truth of why the detectives went to the Simpson residence. They apparently thought that the disclosure of that truth would make the proving of what they believed was a more important truth — that the defendant was guilty — more difficult. Thus, some people believe that the search for one truth in a criminal case can be served by tolerating other half-truths and even lies. But I believe the prosecution's decision to call Detectives Vannatter and Fuhrman to the witness stand may have been the final nail in a coffin that had been built even earlier by the police. That costly decision was thoughtlessly made by prosecutors who have become so accustomed to police perjury about searches and seizures that they did not even pause to consider its possible impact on this jury.

III

Why Do So Many Police Lie about Searches and Seizures? And Why Do So Many Judges "Believe" Them?

When Detective Philip Vannatter testified that O.J. Simpson "was no more of a suspect" than Robert Shapiro, many commentators and pundits concluded that he was covering up the truth. Nearly all said so in private; some said so in public.[1] Even District Attorney Gil Garcetti acknowledged to Harvard Law School students after the verdict that this testimony "was terrible" and that he "couldn't believe Vannatter would say what he did."

Why did Detective Vannatter, who is an experienced detective and witness, think he could get away with so transparent a cover story? As Scott Turow put it: "If veteran police detectives did not arrive at the gate of Mr. Simpson's house thinking he might have committed those murders, they should have been fired."[2]

Yet Detective Vannatter, along with the three other detectives who went to the Simpson house and the supervisor who dispatched them, all swore that they went there simply to "make a notification" to the dead woman's former husband and arrange for the "disposition" of the two small children, not to search for possible evidence of Simpson's complicity in the crimes.[3]

What made this charade even more difficult to understand was the fact that if the police had told the truth, the judges might well have found that the ensuing search was lawful and that its fruits were admissible in evidence under one of several exceptions to the constitutional requirement for a search warrant.[4]

I once asked a policeman, "Why do cops lie so brazenly in search-and-seizure cases?" He responded with a rude macho joke: "Why do dogs lick their balls?" To which the answer is "Because they can." Police know they can get away with certain kinds of common lies. Listen to former New York City criminal court judge Irving Younger discuss a case in which a police officer testified that a drug suspect had just happened to *drop* a small plastic envelope containing marijuana:

Were this the first time a policeman had testified that a defendant had dropped a packet of drugs to the ground, the matter would be unremarkable. The extraordinary thing is that each year in our criminal courts policemen give such testimony in hundreds, perhaps thousands, of cases — and that, in a nutshell, is the problem of "dropsy" testimony. . . . [W]hen one stands back from the particular case and looks at a series of cases, [it] becomes apparent that policemen are committing perjury in at least some of them, and perhaps in nearly all of them.[5]

Judge Younger explained how the Supreme Court's 1962 decision in *Mapp v. Ohio* — which ruled that evidence obtained in violation of the Constitution had to be excluded from state as well as federal trials — caused this epidemic of police perjury.

Before *Mapp* the policeman typically testified that he stopped the defendant for little or no reason, searched him and found narcotics on his person. This had the ring of truth. It was an illegal search but the evidence was admissible because *Mapp* had not yet been decided. Since it made no difference, the policeman testified truthfully. After the decision in *Mapp*, it made a great deal of difference. For the first few months, New York policemen continued to tell the truth about the circumstances of their searches, with the result that the evidence was suppressed. Then the police made the great discovery that if the defendant drops the narcotics on the ground, after which the policeman arrests him, the search is reasonable and the evidence admissible. Spend a few hours in the New York City Criminal Court nowadays and you will hear case after case in which a policeman testifies that the defendant dropped the narcotics on the ground, whereupon the policeman arrested him. Usually the very language of the testimony is identical from one case to another.[6]

Despite his certainty that this kind of "dropsy" testimony is often false, even Judge Younger felt that he had no choice but to accept the policeman's testimony *in the particular case he was deciding,* since it was his word against that of the drug dealer. He came to this decision "reluctantly," because of his belief that "our refusal to face up to the 'dropsy' problem soils the rectitude of the administration of justice." But his bottom-line message to the police was loud and clear. Even a judge who is courageous enough to blow the whistle on the pervasiveness of police perjury *in general* is not willing — or able — to do anything about it *in a particular case.* He will accept "dropsy" testimony as truthful in the case before him. And the police officer in that case will chuckle at the judge's minilecture and go on with business as usual, confident in the knowledge that his perjured testimony will result in the conviction of a guilty and despicable drug dealer.

Everyone is happy with this result. The cop gets credit for a good drug bust. His supervisor's arrest statistics look good. The prosecutor racks up another win. The judge gets to give his little lecture on "rectitude" without endangering his reelection prospects by actually freeing a guilty criminal. The defense lawyer collects his fee in dirty drug money, knowing that there is nothing more he can do. The public is thrilled that another drug dealer is off the street.

It is this benign attitude toward police perjury in the context of search and seizure that makes it so acceptable — indeed so essential — a part of our criminal justice system. As Judge Younger further explained:

> Policemen see themselves as fighting a two-front war — against criminals in the street and against "liberal" rules of law in court. All's fair in this war, including the use of perjury to subvert "liberal" rules of law that might free those who "ought" to be jailed.... It is a peculiarity of our legal system that the police have unique opportunities (and unique temptations) to give false testimony. When the Supreme Court lays down a rule to govern the conduct of the police, the rule does not enforce itself.[7]

It takes judges to enforce these rules, and there are too few judges — especially among those who must stand for reelection — with the courage to free a guilty defendant because the policeman who arrested him violated the Constitution. Even fewer judges are willing to look a policeman in the eye and say, "I don't believe you. I think you are lying."

But virtually all judges who listen to or review police testimony on a regular basis privately agree with what Judge Alex Kozinski of the United States Court of Appeals for the Ninth Circuit publicly stated: "It is an open secret long shared by prosecutors, defense lawyers and judges that perjury is widespread among law enforcement officers," and that the reason for it is that "the exclusionary rule . . . sets up a great incentive for . . . police to lie to avoid letting someone they think is guilty, or they know is guilty, go free."[8] Numerous academic studies, commission reports, and anecdotal accounts have confirmed the pervasive nature of police perjury in search-and-seizure cases. I believe it is fair to characterize the prevalence of police perjury in such cases as law enforcement's "dirty little secret."[9]

Here, for example, is what the Mollen Commission — established to look into cases of police corruption — said in 1994 about New York City's police department:

The practice of police falsification in connection with such arrests is so common in certain precincts that it has spawned its own word: "testily-ing." . . . Officers also commit falsification to serve what they perceive to be "legitimate" law enforcement ends — and for ends that many honest and corrupt officers alike stubbornly defend as correct. In their view, regardless of the legality of the arrest, the defendant is in fact guilty and ought to be arrested.[10]

The report then went on to describe how

officers reported a litany of manufactured tales. For example, when officers unlawfully stop and search a vehicle because they believe it contains drugs or guns, officers will falsely claim in police reports and under oath that the car ran a red light (or committed some other traffic violation) and that they subsequently saw contraband in the car in plain view. To conceal an unlawful search of an individual who officers believe is carrying drugs or a gun, they will falsely assert that they saw a bulge in the person's pocket or saw drugs and money changing hands. To justify unlawfully entering an apartment where

84

officers believe narcotics or cash can be found, they pretend to have information from an unidentified civilian informant.[11]

The traffic violation pretext is precisely the kind of tactic that Detective Mark Fuhrman bragged to Laura McKinny he would employ if he saw a racially mixed couple driving down the street.

Even more troubling, in the Mollen Commission's view, "the evidence suggests that the . . . commanding officer not only tolerated, but encouraged, this unlawful practice." The commission provided several examples of perjured cover stories that had been suggested to a young officer by his supervisor:

Scenarios were, were you going to say (a) that you observed what appeared to be a drug transaction; (b) you observed a bulge in the defendant's waistband; or (c) you were informed by a male black, unidentified at this time, that at the location there were drug sales.

QUESTION: So, in other words, what the lieutenant was telling you is: Here's your choice of false predicates for these arrests.

OFFICER: That's correct. Pick which one you're going to use.[12]

Nor was this practice limited to police supervisors. As the Mollen Commission reported:

> Several former and current prosecutors acknowledged — "off the record" — that perjury and falsification are serious problems in law enforcement that, though not condoned, are ignored. The form this tolerance takes, however, is subtle, which makes accountability in this area especially difficult.[13]

But, as the Mollen Commission further observed: "Testimonial perjury cases are often extremely difficult to prove" against policemen because they are trained witnesses who are careful not to lie when there is hard evidence to contradict them — which there rarely is. They are also protected by the "blue wall of silence."

"The blue wall of silence" is a code that forbids one policeman from testifying against another and requires policemen to "back up" a fellow officer, even if they know he is lying. The Christopher Commission, which studied the Los Angeles Police Department in the wake of the Rodney King beating, found such cover-up behavior to be a real problem.[14]

The Fuhrman tapes confirmed the existence of this mentality. Fuhrman described the attitude of the LAPD's Internal Affairs office as follows:

Now, it's funny because guys in Internal Affairs go, Mark, you can do just about anything. Get in a bar fight. We'd love to investigate just some good ol' boy beating up a nigger in a bar.

No problem, not even any marks, Dana. Just body shots. Did you ever try to find a bruise on a nigger? It is pretty tough, huh?

Fuhrman then told how old-time police officers will cover for each other:

Why don't you give them the 77th lie detector test? You know, everybody — and a bunch of guys will laugh — old timers, you know. And then one kid will ask his partner, "What's that?"

You keep choking him out until he tells you the truth. You know, it is kind of funny. But a lot of policemen will get a kick out of it. Anyway, so you are in the shadows like that.

Finally, he described how he would tamper with evidence by turning an old injection scab on a drug-user's arm into a fresh needle mark:

So if that's considered falsifying a report, and if . . . you find a mark that looks like three days ago, pick the scab. Squeeze it. Looks like serum's coming out, as if it were hours old. . . . That's not falsifying a report. That's putting a criminal in jail. That's being a policeman.

Every objective study of police perjury has come to the conclusion that police perjury is widespread and condoned.[15] And the problem is rampant in most parts of the country. In upstate New York, for example, the FBI has proved that state troopers "faked fingerprint evidence on a routine basis" between 1984 and 1992. What the troopers did with fingerprints was strikingly similar to what the defense alleged the police did with blood in the Simpson case. According to prosecutors, "they would take a suspect's fingerprints from either a police station booking card or an object the suspect was known to have touched, and then would claim to have found the fingerprint at the crime scene." A special prosecutor who was appointed to investigate "thousands of cases in all 11 state police barracks" says that he "continues to be surprised by the extent of the corruption." But the special prosecutor is running into the "blue wall of silence." Indeed, he now believes that most of the corrupt policemen will escape prosecution because some of their colleagues "have done everything they possibly can to frustrate the investigation."

Moreover, the special prosecutor has found that numerous police officials, including supervisors, were involved in either the deliberate planting of fake evidence or in the cover-up. Yet most will escape prosecution, and some who were directly involved with the tampering will still "be working for the New York State Police" when the investigation is completed.[16]

Nor is such corruption limited to rural state troopers. Virtually every large city

— from Philadelphia, to Chicago, to Pittsburgh, to Detroit, to New Orleans, to Boston — has experienced epidemics of evidence planting, false testimony, police cover-ups, and the like. A recent *New York Times* headline read, "Officer Resigns Over False Testimony, but Says His Superior Made Him Lie."[17] The story disclosed a sordid but all too typical tale. A New York City police officer admitted that he had committed perjury at least seventeen times in six criminal cases in which testimony helped send defendants to prison for drug dealing. Thirty-three other officers from the same precinct had also been arrested on a variety of charges, including perjury and illegal searches and seizures.

Now, this officer was claiming that "a senior officer" forced him to give the false testimony. "In fact," he said, "the first time I testified falsely, a superior officer, with two other superior officers present, specifically ordered me to do so and checked up on me several times thereafter to assure that I continued to adhere to what we both knew was a false story so that a drug dealer would go to prison."

Nor did such police conspiracies and cover-ups end at the "senior officer" level.

It is inconceivable that most assistant district attorneys prosecuting these drug dealers were not aware of the police perjury. They closed their eyes to it, thereby implicitly encouraging it.

That is why the rest of the story was no surprise. The cop who admitted he lied on seventeen occasions was not going to be prosecuted. The district attorney claimed there were "mitigating circumstances." There almost always are. The district attorney's office is generally afraid that if the cops are prosecuted, they will blow the whistle on members of that office who were aware of the perjury. Most cops who lie have that ace in the hole. They can testify against the very prosecutor's office that is empowered to arrest them. That is why so few cops are ever indicted for perjury.

There was another mitigating factor in this case that speaks volumes about the pervasiveness of police perjury in certain kinds of cases and its widespread acceptance by many police officers. A cop who was working undercover for the Mollen Commission said he feared that if he did not lie, the other cops would immediately suspect that he was working undercover, because *real cops do lie*. Fuhrman said the same thing on the tapes, when he railed against one of his partners who refused to lie, accusing him of not being a real cop.

FUHRMAN: He doesn't know how to be a policeman. "I can't lie." Oh, you make me [expletive] sick to my guts. You know, you do what you have to do to put these [expletives] in jail. If you don't [expletive] get out of the [expletive] game. He just wants to be one of the boys. But he doesn't want to play. You know? Pay the dues.

MCKINNY: So how does he deal with it?

FUHRMAN: He doesn't lie.

MCKINNY: . . . Says he's not going to lie.

FUHRMAN: Uh-huh. Not a policeman at heart. He's considered one of the good guys.

MCKINNY: He won't take any suspension at all?

FUHRMAN: He'll say, he said to me once. He goes, "I got a wife and kid to think of." I says, "[Expletive] you. Don't tell me because you got a wife and a kid. . . . You're either my partner all the way or you get the [expletive] out of the car. We die for each other. We live for each other. That's the way it is in the car. You lie for me up to six months' suspension. Don't ever get fired for me. Don't get indicted for me. But you'll take six months for me 'cause I'll take it for you. If you don't, get the [expletive] out of here."

MCKINNY: Why do you talk to your partners like that?

FUHRMAN: It shouldn't have to be said.

It is widely accepted that if the Rodney King beating had not been captured on videotape, the police testimony would have been decidedly different from what was seen by millions of people around the world. Indeed, it is known that some policemen carry a "spare" knife or "Saturday night special" to plant on or near an unarmed suspect if they are accused of using excessive force against that person. In the Simpson case itself the first document presented to a court included deliberate police perjury. Detective Philip Vannatter, in seeking a search warrant, swore that O.J. Simpson's trip to Chicago was unplanned, even though he knew it had been planned long in advance of the murders. Judge Ito generously described this statement as "at least reckless" in its disregard for the truth.[18]

I have been writing, teaching, and lecturing about the pervasiveness of police perjury since I first encountered it in the notorious Jewish Defense League murder case in the early 1970s.* In 1982, I set out my version of "The Rules of the Justice Game," which included the following:

Rule III: It is easier to convict guilty defendants by violating the Constitution than by complying with it, and in some cases it is impossible to convict guilty defendants without violating the Constitution.

Rule IV: Almost all police lie about whether they violated the Constitution in order to convict guilty defendants.

Rule V: All prosecutors, judges, and defense attorneys are aware of Rule IV.

Rule VI: Many prosecutors implicitly encourage police to lie about whether they violated the Constitution in order to convict guilty defendants.

Rule VII: All judges are aware of Rule VI.

*This case is described in detail in my book *The Best Defense*.

94

Rule VIII: Most trial judges pretend to believe police officers who they know are lying.

Rule IX: All appellate judges are aware of Rule VIII, yet many pretend to believe the trial judges who pretend to believe the lying police officers.[19]

Following the publication of the Mollen Commission Report in 1994, I wrote an op-ed article for *The New York Times* entitled "Accomplices to Perjury," which began as follows:

As I read about the disbelief expressed by some prosecutors at the Mollen Commission's recent assertion that police perjury is "widespread" in New York City, I thought of Claude Rains's classic response, in "Casablanca," on being told there was gambling in Rick's place: "I'm shocked — shocked!"

For anyone who has practiced criminal law in the state or federal courts, the disclosures about rampant police perjury cannot possibly come as a surprise. "Testilying" — as the police call it — has long been an open secret among prosecutors, defense lawyers and judges.

The article ended on a pessimistic note: "A few cops will be prosecuted, and a quarter-century from now yet another blue-ribbon commission will be 'shocked — shocked' at the pervasiveness of police perjury in the criminal justice system."[20]

My views were echoed by a lawyer who has had long experience with the Philadelphia police. In an interview on the *Today* show, David Rudovsky put it this way:

The accountability starts in the Police Department. But for years, judges and district attorneys have simply been asleep at the wheel in Philadelphia. And unfortunately, the mentality among too many judges, not all, too many district attorneys is the same as the police, the ends justify the means. "And so if they've crossed the line, we'll overlook it."

Rudovsky summed it up as follows:

The problem is police simply in this culture will not report on other police. If they don't do it, seems to me other agencies have to. And that's where the prosecutors come in, that's where judges come in. And unless they change their view of this kind of testimony, we'll see the same scandal in five years in Philadelphia. We've seen it 10 years before, we've seen it 15 years before. Each time it happens, we have the same kind of refrain from the elected officials: a few bad apples. Let's get rid of them.[21]

In light of this widespread knowledge of the reality and pervasiveness of police perjury, and my own discussions of it over the past quarter of a century, I was quite surprised by the reaction to a remark I made about police perjury on *Good Morning America* in the midst of the Simpson case. Mark Fuhrman had just testified at the trial that he had not used the "N" word in the last ten years.

NANCY SNYDERMAN: Mark Fuhrman did hold up yesterday. Were you surprised?

ALAN DERSHOWITZ: No. That's what they are trained to do. Policemen are trained to be cool. They're professional witnesses. The Mollen Commission in New York, after reviewing thousands of hours of police testimony, said, police perjury is rampant in the courts, but lawyers can't get at the perjury unless they can confront the witnesses with their own words. And the irony here —

NANCY SNYDERMAN: You're telling me that police departments tell their detectives that it's OK to lie?

ALAN DERSHOWITZ: Not only do police departments tell their detectives it's OK to lie, they learn it in the Academy. They have a word for it, it's called "testilying." And they do it coolly, and they do it in a way that they can't be broken down unless you can confront them with their own words.

I then explained that in the early 1980s Fuhrman had filed a disability claim in which he acknowledged his racism, his violence, and his use of the "N" word, but that Judge Ito had ruled that F. Lee Bailey could not use this disability claim to impeach him:

These are Fuhrman's own words, and we're not being able to confront him with his own words. And so we get a situation where he says he's not a racist. [Kathleen] Bell [a witness who subsequently testified for the defense] says he is a racist. The jury can't resolve it because they're being denied the tools necessary to resolve these issues.[22]

In talking about the Police Academy, I was paraphrasing a former New York City policeman named Robert Leuci who had testified for the federal government after going undercover to investigate police and lawyer corruption in the 1970s. Leuci said that "Cops are almost taught how to commit perjury when they are in the Police Academy."[23] I had included that quote in my book *The Best Defense* and it had caused little reaction. Nor had the findings of the Mollen Commission, on which I had based the remainder of my comments. I did not anticipate, therefore, that my words would create such a national firestorm. But they did.

The reaction was swift, vociferous, and well orchestrated. The mayor of Los Angeles and its police chief held a rally to condemn my statements. Legislative resolutions were offered in support of the police. Several police organizations tried to have me disciplined for my comments.

The director of the Los Angeles Police Protective League went on television to assure the public that in his "27 years of law enforcement, never, ever" had he even heard of a Los Angeles policeman stretching the truth. He also certified that "Mark Fuhrman did not lie" and that "Vannatter did not lie." Only Dershowitz lied, this man shouted, by telling the public that police often commit perjury in search-and-seizure cases.[24] My office was picketed. I received threatening phone calls. The dean of Harvard Law School was barraged with demands for my dismissal. It was amazing for me to watch the hypocritical posturing by people ranging from a former attorney general of the United States, to retired judges, to police commissioners, to district attorneys, to elected politicians — all of whom knew that I was telling the truth about the pervasiveness of police perjury and its tolerance from on high. I was reminded of the old joke about the Soviet dissident who was arrested for saying that Stalin was stupid. He pleaded not guilty to libel and treason. But the judge said "*That* is not the crime for which you are being charged." "What then *is* my crime?" asked the bewildered dissident. "Your crime," the judge replied in a whisper, "is revealing a state secret."

I felt that I, too, was being accused of revealing a judicial secret, by publicly disclosing a fact well known to everyone in the inner circle of criminal justice, but not widely known to the lay public, at least the white lay public. And my punishment was that some cowards who knew I was telling the truth closed ranks against me and pretended to be shocked by my "irresponsible" breach of the rules of our secret society of lawyers.

Even the dean of Harvard Law School — who would have no reason to know much about the extent of police perjury — felt it necessary to distance himself and the law school from my disclosure. In a form letter he wrote in response to several dozen letters he received from indignant alumni, Dean Robert Clark asserted that "many faculty members disagree with some or all of Dershowitz's public pronouncements." I doubt that many of my faculty colleagues who are familiar with the literature on police perjury disagree with what I have said, although some have told me that they would never have had the guts to say it as straightforwardly as I have. I had always thought that tenure means you don't have to have guts to tell unpopular truths.

One of those who was most vociferous in his condemnation of me was the police chief of Los Angeles, Willie Williams, who should certainly have known better, since before coming to Los Angeles he had headed the Philadelphia Police Department, which had its own perjury and evidence-planting scandal. Several weeks after attacking me, Chief Williams was himself accused of deliberately lying about improperly accepting free hotel rooms in Las Vegas. He then accused members of his own police department of framing him for misconduct he had not committed.

According to *Newsweek* magazine, a group of police officers loyal to ousted chief Darryl Gates targeted Chief Williams by conducting an unauthorized investigation of him, including unlawful surveillance of a trip to Las Vegas, and were now denying it. "This was a rogue operation to get rid of Williams," said an unidentified Los Angeles police source. To put it another way, police officers hostile to Chief Williams — the first African-American police chief of Los Angeles' very white and very racially troubled police department — had conspired to "get" Williams by using unlawful means and were now covering up their conspiracy.[25]

Even after going through the experience of having his own police officers plant evidence in Philadelphia and then being framed by some of his own policemen in Los Angeles, Chief Williams adamantly refused to recognize — at least, publicly — the problem of pervasive police perjury.

On the other hand, William F. Bratton, the police commissioner of New York, recently acknowledged that "testilying" is a "real problem that needs to be addressed." He also placed some of the responsibility squarely at the feet of prosecutors: "When a prosecutor is really determined to win, the trial prep procedure may skirt along the edge of coercing or leading the police witness. In this way, some impressionable young cops learn to tailor their testimony to the requirements of the law."[26] At a conference sponsored by the Criminal Justice Institute of Harvard, Commissioner Bratton — who went to New York City after heading the Boston Police Department — said that police and prosecutors cannot address the problem of testilying "by ignoring it." Bratton "said he agreed with most of what Dershowitz had to say." And while several police chiefs publicly criticized Bratton for agreeing with me, a number privately accepted his assessment.

In November 1995, Bratton announced a new program under which all New York City police officers would be trained to give accurate testimony in court. *The New York Times* tied this decision to the Simpson case:

> The perception that police officers often make false arrests, tamper with evidence and commit perjury has led to scores of acquittals in New York and other cities in recent years, prosecutors and legal scholars said. And that perception was reinforced during the O.J. Simpson trial, when a prosecution witness, Detective Mark Fuhrman, was found to have boasted about tampering with evidence and lying in court to win convictions.[27]

To return to the Simpson trial: Although it was clear to me — and to most observers — that the pretrial search-and-seizure hearings were rife with police perjury, I doubted that the prosecutors would risk calling lying cops to the stand at the trial itself. Judges are more aware than jurors of the pervasiveness of police perjury, but most judges can be counted on by prosecutors to "believe" police witnesses if disbelieving them would cause the case to be thrown out. Juries, on the other hand, are far less predictable — especially if they believe they have been lied to directly.

Before the trial began, I wrote a memo to the defense team urging us to be ready for a "smart move" by the prosecution. The move I anticipated was that the prosecution would decide *not* to call Mark Fuhrman as a witness. I thought that Marcia Clark was smart enough to know that calling Fuhrman would be playing into our hands. He simply brought too much baggage to the case. Indeed, I had speculated that the reason Fuhrman was called off the case within two hours of his arrival at the crime scene was because someone knew that he was trouble. But Fuhrman wormed his way back into the case by accompanying Vannatter, Tom Lange, and Ronald Phillips to the Simpson house, climbing the fence, and finding the glove.

The prosecution could still opt not to call him as a witness (just as the defense eventually opted not to call Rosa Lopez and Mary Ann Gerchas). It would not be entirely risk-free for the prosecution to work around Fuhrman. Had he not been called, the defense would have objected to the introduction of the glove on the ground that the "chain of custody" had been broken. But since it was not Fuhrman who actually removed the glove from the place where it was allegedly found, the prosecution probably would have been able to have its cake and eat it too by introducing the incriminating glove without calling the dangerous witness. The defense would have asked the jury to consider why this witness had not been called, but this kind of "missing witness" argument is rarely compelling.

Whenever I am on a defense team, I try to put myself in the place of the prosecution and think about how I would decide a particular issue. In doing that with regard to Fuhrman, I came away with the clear sense that I would not call him, for reasons both ethical and tactical. Ethically, a lawyer cannot properly call a witness who he or she knows is going to lie. Marcia Clark had to know that Fuhrman was going to lie about not having used the "N" word. She had read his psychological reports, in which he explicitly used the word, had been told about his racism by another assistant district attorney, and was aware that several credible witnesses, with no axes to grind, were prepared to swear they had heard Fuhrman use the word repeatedly. Moreover, *Newsweek* reported that a highly reliable source told them that prosecutors knew Fuhrman lied when he denied using the "N" word.[28]

Even setting aside the ethical considerations, a lawyer should not call a witness who is capable of endangering the entire case and whose testimony is not absolutely essential. Clark did decide not to call Dr. Golden, the pathologist who performed the autopsies, because she believed his testimony would be too vulnerable to cross-examination. He, like Fuhrman, had testified at the preliminary hearing, but unlike Fuhrman he was devastated on cross-examination. Following the preliminary hearing, new information had surfaced about Fuhrman's racism, and I was certain that Clark was smart enough to bite the bullet and not call her expected "star" witness in front of this jury. I was wrong. She made a mistake. She thought she could get away with calling Fuhrman, because prosecutors nearly always get away with calling cops who lie. Juries — especially white juries — tend to believe well-spoken, all-American police officers, even when they are lying. Black juries tend to be a bit more suspicious.

In this case, the white media also seemed to fall for Fuhrman's Boy Scout testimony. *The Boston Globe* reported that "Fuhrman not only withstood Bailey's onslaught, but turned out to be the prosecution's best witness to date."[29] *Time* magazine reported that the defense was "thrown off balance when Fuhrman steadfastly withstood a grueling interrogation."[30] *The Washington Post* assured its readers that Fuhrman had made Bailey's cross-examination look like "a desperate and flimsy patchwork."[31] And the *Los Angeles Times* characterized Fuhrman as having "walked away with few apparent bruises."[32] Most of the black jurors, on the other hand, simply did not believe Fuhrman, even before the McKinny tapes proved they were right.

It is impossible to know for certain whether Marcia Clark would have gotten away with using Fuhrman if the tapes had not surfaced. I remember vividly the call I received from writer Peter Manso telling me that he knew where I could get hold of tapes made by Fuhrman that proved he had lied about not having used racial epithets. I immediately called Johnnie Cochran's office to alert them to this lead, and they told me they were hearing a similar rumor. Eventually, we tracked down Laura McKinny, and the rest is history. Had the tapes not surfaced, we still would have called the live witnesses who testified that they had heard Fuhrman use racial epithets. But Clark would have tried to destroy the credibility and reputations of these good Samaritans, who she had to know were telling the truth. The significance of the tapes lay not so much in the two snippets Judge Ito allowed the jury to hear, as in their very existence, which made it impossible for Clark to challenge the credibility of the live witnesses: Had she done so, Judge Ito would have had to allow more of the tapes to be heard as *corroboration* of the live testimony. At the time Clark decided to call Fuhrman as her witness, she had no idea there were any tapes, and she probably expected the jury to believe the well-spoken cop over the nervous good Samaritan witnesses.

Moreover, cops who lie and prosecutors who tolerate such lies are rarely punished. Judges who pretend to believe lying cops are, of course, never punished. That is why the problem of police perjury persists, and that is almost certainly why Marcia Clark made the decision to risk calling Detective Fuhrman as a witness. Scott Turow believes, and others agree, that this decision contributed significantly to the prosecution's defeat.[33]

The verdict in the Simpson case is a wake-up call about police perjury. As Professor Kathleen Sullivan of Stanford Law School warned, if *judges* do not begin to take police perjury seriously, *jurors* may begin to take the issue into their own hands.[34] That is what Johnnie Cochran urged the Simpson jury to do, and what many Americans believed they did.

Professor Peter Arenella of the University of California–Los Angeles Law School disagreed:

> Johnnie Cochran did make an argument about jury nullification. He suggested that the conviction of O.J. Simpson would endorse Mark Fuhrman's racism, but I think it's absolutely wrong to suggest that in a murder case these jurors would be willing to send such a message, to use this trial as a forum to decry racism.

. . . I watched this trial every day, and there were detectives that lied to this jury. And the jury had to interpret those lies. And unfortunately for the jury, they didn't know how to interpret some of those lies. Vannatter told the jury, "I never considered O.J. Simpson a suspect." Well, of course, the jury understood that Vannatter considered Simpson a suspect. But what the jury didn't know was Vannatter had to do a lie like that at a suppression hearing to get over a Fourth Amendment problem about a warrantless entry. Since they didn't understand the reason for the lie, they read into it greater significance than was really there.[35]

Both of these commentators, and numerous others, agreed on the ultimate issue: that there was police perjury in the Simpson case, that it could have been avoided, and that it seriously hurt the prosecution's case.

Will the Simpson acquittal finally do what half a dozen commissions, dozens of scholarly studies, and a quarter of a century of complaining from me and other civil libertarians have failed to do? Will it finally persuade law enforcement officials — from the attorney general of the United States down to the cop on the beat — that police perjury is not only dangerous to civil liberties, but it is *bad for law enforcement?*

As the district attorney of the New York City borough of Queens, Richard A. Brown, recently put it: "What's important to recognize is the fact that when police officers are perceived to lie, that perception gets into the jury room. You've got to impress upon police officers that they are going to lose cases if the perception exists that they are bending the truth."[36] Although Brown was reacting to New York City Police Commissioner Bratton's acknowledgment of widespread testilying, he could have been talking about the Simpson case — and he could have been lecturing Marcia Clark about how she may well have lost the case by allowing her police witnesses to commit perjury.

Most police perjury is committed by decent cops who honestly believe that a guilty defendant will go free unless they fib about how they gathered the incriminating evidence. In order for the public and policy-makers to realize how police perjury — generally committed in order

112

to save a case — can sometimes backfire and destroy that case, it is important to see how the jury in the Simpson case reacted to the testimony of Detectives Vannatter and Fuhrman.

IV

Were the Jury's Doubts in the Simpson Case Reasonable or Unreasonable?

Most Americans — certainly most white Americans — believe that O.J. Simpson killed Nicole Brown and Ronald Goldman. They also believe that no reasonable jury could have found otherwise. According to a *Washington Post* poll conducted within days after the verdict, 70 percent of white Americans thought Simpson was guilty, and 63 percent thought the jury was biased in his favor.[1] Of the nation as a whole, 60 percent thought Simpson was guilty, 56 percent "disagree[d]" with the verdict, and 51 percent thought that the jury was biased in favor of Simpson. Many Americans view the jury's verdict of acquittal, therefore, as "racist," "wrong," "obscene," "irrational," and "stupid." But in order to convict, the jurors in the Simpson case had to be convinced of his guilt "beyond a reasonable doubt." Perhaps, then, they had decided that this exacting legal standard had not been met and that it was not their job to solve a whodunit but rather to apply the legal standard about which Judge Ito had instructed them. The question still remains: Were the jurors' doubts in this case "reasonable," as that word is defined by the law?

Under what circumstances is a doubt "reasonable"? The U.S. Supreme Court, in an act of abject intellectual cowardice, has declared that the term "reasonable doubt" is self-explanatory and, essentially, incapable of further definition. "Attempts to explain the term 'reasonable doubt' do not usually result in making it any clearer to the minds of the jury,"[2] the Court has declared, which brings to mind Talleyrand's quip that "if we go on explaining, we shall cease to understand one another." Judge Jon Newman of the U.S. Court of Appeals for the Second Circuit recently criticized this approach as follows: "I find it rather unsettling that we are using a formulation that we believe will become less clear the more we explain it."[3] Such a lazy attitude toward the central concept underlying the constitutional presumption of innocence is a bit like the late Justice Potter Stewart's approach to the interpretation of hardcore pornography: I can't define it, but "I know it when I see it."[4]

The problem with "reasonable doubt," however, is that juries do not necessarily know it when they see it because legislatures and the courts have been utterly unwilling to tell them what it is, beyond a few unhelpful clichés. Courts are quite willing to tell juries what reasonable doubt is *not*. A standard instruction reads as follows:

> Proof beyond a reasonable doubt does *not* mean that the state must prove this case beyond all doubt. . . . *Nor* [must the state] prove the essential elements in this case beyond the shadow of a doubt; it does *not* mean that at all. . . . [N]o defendant is ever entitled to the benefit of *any* or *all* doubt [italics added]. . . . The oath that you took requires you to return a verdict of guilty if you are convinced beyond a reasonable doubt. And, members of the jury, equally, your oath requires you to return a verdict of not guilty if you are not convinced beyond a reasonable doubt.[5]

Courts further insist that "reasonable

116

doubt is *not* a speculative doubt, a feeling in your bones. [I]t is *more than* a doubt based on guesswork or possibilities [italics added]."

Some courts that do define reasonable doubt do so in a way that virtually shifts the burden of proof to the defendant. These courts tell the jury that the doubt must be "based on reason," thus excluding a deep *feeling* of uncertainty, or a generalized unease or skepticism about the prosecutor's case. Other courts instruct the jury that the case must be proved with "the kind of certainty that you act on in making your most important personal decisions." This instruction fails to tell the jurors that they are supposed to err on the side of freeing the guilty rather than convicting the innocent. In personal decisions there is no comparable rule. A rational decision-maker goes with the preponderance of the evidence in most instances.

Judge Newman, who surveyed the social science literature on the traditional reasonable-doubt instruction, came to the following disturbing conclusion: "These studies suggest that the traditional charge might be producing some unwarranted convictions. At the very least, the conclusion one draws from such studies is that the current charge in use is ambiguous and open to widely disparate interpretations by jurors." He proposed a simple definition of "beyond a reasonable doubt" as "proof that leaves you firmly convinced of the defendant's guilt."[6]

It is because the typical instructions given by judges on reasonable doubt are so pro-prosecution that many defense attorneys, citing the Supreme Court's dictum, ask that the term not be defined. They prefer to leave its meaning to the common understanding of jurors and to the analogies they can come up with during closing argument. One common example used by lawyers to illustrate that reasonable doubt can come from the gut as well as the mind involves a hunter who sees a distant object that looks like a deer. He takes aim, but then he experiences a sudden uneasiness in the pit of his stomach. He doesn't know why, but he hesitates. Something tells him not to pull the trigger. As he is deciding what to do, the distant object moves and the hunter sees that it is a little girl.

In the Simpson case, Judge Ito did define reasonable doubt in the following way:

It is not a mere possible doubt because everything relating to human affairs is open to some possible or imaginary doubt. It is that state of the case, which after the entire comparison and consideration of all the evidence, leaves the minds of the jurors in that condition that they cannot say they feel an abiding conviction about the truth of the charge.[7]

Were the jurors' doubts in the Simpson case "reasonable" or "unreasonable" under this instruction? We can never know with certainty, of course, because we do not have access to the mental processes of each of the jurors. But consider the following line of reasoning that could have been — and, according to several juror interviews, probably was — employed by jurors in this case.

Begin with Detective Philip Vannatter, an experienced and well-respected homicide detective who was in charge of the investigation. Vannatter arrived at the crime scene at 4:30 A.M. Shortly thereafter, he was told that back in 1985 Detective Mark Fuhrman had been dispatched to the house of O.J. Simpson, the former husband of one of the victims, after the victim had called the police. Four detectives — Vannatter, Fuhrman, Lange, and Phillips — then drove over to the Simpson estate at approximately 5:10 A.M. After failing to rouse anyone by telephone, and after Fuhrman saw blood on the door of the white Bronco parked outside the gate, Vannatter authorized Fuhrman to climb the wall and open the gate.

Thus, one of the first legal issues in the case is the constitutionality of this warrantless entry onto the property of O.J. Simpson. Detective Vannatter swore under oath that when he went to the Rockingham estate, he did not believe Simpson was a suspect. Fuhrman, Phillips, and Lange swore, as well, that the purpose of going to the Rockingham estate was to notify Simpson of the death of his former wife and to make arrangements for the disposition of the children. Finally, their supervisor corroborated the testimony of the four detectives, himself swearing that he had ordered the detectives to go to the Rockingham estate simply to "notify" Simpson.

The jurors did not believe that testimony. Nor did most of the commentators. It was difficult to credit testimony by an experienced homicide detective that he did not suspect the former husband of a brutally murdered woman, even after learning that the former husband had previously been investigated for domestic violence.

Juror Brenda Moran, a forty-five-year-old African-American, "disclosed that the jury came to doubt Detective Philip Vannatter, the man in charge of the investigation." She said that the jury believed that Vannatter lied on the stand when he said that detectives did not consider Simpson a suspect when they went to his home in the hours immediately after the murders.[8] This view was confirmed by Anise Aschenbach, a sixty-one-year-old white juror, who believed that Vannatter "made some misstatements. I don't think he was playing it square."[9]

Not only did the jurors believe they had been lied to by Detective Vannatter, they also believed that they had been the victims of a police conspiracy and cover-up — perhaps not a conspiracy to plant any evidence, but surely a conspiracy to lie about why the four detectives went to Simpson's house and why Detective Fuhrman was authorized to scale the wall and open the gate. After all, five police officers had sworn to the same story — a story the jury simply did not believe. As juror Yolanda Crawford put it: "Not a conspiracy with all the police officers, but maybe with some." When asked whether "a lot of people" would have to have been involved, she replied, "I don't think so," just Fuhrman and a few others.[10] Juror Lionel Cryer expressed a similar view that a small number of police — "maybe one or two" — could have been part of a conspiracy.[11]

The jury thus started out with the realization — new, perhaps, to some; not so new to others — that these policemen were prepared to lie to them and to cover for each other, at least as to certain aspects of the case.

It was against this background of distrust that the jury learned that the same Detective Vannatter, who they believed had lied to them about his reasons for going to Rockingham, had carried Simpson's blood sample around with him for almost three hours, instead of checking it in at the Parker Center or at the nearby Piper Tech, where they were to be stored and analyzed. Standing alone, this bizarre action might not have aroused suspicion, but against the background of his perjury and other factors, it took on increased significance. Juror Brenda Moran told the press that the jury found Vannatter's decision to carry Simpson's blood sample around with him for several hours "suspicious because it gave him the opportunity to plant evidence": "He's walking around with blood in his pocket for a couple of hours. How come he didn't book it at Parker Center or Piper Tech? He had a perfect opportunity. Why walk around with it? He was my biggest doubt. . . . There was an opportunity to sprinkle it here or there."[12]

A journalist summarized his interview with one of the jurors as follows:

In other words, the jury didn't believe four detectives were needed there just to deliver bad news, and once they didn't believe that, jurors say they began suspecting police might have been up to something no good, especially because Detective Vannatter carried Simpson's blood samples around the Simpson mansion.[13]

This combination of factors caused the jurors to look skeptically at other testimony about the Simpson blood sample. For example, Thano Peratis, the nurse who extracted the blood sample from Simpson on June 13, 1994, swore to the grand jury and at preliminary hearings that he had taken 7.9 to 8.1 cc's of blood from Simpson's arm. He was quite precise. Upon being questioned in the preliminary hearings about how much blood he had taken from Simpson, Peratis answered, "Approximately 8 cc's. . . . Well, it could have been 7.9 or it could have been 8.1. I just looked at the syringe and looked and it was about 8 cc's." At the time he gave this sworn testimony, Peratis did not know that it would undercut the prosecution's case, since only 6.5 cc's of Simpson's blood could eventually be accounted for by the prosecution. Much would later be made by the defense of the "missing" 1.5 cc's of the defendant's blood. Nor did Peratis know that three weeks *after* the blood sample was taken, the police would claim to find trace amounts of Simpson's blood on two items on which no blood had been found during the initial investigation, immediately after the murders. These amounts were consistent with the unaccounted-for 1.5 cc's having been sprinkled on the items. The two items were the socks found on the floor of Simpson's bedroom the morning after the murders, and the back gate at Nicole Brown's condominium.

The socks were the more suspicious of these two items. Nicole Brown's blood was also found on the socks, and the defense claimed that it, too, might have been added later. These socks were visually inspected both by prosecution and defense experts, neither of whom saw any blood. Indeed, the official police inventory report said, with regard to the presence or absence of blood on the socks: "none obvious."[14] It was possible that the blood was simply not noticed, but it was also possible that originally no blood was on the socks.

In order to help resolve this mystery, the prosecution announced that it was sending the socks to the FBI lab in Washington in order to have the blood tested for the presence or absence of a preservative called EDTA, which is not present in blood taken from the human body, but is present in blood which has been preserved in a test tube. Thus, the absence of EDTA would conclusively prove that the blood on the socks came directly from Simpson and Brown and not, as the defense was suggesting, from a test tube. The prosecution predicted that "there will be no question that when these tests prove that *there's no EDTA* [in the bloodstains], there will be no question, no one will have a lingering doubt."[15] The prosecution made it clear that an EDTA test produces an either-or result, with no in-betweens or gray areas. "There's only two possible outcomes to this test. There's either going to be EDTA there or there's not going to be EDTA there. And we're willing to accept the outcome, whatever that is. . . . We agree to accept these results in advance."[16]

To the shock of prosecutors, the FBI tests demonstrated the presence of EDTA in the blood found on the socks. They also found no EDTA in the area surrounding the blood on the socks, a result excluding the possibility that laundry detergent used to wash the socks could have explained the presence of the EDTA.[17] That should have ended the matter, according to the prosecution's advance agreement. The presence of EDTA in the blood should have led the prosecution "to accept the outcome," as it said it would, and agree that this blood had to come from preserved reference samples, rather than directly from a human being's bloodstream. But the prosecution withdrew its agreement and changed its tack. An FBI expert, Roger Martz, acknowledged the presence of EDTA, but testified that the amount was consistent with having come directly from a human body.[18] The defense expert categorically disputed that opinion, testifying that any human being whose blood contained that much EDTA — which is an anticoagulant — would "bleed to death."[19]

Again, it is possible that despite this testimony, the blood did come directly from a human body, but it is also possible that the blood came from a test tube of blood preserved with EDTA.

The next suspicious factor was the blood-splatter pattern on the socks themselves. I had always had a keen interest in the socks, since I myself saw them at the police lab just days after the murders. So did Dr. Michael Baden. I am no expert, but he is one of the world's leading forensic patholo-gists, and he did not notice any blood on the socks. Nor did several prosecution experts. Accordingly, I had been suspicious of the socks ever since I first heard that the police had discovered Simpson's blood on them several weeks later.

As soon as I heard of the discovery, I took a pair of white socks from my drawer and insisted that my family watch an experiment. I put one sock on my foot and laid the other flat on a table. I then sprinkled red wine on each sock. I left the one

I was wearing on my foot for ten minutes; then I took it off and laid it on the table next to the other one. On both socks, the sprinkle patterns on the sides on which the wine was sprinkled were relatively similar. But the patterns on the socks' *other* inner side were dramatically different. The sock that I had worn had hardly any wine stain on thc other side, because the wine had mostly dried by the time I removed the sock and the two sides came into contact for the first time. The sock that I sprinkled while it lay on the table had a discernible mirror-image stain on the unsprinkled side, since the wine had seeped through and come in direct contact with the other side. (I must have ruined a dozen pairs of socks showing this to friends, as did other members of the defense team.)

My amateurish experiment was replicated, under laboratory conditions, by one of the world's leading authorities on blood splatter, Dr. Herbert MacDonnell. Although Judge Ito did not allow Dr. Mac-Donnell to report directly on his experiment, he did allow him to answer this question:

Based on your observations of the sock

and based upon your 40 years of experience in this field, sir, are the wet transfer stains you observed on the ankle area of sock 13-A consistent with someone dabbing the sock with blood when it is not being worn by Mr. Simpson and instead spread out and laid flat on a flat surface?

MacDonnell answered the question affirmatively.[20] Again, it was possible that he was wrong and that the blood had been splattered on the socks while they were worn by Simpson. But the prosecution's theory of how the blood got on the socks was beginning to weaken as the result of a series of factors that may have been either coincidental or suspicious.

The suspicious scenario was enhanced by several other items of evidence, or the absence thereof. The socks bore none of the fibers, hairs, dirt, berry juice, or other material that abounded at the crime scene. If the socks had been splattered with blood at the crime scene, why had they not also come in contact with other material in that area? As Dr. Henry Lee, the chief criminologist for the state of Connecticut and one of the world's most renowned forensic authorities, testified in his unique way: "If the shoes have contact the berry, contact the soil or fiber debris, in theory, we should see the transfer."[21]

Even more significantly, the inventory videotape taken by the Los Angeles Police Department to protect itself from claims that anything could have been stolen from the Simpson house showed no socks on the white rug where the police claimed they later found them. Willie Ford, who took the police video of the Rockingham estate, testified that he never saw any socks in the bedroom. Again, there was a possible explanation for this discrepancy — perhaps the chronology was wrong — but it was at least equally consistent with suspicion.

Juror Anise Aschenbach told the media that she was "troubled by the socks that showed up in Simpson's room — first socks that were not there and were not bloody, but then the same socks suddenly appeared with blood on three sides."[22]

The matter of the gate at Nicole Brown's condominium, although not as suspicious as the socks, raised similar questions. No blood was inventoried on the gate during the original search. Simpson's blood was found on it approximately three weeks later. Here, too, there was EDTA in the blood, and not on the control area adjoining it. And it had high concentrations of DNA — higher than those in the blood found immediately after the crimes. This was suspicious — according to the experts — because if the blood had been exposed to the elements for several days, it would have been degraded by the weather, especially sunlight and moisture. Juror Aschenbach specifically mentioned the blood "on the back gate," as did jurors Crawford and Cryer; Mr. Cryer said he thought the "possibility strongly existed" that the blood might have been "planted."[23]

Had the five detectives been more candid with the jury about the original search, it is certainly possible that the jurors might have discounted all these suspicions as coincidental. After all, in life — unlike in literature   innocent coincidences do occur. But this was a prosecution based on inferences from evidence that the prosecutors argued could not be explained as coincidental. The jury was thus thinking about the power of circumstantial inferences and the likelihood of a series of coincidences.[24]

Finally, there was the unsworn videotaped interview with the nurse who extracted the blood from Simpson. Recall that nurse Peratis originally testified under oath that he removed 8 cc's of Simpson's blood, which Detective Vannatter then carried around with him, and of which only 6.5 cc's could be accounted for by the prosecution. Peratis's sworn testimony about the 8 cc's thus became a linchpin of the defense case. Near the very close of the prosecution's rebuttal case, the prosecutor got the trial judge to issue a highly questionable ruling allowing the introduction of an unsworn and un-cross-examined videotaped "discussion" between a prosecutor named Hank Goldberg and Thano Peratis, in which Peratis conveniently remembered that he actually took only 6.5 cc's of Simpson's blood, rather than the eight cc's he originally swore he took.

It was doubtful that the jurors believed this bit of revisionist history. Indeed, taken together with the police perjury about the search and seizure, it may have led them to view the series of "coincidences" involving the blood, the socks, and the gate with even greater suspicion.

If the jurors experienced some doubt about how the late-discovered blood got on the socks and the gate, was this doubt necessarily "unreasonable," "emotional," "racial," or in any other way improper? We will, of course, never know how each of the jurors actually analyzed this important issue. But I do not believe the case can be made that doubts about the prosecution's theory that the blood was left on the socks and gate by Simpson during the crime were necessarily unreasonable ones. I believe that many reasonable jurors, of all races and backgrounds, would have experienced doubts about this blood evidence, provided their minds were also open to the possibility that police do sometimes tamper with or enhance evidence, especially when they believe the defendant to be guilty.

We do not know whether these jurors were aware of the evidence-tampering scandals in New York, Philadelphia, and other places. We do not know whether any of them might have learned from "pillow talk" that Detective Fuhrman had bragged about tampering with, and even making up, evidence against African-Americans. We do not know whether any of the jurors might themselves have experienced, or knew others who had experienced, police misconduct. But the jurors had good reason to believe, after all, that there was a police conspiracy to tell a cover story about the search and seizure in this very case, a conspiracy that might have involved at least five officers, one a high-ranking lieutenant. Even fewer police would have been needed to sprinkle some blood on the socks and gate. That does not mean a juror should necessarily have concluded that the police definitely put the blood there. It would mean he or she could not be absolutely certain they did not. As Dr. Henry Lee put it in a related context: "Something wrong." Several of the jurors pointed to this testimony as persuasive.

However, such a reasonable doubt about two items of evidence would not necessarily lead to a reasonable doubt about Simpson's guilt. After all, if there were no doubt that the remaining evidence had been untampered with, and that this remaining evidence, *taken alone,* would prove the defendant's guilt beyond a reasonable doubt, should not a reasonable jury still convict? That is one of the most interesting questions raised by the above scenario. And there are several possible answers.

One possible approach the jury might

have taken was to compartmentalize the evidence in order to be able to consider entirely separately the evidence that it believed might have been corrupted, and the evidence that it did not believe was corrupted. That is what the prosecution asked it to do with respect to the testimony of Detective Fuhrman — namely, to believe that he lied about using the "N" word, but told the truth in the rest of his testimony, especially the part corroborated by others. One problem with this formulation, however, is that the corroboration for much of Fuhrman's testimony came from the very police officers whose testimony about search and seizure was, the jury believed, a cover story. The other problem was that the prosecution could not easily compartmentalize the evidence so neatly. Once the jurors were ready to question the blood on the socks and the gate, they were naturally more suspicious of the other evidence.

Consider, for example, the glove found behind Simpson's house. That important piece of evidence — unlike the socks and gate — was seen to have blood on it from the moment it was allegedly found by Fuhrman on the morning of the murders. Yet it, too, raised suspicions on the part of several jurors.

This highly incriminating glove was suspicious for several reasons. First, it was found in an unlikely place, which prosecutors could never explain satisfactorily. At first they argued that it was accidentally dropped by Simpson as he climbed over the wire fence from a neighbor's adjoining yard. When an analysis of the surrounding vegetation showed that to have been impossible, the prosecutors changed their theory. Now they claimed that Simpson had deliberately thrown the glove behind his house in order to hide it. But when they realized how preposterous it was to argue that a killer who had successfully hidden the murder weapon and his bloody clothes would deliberately throw the single most incriminating item of evidence, and the easiest to dispose of, in the first location any good detective would (and did) look, they abandoned that theory as well. Finally, they asked the jury to believe a variation of this "dumb defendant" theory: namely, that Simpson went behind his house to bury all the incriminating evidence — the knife, the clothes, and the glove — in his own backyard, but that he banged his head on the air conditioner, which caused him to drop only the glove and change his mind about the rest of the evidence.[25]*

None of this made much sense. That does not mean, of course, that it didn't happen. People do dumb things. But in combination with other suspicious circumstances, it gave rise to doubts about whether the glove was found by Fuhrman or planted by him. These other circumstances included the absence of any blood around the glove, the absence of any bruise on Simpson consistent with his having hit his head against the air conditioner, and the fact that the glove was still damp from blood when the glove was found.

This last circumstance was especially difficult to explain since there was no rain, dew, or moisture on the night in question. Had the glove been dampened by blood at about 10:30 P.M. and dropped behind Simpson's house at 10:45 P.M., it would have been bone dry by about 6:15 A.M., when Fuhrman claimed he found it, since blood dries quickly in the night air. But the glove would still have been damp if the following had occurred: Fuhrman, after

---

*Yet another variation was that Simpson dropped the glove while trying to enter a side door. But the position of the glove undercuts that theory.

being told by Lieutenant John Rogers at 2:30 A.M. that he was no longer on the case, walked alone outside the crime scene, furious that he had been taken off the only big case of his career. Alone and outside the crime scene, he found the second glove, which had been dropped by the escaping killer. Deciding that this glove was the key to keeping himself on the case, he pocketed it (or placed it in his sock or in a case) and figured out a way to get to Simpson's house, offering to drive the other police officers there.

Once at the Simpson house, he again wandered off by himself, saw the white Bronco, got inside and identified it as Simpson's, either on purpose or accidentally smeared some blood from the glove (or from his shoes) on the inside of the Bronco, and then returned to the other officers, reporting that he had found blood on Simpson's Bronco.* He then climbed the wall, let the others in, and talked to Kato Kaelin, who told him that he had

---

*While Fuhrman testified that the Bronco was parked "a little askew," "a little unusual for that type of parking," police photographs later showed that there was nothing unusual about the way it was parked. This led to the suspicion that Fuhrman might have entered the Bronco and moved it.

heard three bangs near the air conditioner. Fuhrman then went behind the house — again alone — and planted the glove. The glove was still damp because it had not been exposed to the night air.

Again, I did my own amateurish experiment to test this hypothesis, using gloves, red wine, and a plastic sandwich bag. It demonstrated the scenario's plausibility. Accordingly, we commissioned an experiment to test it scientifically. The scientist took two identical gloves and sprinkled precisely the same amount of blood on each as was found on the glove Fuhrman discovered. One glove was then placed outdoors for several hours under conditions replicating the conditions on the night of June 12, 1994. The other was placed in a bag for most of that time. The first glove was bone dry. The second was damp. Just as my sock experiment did not prove tampering, this does not prove conclusively that the glove was planted. But taken together with the other suspicious circumstances, and with the glove's finding by a man the jurors knew had lied to them about at least two other matters, the fact that the glove was damp may have led several of them to doubt that Fuhrman was telling them the truth about finding the glove.

Judge Ito invited the jurors to disbelieve *all* of Fuhrman's testimony when he instructed them that "a witness who is willfully false in one material part of his testimony *is to be distrusted* in others. You may reject *the whole testimony* of a witness who has willfully testified falsely as to a material point unless from all the evidence you believe the probability of truth favors his . . . testimony in other particulars [italics added]."[26]

Remember, Fuhrman's testimony about finding the glove was uncorroborated. It depended entirely on believing Fuhrman alone. Juror Aschenbach was asked: "If another police officer had discovered the glove, someone without Mark Fuhrman's background, would that have made a difference to you?" She responded in the affirmative, stating that Fuhrman "was a big issue for me."[27] She explained: "Well, seeing the type of character [I] thought it was so possible that he would plant the glove." That possibility also led Aschenbach to wonder about the blood in the Bronco: "That same evidence [may] have gotten into the Bronco — he was there, too, that — that whole portion of it, you know, I couldn't depend on it, so I had to discard it."*

The prosecution relied heavily on the unlikelihood that Fuhrman would have planted the glove without even knowing that Simpson was a realistic suspect. Perhaps Simpson had an airtight alibi; if so, Fuhrman would have been caught in his frame-up. But this argument was particularly unconvincing. Fuhrman was, after all, caught on tape making the most self-destructive (and case-destructive) statements imaginable. Moreover, Fuhrman's hatred for blacks married to whites was anything but rational. Back in 1985, when he was called to the Simpson house by Nicole Brown, he may have been furious that he could not arrest Simpson, because it is not a crime to smash the windows of one's own car. As soon as he learned who

*Besides arguing that the glove may have been planted, the defense noted several irregularities in this evidence. First, surprisingly little of a black man's limb hair was found on it, considering that Simpson was supposed to have owned and worn it for four years. Second, the glove was handled by Collin Yamauchi in the lab immediately after some blood spurted from Simpson's reference blood tube, and it is possible that Yamauchi did not even change gloves after the mishap. The very low DNA presence in the blood on the glove was consistent with this type of lab mishap transfer, as was the location of the blood.

the female victim was in the 1994 murders, Fuhrman may have been convinced that Simpson had killed his former wife — and that this time that "N" was not going to get away with it.

Moreover, Fuhrman did not actually "find" the glove until *after* he spoke to Kato Kaelin, from whom he may have learned the basic facts as to Simpson's whereabouts. The fact that Fuhrman testified that he did not know Simpson's whereabouts at the time should obviously have been viewed with great skepticism. Then there were the three bangs. Everything was fitting neatly into place. It may have sounded perfect to a man who had previously planted evidence against "N"s and gotten away with it. So Fuhrman went alone to the spot where the bangs were heard; he dropped the glove and called his fellow officers. He would not have trusted them to cover up the planting of evidence, since two of them were not cops he had worked with before. Probably, though, virtually any Los Angeles cop could have been trusted with a cover story for a search and seizure.

Did this actually happen? No one will ever know for certain. Is there evidence that the glove could have been planted and that Fuhrman had the opportunity and motive to plant it? Absolutely: the dampness of the glove; the absence of blood near the glove; the fact that the glove didn't fit Simpson; the presence of an unidentified Caucasian hair on the glove;* the fact that Fuhrman was alone both outside the crime scene and when he "found" the glove; the failure of the prosecution to articulate a plausible theory about how Simpson could have dropped the glove; the perjury of Fuhrman on other matters; and his virulent racism and boasts that he would frame black men involved with white women.

A juror who believed that five policemen conspired to lie about the search in this case and who believed that police might have planted the blood on the socks and gate could well have a reasonable doubt about whether Fuhrman told the truth when he said he found the glove behind Simpson's house.

This seems to be precisely how juror Anise Aschenbach — the white juror who initially voted against Simpson and still believes he may have committed the murders — seems to have analyzed the evidence.

*The hair did not match Fuhrman's.

143

After becoming convinced that Vannatter was not "playing it square" and that Fuhrman could not be believed, Aschenbach concluded: "I didn't feel good about the evidence. There was so — so much doubt was thrown into it, you know, with the possibility of Fuhrman, you know, possibly planting the glove, you know; plus that same evidence maybe getting into the Bronco. You know, that disturbed me a lot. The way it was collected disturbed me a lot. I think the defense did a lot to, you know, make me doubt the credibility of [the prosecution's] best evidence, which was blood and trace evidence." Although she was not certain that evidence was planted, Aschenbach said: "If we made a mistake, I would rather it be a mistake on the side of a person's innocence than the other way."[28] This was the juror we referred to as "Henrietta Fonda," because she had previously turned a jury around from an eleven-to-one vote for acquittal to a twelve-to-zero vote for conviction.

Another juror, Sheila Woods, also focused on the glove. On the *Today Show*, Katie Couric asked her:

What was the most questionable piece of evidence, in your view?

MS. WOODS: The Rockingham glove. The way it was found by Detective Fuhrman on a small, narrow walkway behind Kato Kaelin's bedroom. That walkway was lined with leaves; however, the glove was wet and sticky when found, and there was no evidence of blood in any area surrounding that area. There was testimony that — from Professor MacDonnell, who conducted his own experiment regarding drying times of the glove with his own blood samples, and it was shown that the glove should have dried within three to four hours. However, the glove was still wet and sticky when it was found.

COURIC: In fact, the-the-the wet and sticky — or the — I think they said moist and sticky . . .

MS. WOODS: Yes.

COURIC: . . . glove, those were two very important words in the minds of the jurors, weren't they?

MS. WOODS: They — it was.

. . . .

COURIC: . . . But do you think he had an opportunity or the opportunity to plant that glove?

MS. WOODS: It is a possibility. He was

145

one of four detectives that went over to Rockingham to inform Mr. Simpson of the death of his ex-wife. The other three detectives were in the residence talking with Arnelle Simpson and Kato Kaelin while Detective Fuhrman was nowhere to be found.

. . . .

COURIC: . . . but proved that Mark Fuhrman did in fact plant this glove?
MS. WOODS: No, there was no proof.
COURIC: You just thought it was within the realm of possibility?
MS. WOODS: Yes.[29]

Let us now assume that a given juror believed, or had a reasonable doubt, that the police may have planted the blood on the socks, the blood on the gate, and/or the blood on the glove. Let us assume that the jurors believed that Detectives Vannatter, Fuhrman, Lange, and Phillips lied about why they went to Simpson's house and entered his property without a warrant. Surely, even all this does not necessarily prove that Simpson was innocent of the murders. It is certainly possible that the police could have tried to frame a guilty defendant. Indeed, police who do tamper with evidence probably do so more often when they believe the defendant to be guilty than when they believe him to be innocent. Of course, the fact that police believe that a defendant is guilty does not necessarily mean he *is* guilty.

There are several possible ways a jury could deal with the remaining evidence after concluding (or having a reasonable doubt) that some of it was corrupted. First, the jury could simply act as if the corrupted evidence had never been introduced. Many commentators stated that this is precisely what any reasonable juror should do. They argue that the remaining evidence, standing alone, proved Simpson's guilt beyond a reasonable doubt, and they point to incriminating evidence found at the crime scene, including Simpson's blood, a hat bearing hair consistent with Simpson's, shoe prints the same size as Simpson's, and a left glove that resembled one Simpson was seen wearing on tapes of a football game. This crime scene evidence — standing alone, without any of the questionable evidence found at the Simpson estate — would establish Simpson's guilt, according to these observers. In addition, there was other evidence, such as Simpson's blood drops at his estate, which could not have been corrupted by the police, as well as the blood found in the Bronco, which included Simpson's, Goldman's, and Brown's. Then there was the time line, which established opportunity. Finally, there was the history of spousal discord, which established motive. The commentators who argue that the uncorrupted evidence should have been independently considered, without taking the arguably corrupted evidence into account, point to the above items standing alone as enough to establish Simpson's guilt.

The fallacy in their reasoning is that this evidence *did not stand alone.* No reasonable juror could totally ignore the fact that *this* evidence was gathered by the same police department that might have tampered with the other evidence, and that it was presented by the same prosecutor's office that might knowingly have presented perjured testimony in support of the search of the Simpson estate. Any reasonable juror who believed that several police officers might have lied to them about *some* of their actions and tampered with *some* evidence could not simply ignore those beliefs in assessing the rest of the evidence. *All* the police evidence and testimony would now come before the jurors bearing a presumption, or at the very least a suspicion, that it had been corrupted. Perhaps the prosecutors could have overcome that presumption or suspicion, but it would not have been easy. After all, policemen who are deemed willing to lie and tamper with respect to some evidence should not be deemed unwilling to lie and tamper with respect to other evidence.

Moreover, some of the prosecution's evidence, even standing alone, did not present all that compelling a circumstantial case. The hair found in the hat was consistent with the hair of a great many black men, and the fibers were inconclusive. The defense argued that hair and fiber are "weak association" evidence — they do not "match" an individual as narrowly as blood evidence. But even if the hair and fibers were Simpson's, it was not surprising. Simpson was a frequent visitor to the Bundy residence; strands of his hair and fibers from his clothing were all over the place. They could have been spread around the crime scene and onto the victims by Nicole Brown's dog, or by blankets from the house that were used to cover the crime scene. Or they could have been mixed together when crime evidence was stored in the same box during the investigation.

Simpson's shoe size is shared by millions of men. The defense noted that this, too, is "weak association" evidence, consistent with any large man. The prosecution never established that Simpson owned or wore the type of shoe that matched the print.

The presence of Simpson's degraded and discolored blood near a residence where he spent a great deal of time playing with kids, dogs, bikes, and so on, would seem consistent with his earlier, innocent presence there. The defense also argued that investigator Dennis Fung had left this blood in a hot car for four hours, "cooking" it and degrading the DNA. When the blood finally got to the lab, Yamauchi handled the swatches at the same time as he did a reference tube of Simpson's blood, not following the proper procedure of changing gloves and washing down between handling separate samples. Thus, the swatches could have been cross-contaminated in the lab, creating a false positive match with Simpson. In addition, the swatches were never sent for the EDTA preservative testing which might have indicated whether they were planted from laboratory samples. A few blood drops near Simpson's own house would hardly be enough to convict, since it is quite natural that traces of someone's own blood should appear around his house as a result of minor cuts and scrapes. Moreover, Simpson told the police — before he knew about the prosecution's evidence — that he had cut his finger while retrieving his cellular phone from the Bronco.

And the glove didn't fit.

The strength of the prosecution's case was that *so many* pieces of evidence — any of which independently would be consistent with innocence — *all* failed *to exclude* Simpson. Quantity thus mattered, along with quality. To the extent that the quantity of the prosecution's evidence was lessened by the quality of the evidence believed corrupted, the prosecution's circumstantial case was weakened considerably. For example, the jury may have discounted the blood found in the Bronco, suspecting that it could have been placed there — deliberately or accidentally — by Fuhrman or another officer who had first stepped in the blood at the crime scene and then entered the Bronco to search or move it. The defense pointed out that there was very little blood in the car, considering that the perpetrator was supposed to have gotten into it immediately after the bloody killings. The defense also claimed that the amount and location of the blood were more consistent with it having been planted by Detective Fuhrman, who had plenty of opportunity when the Bronco was not well secured by police. The blood on the floor was consistent with the victims' blood having gotten on Fuhrman's shoes at the crime scene, moistened by grass wet from sprinkling, and transferred to the floor while Fuhrman sat in the car. The blood on the console was consistent with Fuhrman having wiped a glove there. And the blood on the door could have come from a cut on Simpson's hand, made by a sharp edge on his cellular car phone.

Juror Aschenbach said that without the powerful sock, glove, gate, and Bronco evidence, the other far more "circumstantial" evidence — the hair, the shoe prints, the left glove, and Simpson's own blood at both locations — were more subject to innocent explanations, even if considered together. If a juror were also to discount much of the blood evidence because of the negligence of those who collected and processed it, the circumstantial inference of guilt would weaken even further. But considerable doubt would exist even if jurors concluded that *all* the blood was properly collected and correctly identified with its source through DNA testing or conventional serological testing. If jurors reasonably believed that correctly identified blood might have been corruptly planted (or negligently smeared) on the socks, the glove, the gate, and the Bronco, then this could constitute sufficient doubt to warrant an acquittal.

This was a complex case, not easily categorized as solely circumstantial in nature. It had some of the weaknesses of an "eyewitness" case (the credibility of witnesses) as well as some of the weaknesses of a circumstantial case (the consistency of much of the evidence with both innocence or guilt). To convict, the jury had to reach two separate conclusions: First, it had to decide which of the "circumstantial" evidence was uncorrupted — that is, which of the police who testified about it were telling the truth; second, it had to conclude that the uncorrupted "circumstantial" evidence led to only one reasonable conclusion — namely, the defendant's guilt. To the extent that it believed more of the evidence may have been corrupted, it would be less likely to conclude that the remaining evidence was inconsistent with an innocent explanation. That was the prosecution's burden — and its dilemma.

Nor, apparently, was the jury helped much by the prosecution's evidence of opportunity and motive. The time line, which purported to show that Simpson *could have* committed the murders in the time available, was, at best, ambiguous. The defense made a powerful showing that Simpson could not have committed two brutal and bloody murders, cleaned himself up, and gotten back home in the time between the wails of the dog and the three bangs on the air conditioner. In any event, to the extent that the prosecution was relying on the "testimony" of the two Katos — the dog who wailed and the houseguest who heard the three bangs — it was not operating from strength.

As to the motive, the jurors were apparently not impressed with the prosecution's domestic discord evidence. Men who abuse rarely kill (although men who kill have often abused), and these jurors were not persuaded that a single episode of violence five years earlier — the only such evidence the jury heard — and several other nasty incidents proved that O.J.

Simpson murdered Nicole Brown and Ronald Goldman.

It is likely therefore that the thinking of some of the jurors went something like this:

1. We believe that five policemen lied to us about the search.

2. We suspect that Vannatter may have sprinkled the socks and the back gate with some of the Simpson blood he was carrying around. Although we can't be sure, this does seem possible in light of the discrepancy over the amount of blood originally taken, the absence of blood in the original reports, the absence of the sock in the inventory video, the blood-splatter pattern on the socks, the presence of EDTA, and the high concentrations of DNA only in the late-discovered blood.

3. We cannot believe anything Detective Fuhrman told us, especially if it is not independently corroborated. He lied to us, and he is a racist. Although it may seem unlikely, we must suspect the possibility that Fuhrman planted the glove. He did have the opportunity and the motive. It is suspicious that no blood was found near where Fuhrman said he found the glove. And the glove didn't fit Simpson. We saw that with our own eyes.

4. There is a lot of other evidence pointing to Simpson's guilt over and above the three suspicious items mentioned. But our suspicion about these three items leads us to view the remaining evidence with skepticism. If we believe all the remaining evidence is uncorrupted, that might be enough to convict. But we have some doubts about the blood in the Bronco, and maybe some of the other evidence. And we heard a lot of conflicting expert testimony about the way the blood was collected and analyzed. We believe Dr. Lee when he said, "Something wrong."

5. Taken all together, the case just leaves an uncomfortable feeling. Some of the evidence may have been corrupted; other evidence may have been tainted by negligence; we don't know whom to trust or believe; and the evidence that is undisputed is just too ambiguous.

6. The judge instructed us that if we believe that a witness lied about one issue, we should view the rest of his testimony with suspicion and are even free to reject it all. And the defense asked us to apply that general principle to the prosecution's case as a whole. As Dr. Henry Lee put it, "If I order — goes to a restaurant, order a dish of spaghetti. While eating the spa-

ghetti, I found one cockroaches. I look at it. I found another cockroaches. It's no sense for me to go through the whole plate of spaghetti, say, there are 13.325 cockroaches. If you found one, it's there. It's a matter of whether or not present or absence."[30] In other words, if we believe that *some* of the prosecution's evidence was deliberately corrupted, we should view the rest of its case with suspicion. That sounds reasonable. We really have lost confidence in the police witnesses and in the prosecutors who presented them. And remember that Marcia Clark, in her closing argument, talked about how she became a prosecutor because she wanted to call only witnesses she believed were telling the truth. That was a strange argument coming from the woman who called Fuhrman, Vannatter, and the other police who conducted the search.

7. Therefore, while we are not necessarily convinced that Simpson is innocent, we have a reasonable doubt about his guilt.

Some interviews with the jurors suggest that this may have been how at least a few of them reached their verdict. If, in fact, something like this process of reasoning was employed, can it fairly be said that these jurors acted irrationally, emotionally, racially, or unjustly?

It is, of course, possible that other jurors reached the same verdict by quite different reasoning. Consider the following alternative scenario. Several jurors agree as to Steps 1 (the cops lied about the search, 2 (Vannatter may have sprinkled Simpson's blood on the socks and gate), and perhaps even 3 (Fuhrman may have planted the glove). But they disagree about the rest of the reasoning, believing instead that the remaining evidence does prove Simpson's guilt beyond a reasonable doubt. *In other words, they conclude that the police tried to frame a guilty defendant.* Despite their belief that the defendant is guilty, they refuse to convict, on the ground that it would be wrong to convict any defendant against whom the police deliberately planted evidence. One black juror, Lionel Cryer, has submitted a book proposal in which he says that he was convinced that several policemen lied on the stand and "attempted to frame a murderer." Such a decision would be a form of jury nullification, but *a very different form* than most of the commentators have been discussing. It would not be race-based jury nullification (although it is never possible to enter the minds of the jurors to be certain that race played absolutely no part in the decision). It would be jury nullification of a kind that has legitimate roots deep in our history.

Jury nullification "occurs when a jury — based on its own sense of justice or fairness — refuses to follow the law and convict in a particular case even though the facts seem to allow no other conclusion but guilt." The Honorable Jack B. Weinstein, United States district judge for the Eastern District of New York, has argued:

> The legitimacy of the jury process demands respect for its outcomes, whatever they may be. Attempting to distinguish between a "right" outcome — a verdict following the letter of the law — and a "wrong" one — a "nullification" verdict — can be dangerous, and this endeavor depends largely upon personal bias. Nullification is but one legitimate result in an appropriate constitutional process safeguarded by judges and the judicial system. When juries refuse to convict on the basis of what they think are unjust laws, they are performing their duty as jurors.[31]

Jury nullification has both deep roots and a vibrant history in American jurisprudence. In 1895, the Supreme Court recognized the jury's power to nullify. It ruled that judges could not overrule jury acquittals even if they appeared to have been reached in the face of overwhelming evidence of guilt.[32]

During the nineteenth century, jury nullification emerged in a racial context. Northern juries would use nullification to undermine the effects of fugitive slave laws. Juries were so unwilling to sentence fugitive slaves to death that the overwhelming numbers of acquittals led Congress and state legislatures to reject mandatory death penalty schemes.[33] In the 1960s and 1970s, antiwar activists and black activists like Martin Luther King, Jr., urged jury nullification as a partner to civil disobedience to fight against the Vietnam War and segregation. At the same time as Martin Luther King was urging civil disobedience and nullification to challenge segregation policies, all-white juries in the South used nullification to free murderers of black civil rights workers.[34]

Sometimes juries nullify when they disagree not with the law itself, but with how the law is being enforced. They object to the procedure rather than to the substance of the law. As Judge Weinstein put it: "Some juries want to follow the law but think that the police and society are so biased that they find it difficult to consider law enforcement officers credible."[35] Instead of policing laws, the juries police the law enforcement officials. One contemporary manifestation of jury nullification that is applauded most loudly by some of the same people who are complaining most bitterly about the Simpson verdict occurs in the context of the "battered woman syndrome." Although the law of self-defense is clear — a battered woman may kill or maim her batterer only if her life is in imminent danger and she has no other option, such as leaving or calling 911 — several juries have acquitted battered women who did not meet these stringent criteria. The Lorena Bobbitt case was an unusual example. More typical have been the acquittals of several battered women who have shot their batterers while the men were sleeping.[36]

The form of jury nullification that may have been employed by some jurors in the Simpson case — the refusal to convict a defendant who they believed guilty but who had also been "framed" by the police — draws some support, as well, from judicial authority. This form of nullification is related to the exclusionary rule, the "shock the conscience" test, and the "outrageous governmental misconduct" defense, all of which require the release of guilty defendants in order to send an important message to the police.[37] Appellate courts will sometimes reverse a conviction, despite the presence of otherwise sufficient evidence, if it is later discovered that some of the evidence was planted or perjured testimony.[38]

Recently in Philadelphia, an evidence-planting scandal was uncovered. Several rogue cops had planted drugs on innocent as well as guilty targets. The Philadelphia District Attorney's Office is now reviewing all the cases in which these cops were involved. In a television interview in October 1995, District Attorney Lynn Abraham said that even Jack the Ripper would have to be set free if the police planted evidence against him.[39]

The prosecution accused Johnnie Cochran of seeking precisely this kind of jury nullification when he asked the jury to "stop" the kind of police behavior that had occurred in this case. Judge Ito ruled that

Cochran had stayed just within the bounds of proper argument.[40]

An idea resembling this form of jury nullification may well have been at work in the minds of at least a few jurors. Some — consciously or unconsciously — may have employed a combination of the above scenarios. For example, some jurors may have believed, at a rational level, that the remaining uncorrupted evidence did logically prove Simpson guilty; but they may have had a gnawing feeling of uncertainty or discomfort about voting to convict in a case where they believed there had been police perjury and evidence planting. The same black juror who wrote that police may have tried to "frame a murderer" also said that, although he believed "Simpson was possibly guilty," he simply could "not believe the police who gathered the evidence."

I wonder how many people, if they were serving on a jury in a less emotionally charged case than this one, could bring themselves to vote for a conviction if they believed that the police had deliberately planted false evidence — even if they also believed the defendant was almost certainly guilty. I have asked this question of an assortment of friends, colleagues, students, and relatives of all political persuasions. The answers have been varied, but many people — including some conservatives — have acknowledged that they would have a hard time voting for a conviction if they truly believed that the police had deliberately tampered with evidence, even if they were also convinced the defendant was guilty. A few weeks after the verdict, I asked for a show of hands on this question from a group of six hundred criminologists during a panel discussion on the Simpson case. The vast majority of this largely white, highly educated group said they could not convict a defendant if they believed the police tried to frame him, even if they believed he was also guilty. One of my closest friends, an Orthodox Jew with a rather conservative law-and-order bent, told me that he had served on a jury in a case involving a defendant who was obviously guilty of drug dealing. But the jurors concluded that the police lied to them and acquitted the dealer. Reasonable people may disapprove of this genre of jury nullification, but it is well within the tradition of what American juries have done for centuries.

I recently asked a friend of mine who is a judge whether he thought such jury nullification was proper. He quickly said no. I then asked him what he would do *as a judge* if he concluded that the police had planted evidence against a convicted defendant he believed guilty. "I'd throw the conviction out," he said. "Even if you knew the defendant was guilty?" I pressed him. "Absolutely," he replied. I asked him what the difference was. He responded: "I'm a judge. It's my job to make sure the system isn't polluted by evidence tampering." Perhaps some of the jurors also believed, as Professor Kathleen Sullivan surmised, that it was their job to keep the system free of perjury and evidence planting.

It is impossible, of course, ever to exclude the possibility that race, or other improper factors, may have played a role in the thinking of some jurors. One reason why the Supreme Court has been so concerned about the racial makeup of juries is its realization that race sometimes does matter, as do gender, religion, and other identifying features of the defendant, the victim, the jurors, the lawyers, and the judge. But the important point here is that this unpopular and much-criticized jury verdict can be explained without reference to race, even though the possibility that race had an impact can never be totally excluded.

In sum, I believe that the prosecution put on a case it knew to be partially false, in order to prove what it honestly believed to be the true guilt of the defendant. This is all too typical of what prosecutors often do. The difference is that this time the jury did not let them get away with it. In the end, the jurors concluded that the defense had put on a more honest case than the prosecution. The defense did not call potential witnesses who raised credibility problems, such as Rosa Lopez and Mary Anne Gerchas, relying instead primarily on scientific experts who generally testify for the prosecution. The prosecution relied primarily on police officers, several of whom the jury believed were lying. The defense consciously worked at maintaining its comparative credibility with the jury. Its jury consultant provided ongoing information on this issue: "By the end of the case, all the prosecution attorneys ranked lower than the defense lawyers on the perception of honesty," according to the "shadow" jurors, who were hired by the jury consultant to watch the trial and give their reactions.[41]

Whether Simpson did or didn't commit the murders — whether the verdict found ultimate "truth" or "falsity" — I am confident that the jury's unanimous acquittal in this case will promote truth in the long run, by sending a powerful message that business as usual will not always be tolerated. "Business as usual" is prosecutors' use of some police witnesses they know, or at least strongly suspect, are lying about some of the facts in order to prove the guilt of a defendant they "know," or at least believe, to be guilty. "Business as usual" is judges pretending to believe these lying police witnesses in order to avoid excluding evidence that proves to them that the defendant committed the crime.

What was unusual about the Simpson case is not that prosecutors who believe the defendant was truly guilty were willing to use some false testimony by policemen to secure a guilty verdict. Nor was it unusual that judges pretended to believe the false testimony. What was unusual is that a wide variety of circumstances came together in this case to lead the jury to disbelieve the lying police officers, to distrust the prosecution's case, and to find a reasonable doubt. These circumstances included the resources available to the defense, which enabled it to challenge aspects of the prosecution case that usually go unchallenged; the decision by the prosecutor to try this case in a location where a jury could be selected that was more receptive to the defense challenges; the combination of incompetence, perjury, and suspicious actions by several police officers; recent events in Los Angeles, which created a climate of suspicion against the Los Angeles police and prosecutors; the luck of the Fuhrman tapes surfacing, coupled with the resources of the defense, which enabled it to obtain these tapes through litigation in North Carolina;* and some very bad mistakes by Marcia Clark and some of her colleagues.

Each of these factors may have led to reasonable doubts in the minds of jurors, even some who may still believe that Simpson probably did it. Other jurors may have refused to convict even though they had no reasonable doubt about Simpson's guilt, because they believed that the police may have tried to "frame" a guilty man. Yet other jurors may have concluded, on the basis of the evidence they saw and heard,

*The woman who made the tapes, Laura Hart McKinny, resisted turning them over and the defense had to send a legal team to her home state to secure them.

that Simpson was innocent.

Different jurors, exposed to the same evidence but with dissimilar life experiences, might have voted to convict. That is the nature of the American jury system. This jury's verdict was well within the tradition of American justice and does not warrant the racist and elitist epithets thrown at it by people who believe the system failed.

V

Did the Jurors View the Evidence Through the Prism of Race More than of Gender?

"This is a story about race and gender and how they intersect," observed a professor of women's studies.[1] "It's about a black man married to a white woman being judged by black women." Although most of the media focused on the race component of the Simpson trial, some observers saw "women . . . at the center of the spectacle: Nicole Brown Simpson, the battered and murdered ex-wife; Marcia Clark, the lead prosecutor; the female-dominated jury; and then, in televised images after the acquittal, black women smiling to the heavens, thanking Jesus, and white women, sobbing, unable to speak."[2]

The jury that took four hours to acquit included nine blacks, but it also included ten women — eight of whom were black.

The racial composition of the jury was not entirely accidental. A decision by District Attorney Gil Garcetti early in the case made it all but inevitable that the jury would be largely black. Garcetti had the option of trying Simpson in Santa Monica. Instead he chose downtown Los Angeles, where the jury pool is largely black. There is much speculation about why he did so; the reasons suggested range from convenience, to security, to media accessibility. Pulitzer Prize–winning journalist William Lockman reported:

> Politically, Garcetti preferred a predominantly black jury to deliver the guilty verdict he thought he had in the bag (and he knew that all-black and predominantly black Los Angeles juries regularly send black defendants to the penitentiary, even to the gas chamber). After the Rodney King fiasco, Garcetti didn't want O.J. Simpson being found guilty by a predominantly white jury. So from the beginning race played a factor because people deliberately played to it.[3]

Garcetti insisted that the racial composition of the jury had nothing to do with his decision to move the trial downtown. But commentators both during and after the trial suggested additional motives:

> The decision to move the case downtown was made, [Garcetti] said, principally because "Santa Monica doesn't have the physical facilities to handle this type of case." At the time, however, Garcetti said privately that he believed a conviction handed down by a mostly white Westside jury would "lack credibility."
> ... [T]his case was brought downtown so that Gil Garcetti, our District Attorney, could micro-manage it.[4]

One experienced Los Angeles criminal defense attorney, Harland Braun, actually saw a largely black jury as increasing the odds for a conviction:

> I think it assists the prosecution to have a lot of blacks. . . . [I]f there were just a few blacks on the jury they would have risked being polarized against the others, but because they are a majority, then the spotlight is on you: "Are we going to look like a bunch of nincompoops or are we going to look

responsible?" . . . The blacks might feel an impetus to convict, to prove they aren't racially motivated.[5]

Garcetti also wanted the trial downtown in order to get an indictment through a grand jury proceeding instead of a preliminary hearing. That would have been a great advantage for the prosecution, because grand jury proceedings are secret and the defense does not participate; thus, the prosecution could secure its indictment without revealing its case to the defense prior to the trial. The only grand jury in Los Angeles County sits downtown, so that's where Garcetti moved the trial. But, unexpectedly, the defense team succeeded in getting the grand jury dismissed because of concerns that it had been tainted by the publicity surrounding the trial — publicity generated in large part by Garcetti's office and the Los Angeles Police Department. Having selected downtown as the venue for this trial, prosecutors then tried to challenge as many of the black jurors as they could while obeying the Supreme Court's prohibition against using race as a criterion for peremptory strikes. Of the ten peremptories the prosecution used, eight were against blacks.[6] Even once the trial was under way, they succeeded in removing several black jurors who they believed might be favorable to Simpson.[7] The defense also tried to shape the jury in order to favor its position — a tactic common in jury trials, both criminal and civil.

The high number of women jurors was largely an accident, although the defense thought long and hard about the potential impact of so many women in a case which the prosecution was determined to try as one of spousal abuse leading to murder. As one of the prosecutors put it: "In our team's opinion, this case at its heart was a case of domestic violence."[8] The prosecution set out to prove that, as one prosecutor put it, "a slap is a prelude to homicide."[9]

The defense was of two minds on what we called the spousal discord evidence. On the one hand, we were convinced from the very beginning that the prosecutors' emphasis on what they called "domestic violence" was a show of weakness. We knew that we could prove, if we had to, that an infinitesimal percentage — certainly fewer than 1 out of 2,500 — of men who slap or beat their domestic partners go on to murder them. We also knew that we had another ace in the hole. Early in the case, we retained the world's leading authority on the "battered woman syndrome," Dr. Lenore Walker, the psychologist who coined the term and did much of the research leading to its scientific acceptability.[10] I knew Dr. Walker's work well, since I have long been interested in the battered woman syndrome as it relates to self-defense. I have taught this issue for years, litigated cases on behalf of battered women, and written on the subject.

I had recently debated Dr. Walker on an expanded edition of *Nightline*, and we had remained in contact. So when I was brought in on the Simpson case, I immediately suggested that we take the preemptive step of retaining her expert services. I knew from having read her work that Dr. Walker would have to conclude that O.J. Simpson did not have the characteristics her research had found to be associated with the classic batterer, and that she would have to agree with our assessment that no scientifically accepted research existed that could lead to the conclusion that Simpson fit any profile of a domestic murderer.

We were confident, therefore, that we

175

could win any *rational, academic,* or *scientific* debate over the relationship between Simpson's prior domestic discord with Nicole Brown and her subsequent brutal murder. But we realized that domestic violence is not always an issue that is debated rationally, academically, and scientifically. It is a hot-button issue, especially among many feminists. It is also a political issue, as Gil Garcetti made clear at every opportunity. We also knew that the prosecution wanted to introduce as much evidence of domestic violence and discord as the judge would allow. This was for two separate, although overlapping, reasons. The first was the direct relevance of the abuse evidence to the question of who committed the murders. As the prosecution put it, these incidents showed "motive" and "identity." That is, a history of abuse proved, according to the prosecution, that the abuser had the motive to kill and therefore that it was he, rather than some unidentified stranger, who killed his former wife and abuse victim.[11]

The second reason why the prosecution wanted to introduce as much evidence as it could about how Simpson treated his wife was to destroy the generally positive image he had previously enjoyed in the community. In the days following the murders — before the police released the notorious 911 tape to the media — there was widespread disbelief that a "nice man" like O.J. Simpson could have committed these awful killings. On the Larry King show of June 14, 1994, on which I appeared as a commentator, having not yet been asked to join the defense team, I listened to Michael Jackson, the perceptive Los Angeles radio talk-show host, describe the public reaction: "I have never met anybody — and I've been speaking to people all day long on this particular issue — who has any dislike for O.J. Simpson. They desperately want him to be not guilty."[12] Nor was this positive perception limited to black callers: "I can only speak as a white male. I don't think we look at him and think, 'Hi, there's a nice black man.' We look at him and think, 'There's a great guy.' At least, that was the image."

As soon as the 911 tape was aired on June 22, 1994, this positive perception changed dramatically. Even though the tape revealed no physical violence toward Nicole Brown — indeed, she said no when asked if she had been struck, and "I don't know" in response to the 911 operator's query "Do you think he's going to hit you?"

— it showed a side of Simpson that the public had never seen. Most of the public began to dislike the person who could be heard screaming "I don't give a shit anymore. . . . I'm not leaving. . . . I'll leave here with my two fucking kids, is when I'm leaving." Many people who heard the 911 tape no longer wanted Simpson to be innocent.

It was this phenomenon — known in the law as the "bad man theory" — that we most feared, because it operates subconsciously for the most part. It predisposes a juror to believe evidence of guilt and to disbelieve evidence of innocence.

> The danger of [bad man] evidence . . . is jury confusion: that the jury, despite instructions from the court, will consider the character of the defendant as probative of the question of guilt of the instant crime. . . . The bad man theory (he did it before . . .) is almost unavoidable.[13]

The prosecution understood this phenomenon as well. When a woman has been brutally murdered, any evidence that she was previously mistreated by her former husband will make that man look horrible in the eyes of the public and the jury, regardless of whether it bears on whether he killed her. That is why the prosecution in the Simpson case tried so hard to admit evidence of at best marginal relevance to the murder — evidence such as a joke Simpson told while making a workout video, a dream he allegedly recounted to an acquaintance named Ronald Shipp, and an episode at a bar during which he allegedly grabbed his wife's crotch and said, "This belongs to me." These episodes, seen in the context of their victim having subsequently been murdered, made Simpson look terrible. And the reason courts generally exclude such "bad man" evidence is that it poses a danger that some jurors might interpret other ambiguous evidence as showing that the "bad" defendant is guilty even if he is innocent of the crime for which he is standing trial.

We understood these risks and we tried to diminish them by limiting the evidence of spousal discord the judge would allow the jury to hear. Because of my academic expertise in this area, I was placed in charge of writing the legal briefs on this and related issues. We told the court that very recent data on battered women reveals that a woman is battered by a man every 12 or 15 seconds. . . . That translates into 2,102,400 (1 every 15 seconds) to 2,628,000 (1 every 12 seconds) beatings a year. Some studies even estimate that as many as 4 million women are battered annually by husbands or boyfriends. . . . Yet in 1992, according to the FBI Uniform Crime Reports, a total of 913 women were killed by their husbands, and 519 were killed by their boyfriends. In other words, while there were $2\frac{1}{2}$ to 4 million incidents of abuse, there were only 1,432 homicides. Some of these homicides may have occurred after a history of abuse, but obviously most abuse, presumably even most serious abuse, does not end in murder. In fact, the ratio of murders to batterings is somewhere between .0006 to 1 (1,500 murders to 2,500,000 "batterings") and .000375 to 1 (1,500 murders to 4 million "batterings").

It is, of course, also true that a high proportion of women who have been battered by their husbands or boyfriends and are then found dead were killed by these batterers, but it is equally true that a high proportion of women who have *not* been battered and are found dead were killed by their husbands or boyfriends. The reality is that a majority of women who are killed are killed by men with whom they have had a relationship, *regardless of whether their men previously battered them*. Battery, as such, is not a good independent predictor of murder. Prior relationship — with or without battery — is a fairly good after-the-fact indictor of who killed any murdered woman. But of course, no jury would ever be allowed to infer that a man murdered his ex-wife just because he had been involved with her.

The relationship between battery and murder is a complex one, and we argued that the jury could easily become confused and ascribe too much weight to the history of spousal discord in this case. Yet Judge Ito ruled that "Evidence of defendant's prior assaults upon Nicole Brown Simpson may be admitted at trial as to the issues of motive, intent, plan and identity." But he also agreed to consider each alleged incident of discord individually before allowing the jury to hear about it.[14]

Early on in the pretrial preparation, I surprised the defense team by predicting that the prosecution might begin its case with the spousal abuse evidence, rather than the physical evidence. Traditionally, murder cases are presented through the "flashback" technique. The prosecution begins with the dead bodies — the autopsy, the cause of death, the crime scene evidence — and works backward toward the dcfcndant. In this case we hoped the prosecution would fall into the trap of presenting the case chronologically, beginning with the history of the Simpson relationship and marriage. We believed that by putting on their most speculative evidence first, the prosecution would be frittering away the considerable advantage it had in going first — and last. The first days of evidence are thought to have the greatest impact on the jury, along with the last word, especially in close cases.

With both our public statements and our court papers, we lured the prosecution into believing that we feared the spousal discord evidence most. We knew that Garcetti was anticipating a tough reelection race and that he would milk the domestic abuse aspect of this case for everything it was worth in order to appeal to women voters. In his press conferences, he focused heavily on this politically powerful issue. Marcia Clark, too, emphasized this aspect of the case. Indeed, there was much speculation that Clark had been selected as lead counsel in part because of her experience and interest in cases involving violence against women. She had won a murder conviction against the man who killed TV actress Rebecca Schaeffer after having stalked her for three years.

Before Johnnie Cochran was brought on board as head trial counsel, we thought long and hard about the advantages of retaining a woman to play a prominent role on the trial team, especially on the issue of spousal discord. We revisited that question after the jury was selected and so many women appeared on it. We decided that if we were to select a woman for these reasons, we would be playing into the prosecution's theory that this was indeed a domestic violence case. From its very beginning to its closing arguments, we regarded this case as essentially forensic in nature: Did the prosecution's physical evidence and the way it was gathered, tested, and testified about prove the defendant's guilt beyond a reasonable doubt? We opted therefore to create a trial team with experience in forensics (Barry

Scheck, Peter Neufeld, Robert Blasier) and in examining police witnesses (Johnnie Cochran, F. Lee Bailey, Robert Shapiro). Several women played important roles (Shawn Chapman, Sarah Kaplan, and jury consultant Jo-Ellan Demetrius) but there was no attempt to highlight the role of women or to assign them specially to the domestic discord area.

The prosecution fell into our trap and devoted the first ten trial days to a parade of witnesses who recounted the eighteen-year relationship between Simpson and Nicole Brown. Meanwhile, the evidence the prosecution could present on domestic discord had been severely reduced. In pretrial rulings on the admissibility of this evidence, the prosecution withdrew evidence of eighteen out of its initial list of fifty-nine domestic abuse "incidents," realizing that they were of slight relevance and would not likely be admitted. Judge Ito disallowed evidence of a further twelve incidents. Ten others were so innocuous that the defense did not even contest their admission. This left the prosecution with nineteen incidents, many of which were of very questionable relevance and only two of which involved any physical contact between Simpson and Brown. Besides the joke and dream evidence, they also included a threat by Simpson to report Nicole for tax evasion, and two occasions when Simpson left flowers at her home.

Later in the trial, when it realized that the domestic discord evidence it was presenting had not made much of an impression on jurors who had been dismissed, the prosecution dropped still more of its domestic abuse witnesses. In the end, it was able to show only *one* incident of physical violence, which took place following a New Year's Eve of heavy drinking in 1989 — five and a half years before the murder. Indeed, the defense had Nicole Brown's deposition (taken during the subsequent divorce proceedings), in which she herself acknowledged that this was the only incident of physical violence.

The public saw a very different picture. All the prosecution evidence that was admitted, and much that was not, appeared in the media. The public heard allegations that Simpson once slapped Nicole at a beach, that he pushed her out of a slow-moving car in a parking lot, and that Nicole, afraid Simpson was stalking her, contacted a battered women's center days before her death. Also revealed — by the

National Enquirer — after the verdict, were the purported contents of a diary kept by Nicole Brown in connection with her 1992 divorce from Simpson, detailing further alleged abuses.[15]

It should not be surprising, therefore, that much of the public regarded Simpson as a chronic wife beater with a long and uninterrupted history of spousal abuse. The jury, on the other hand, heard about a man who was occasionally rude to his wife, who argued with her, and who hit her once, after a New Year's Eve of drinking. We will never know for certain which of these portrayals comes closer to the truth, since the episodes reported in the media were not testified to under oath or subjected to cross-examination. Nor has Simpson given his account of the relationship and presented his counterevidence.

Neither the picture the jury saw nor the one the public viewed was a pretty one. There is never any justification for domestic violence. But neither is there any scientifically accepted evidence that domestic abuse — even of the sort attributed to Simpson in the worst-case scenario — is a prelude to murder. The evidence of spousal abuse that Judge Ito allowed the jury to hear — and he was quite favorable to the prosecution in his domestic abuse rulings — presented a weak and speculative case for concluding, without more evidence, that Simpson had escalated from hitting to murder. As a matter of empirical scientific fact — as distinguished from lawyers' rhetoric — a slap is rarely a prelude to murder.

But there was, of course, more, much more. Even the prosecution would not have brought this case to trial if the only evidence had been that Simpson had previously hit his murdered ex-wife. It was the *combination* of spousal abuse evidence (allegedly proving motive and pattern), the forensic evidence (allegedly proving identification) and the time line (allegedly proving opportunity) which made the prosecution's "mountain of evidence" so high.

We made the judgment early on that if we could challenge the forensic evidence and use the time line to our advantage, we would not have to worry about the domestic abuse evidence. In any event, there was not much we could do about it. We certainly did not want to highlight it. Nor did we want to be in the position of denigrating it, especially in front of a largely female jury. We eventually decided not to call our expert witness, Dr. Lenore Walker, in order to avoid emphasizing this issue or inviting the prosecutors to call an expert of their own. We had a sense, confirmed by our jury expert, that the prosecutor had seriously misread this jury by assuming that the women jurors would view its forensic and time line evidence through the prism of spousal abuse rather than through the more relevant lens of race and of distrust of the Los Angeles Police Department.

The Anita Hill–Clarence Thomas conflict of 1992 had convinced many observers that many black women — and our jury had eight — see the world more through the prism of their experiences as blacks than through the prism of their experiences as women.[16] Although all such generalizations are suspect, we had no choice but to make some judgment on this issue. Because we had a jury expert, we could focus more on the *particular* black women jurors in the box, rather than on the generality of black women. But because we had only limited information about our jurors, we still had to generalize a bit.

I have always believed that race is a salient characteristic in our criminal justice system. Race matters in how one is treated from the initial encounter with the police to the gubernatorial decision whether to commute the death sentence. For more than a quarter of a century, race has been a central concern in my first-year criminal law course at Harvard Law School. I tell my students that to study criminal justice in America while omitting the impact of race is to blink at reality. Many criminal law teachers deliberately omit controversial issues, such as race and gender, from their courses. Especially if they are white and male, they regard classroom discussions of these hot-button issues as no-win situations. Most of those who do allow discussion of these issues stay above the fray, allowing the students to "vent" their frustrations but rarely expressing their own views. I take the opposite tack. Since many students are reluctant to express views in class which may be "politically incorrect," I go out of my way to play the devil's advocate whenever controversial issues are discussed.

Most of my students are aware of my strong personal views on race, especially as relevant to the death penalty, since I began writing about that issue even before I became a professor. When I was a law clerk for Justice Arthur Goldberg on the Supreme Court, I was responsible for a memorandum which raised the first challenge to the constitutionality of capital punishment as racially discriminatory.[17] That memorandum eventuated in a dissenting opinion by three justices — Goldberg, Brennan and Douglas — that for the first time in American judicial history raised questions about the constitutionality of the death penalty and invited the bar to begin to challenge it, especially in racially discriminatory contexts.

Over the next quarter of a century, I have fought against the disparate application of the death penalty based on the race of the perpetrator and assailant. In a *Nightline* debate on the eve of the Supreme Court's most important decision on this subject, I took the position that the death penalty, as administered, violates the "equal protection" clause of the Constitution because a black man who kills a white is far more likely to be executed than a white man who kills a black.[18]

The attorney general of Georgia, Michael Bowers, responded that it "so happens that the highly aggravated cases will generally involve, or to a higher degree involve, white victims, while those with more mitigating circumstances, or more highly mitigated, will more likely involve black victims." I replied that this did not just "so happen" — it was "not a coincidence." Instead, "it reflects a kind of racist ideology. It says that when a white person is killed, we perceive the circumstances as more aggravated than when a black person is killed. . . . [W]e look at cases through the lens of our own perspectives."

It is interesting that some conservatives who are now confident that the Simpson verdict was based on black racial bias are the same conservatives who argue against blaming disparate death penalty verdicts on white racial bias. The statistical evidence is clear: Predominantly white juries impose the death penalty far more frequently on blacks who kill whites than on whites who kill blacks. When our equal protection challenge was brought to the Supreme Court on the basis of these statistics, many conservatives were quick to argue that we cannot know *for certain* that race was the determining factor in these sentences. In my *Nightline* debate with Attorney General Bowers, he discounted the statistical proof and demanded proof that each particular juror "intended" to discriminate on the basis of race. I responded as follows:

> The [Attorney] General says that it doesn't matter what the statistics show, unless you can show in a particular case that the jurors sat there and said, "We're going to consider race." Well, we can't get into the jury box; we can't get into the jury mind. The only way we can figure out what juries and prosecutors and judges are using — whether intentionally or unintentionally — is to look at a mass of cases. If, for example, some employer has a pattern of never, never hiring a black — always preferring the white — we can't know in any particular case that the white wasn't more qualified than the black, but nonetheless, the courts around the country say, "That's enough for us."[19]

All people — white, black, Hispanic, Asian, Jewish, male, female, gay, heterosexual — view the world through the prism of their experiences. I am even prepared to believe that the original twelve jurors from Simi Valley who voted to acquit the Los Angeles policemen caught on videotape beating Rodney King honestly saw that videotape differently than did the twelve Los Angeles jurors who subsequently convicted the same cops of essentially the same crime on the basis of the same evidence.

The social science research supports this conclusion, *both* for white jurors *and* for black jurors. Darnell Hunt, a sociology professor at University of Southern California, set up separate black and white focus groups to test their perceptions of the same evidence in the Simpson case. His preliminary conclusion was that "based on their respective life experiences in our still largely segregated society, blacks and whites often perceive the same event or individual in different ways."[20] Vanderbilt University law professor Nancy J. King, in her review of the effect of race on jury verdicts, concluded that, "studies . . . confirm that juror race affects jury decisions in some cases."[21] Two frequent findings are (1) that blacks are more likely to acquit than whites, and (2) that both blacks and whites are more likely to acquit defendants of their own race than those of other races.

A significant number of studies have found that white jurors are more likely than black jurors to convict black defendants and that they are also more likely to acquit defendants charged with crimes against black victims.[22]

One mock-juror study found that black jurors were more likely to acquit defendants of either race, and white jurors were especially resistant to developing reasonable doubts about black defendants during deliberation.[23] Other such studies have found that both black and white jurors favor defendants of their own race. White subjects in these studies were more likely to find a minority-race defendant guilty than they were to find an identically situated white defendant guilty.[24]

One survey, surprisingly, found that black jurors — and especially black females — were *more* predisposed to convict defendants.[25] On the other hand, a 1984 archival study of the relationship between racial composition and verdicts in Dade County, Florida, found that "juries with at least one black juror were less likely than all-white juries to convict black defendants."[26]

The social science data also confirmed our view that in the Simpson case a largely white jury would be less receptive to our planned attack on the credibility of certain police officers than would a largely black jury. Each juror brings to the deliberations what researchers call interpretive bias: "This form of bias arises from the composition of the jury and from the varying perspectives that jurors bring to the court even without any specific knowledge of or connection to the case."[27] The prosecution of Washington, D.C., mayor Marion Barry is cited as an example of this "interpretation filter":

The pretrial publicity in that case included a videotape of Barry smoking crack cocaine in a hotel room, to which he was lured by a sometime girlfriend who was cooperating with federal investigators. A common effect of that videotape on white citizens of Washington, D.C., was that it led them to conclude that Barry was caught redhanded and was indisputably guilty. On the other hand, many black citizens saw in that same video a black public official entrapped by white agents, a man who deserved more empathy than blame. Each group developed a specific bias from its exposure to the pretrial publicity, but that specific bias varied greatly depending upon the observers' different interpretive perspectives.[28]

The two trials of the police officers who beat Rodney King are another obvious example of this filter effect.

No one group's interpretive bias is necessarily any less accurate than that of others: "All jurors are members of certain groups (religious, racial, economic, gender, regional) that influence their perspectives on human events. General bias in one direction is not any more objectively incorrect than is an equally strong general bias in the opposite direction."[29] Other researchers echo these themes:

Recent studies investigating juror decisionmaking have concluded that each juror, using her own life experiences, organizes the information she receives about a case into what for her is the most plausible account of what happened and then picks the verdict that fits that story best. Jurors may interpret the same evidence differently depending on which stories they choose. Because racial background may influence a juror's judgment of whether any given story is a reasonable explanation of events, black and white jurors may reach different conclusions after evaluating the same evidence.[30]

The consensus seems to be that race is more likely to affect juror verdicts indirectly, through perceptions of the evidence, than directly, through explicit racial favoritism. This way of looking at the impact of race on jury verdicts explains a common finding in several juror research studies. In some mock-juror studies, researchers systematically vary the strength of the evidence in the simulated trials. The results reveal that race strongly affects verdicts only when the evidence is inconclusive, neither very strong nor very weak.[31]

This suggests that, contrary to the views of prosecutor Marcia Clark and others, jurors do not necessarily "vote their race" by disregarding strong evidence. Instead, their life experiences condition their view of the evidence, and that view in turn influences their verdict.

One particular element of the life experience of many blacks, likely to affect their views of criminal evidence, was central to the Simpson case. Many black jurors did not need to hear the Fuhrman tapes in order to accept the possibility that the police would lie and tamper with evidence in order to set up a black man. Many blacks, in Los Angeles and elsewhere, experience racist police harassment regularly. They also encounter more subtle discrimination from white-dominated authorities on a daily basis.

> Rare is the African-American who cannot relate a tale of having been stopped by police in an affluent neighborhood or followed closely at the heels around a clothing store. As [black Harvard law professor Charles Ogletree] recently put it, "If I'm dressed in a knit cap and hooded jacket, I'm probable cause." One consequence of such treatment is that the attitudes of blacks and whites toward police diverge markedly.[32]

This difference was recently confirmed, in a way directly relevant to the Simpson case, by a study of eight hundred former jurors. This study found that "forty-two percent of whites believed that, given a conflict between a law enforcement officer and a defendant, the police officer should be credited. Only twenty-five percent of African-American jurors interviewed felt that the police officer's testimony should be believed."[33]

Evidence of the misdeeds of detectives Vannatter and Fuhrman directly implicated these attitudes and beliefs of black jurors. According to many researchers and scholars, the most important verdict-affecting belief that black citizens bring to the jury box is an appreciation that the police may lie, tamper with evidence, and violate constitutional rights in order to investigate and prosecute a defendant — especially a black defendant. For whites, on the other hand, police perjury is a concept largely outside their realm of experience. "For whites, such a situation could only be imagined."

It may well be the case that in some instances minority jurors have a fuller, more realistic picture of the criminal justice system and its vagaries than do members of the white mainstream. Given their disparate experiences of law enforcement, middle-class white jurors are more inclined than African-Americans to believe that police officers always tell the truth, act with integrity, and protect the innocent.

Much of the white United States had a very difficult time believing the possibility that the O.J. blood evidence in the trial was suspect. . . . Most of black America did not. That's because most of us know, or know of, somebody who has been through some kind of funky business with the police trying to make their arrests air-tight. Mark Fuhrman was not nearly the shock for black people as he seemed to be for whites.[34]

As *The New York Times* asked rhetorically in an editorial about "police thuggery" in cities ranging from Los Angeles to New Orleans and Philadelphia:

What must it be like to grow up in a neighborhood where the only difference between police and out-and-out criminals is that the police wear uniforms? More and more Americans are finding out. The effect on communities, and on the attitudes of jurors, is corrosive. . . . The children who witness police lawlessness will one day grow up to be jurors. No one should be surprised when they take a jaundiced view of police testimony.[35]

What about the gender of the jurors and the domestic violence evidence? Commentators have concluded that "race must have trumped gender in the jurors' minds."[36] The prosecution made an appeal to the jurors — of whom ten out of twelve were female — to sympathize with Nicole Brown, especially by introducing evidence of her past domestic abuse at the hands of O.J. Simpson. The defense, in turn, introduced to the jury — nine of whose members were black — evidence of racially motivated evidence tampering, perjury, and constitutional violations in the investigation and prosecution of the killings. If the defense's appeal was more effective, many have concluded, it must be because the racial bias of the jurors outweighed the strength of their identification with battered women.

That women — black or white — with presumably so much in common could see the verdict so differently suggested that the racial wall was higher and thicker than anyone had imagined.

The "not guilty" verdict suggests that the women on the jury identified more with the racial issues raised by the defense than the gender issues of domestic violence outlined by the prosecution.[37]

These analysts seem to be assuming that the black jurors on the Simpson jury somehow had their powers of reason swamped by their racial identities, or that identification with the defendant and racial solidarity must have motivated the verdict, regardless of the evidence. But race and gender may have affected the jurors' deliberations in more subtle, and less overt, ways.

First, commentators who argue that "race trumps gender" may be correct in the sense that race makes much more of a difference in many black jurors' perceptions and beliefs than gender does. Under the cultural-experience explanation of juror "biases," this makes perfect sense. The everyday experiences of blacks and whites are far more different than are those of men and women of the same race. From day to day, men and women of the same race associate with each other and with many of the same people. Although their experiences and beliefs do differ, they also overlap a great deal. By contrast, blacks and whites are almost fully isolated from each other in many parts of our society. They live in different worlds, whereas men and women with the same racial and socioeconomic characteristics inhabit pretty much the same world. So it is no wonder that black jurors bring more radically different perceptions into the jury room, which in jury research show up as more pronounced differences across race than across gender.[38]

Many black women find that racism is a more pronounced force in their lives than sexism:

> While to many black women sexism pales in the face of racism, white women, unburdened by race in a predominantly white society, are freer to focus on sexism. But that often leaves them perplexed when black women break ranks, maybe even to their own detriment, as when many sided with Clarence Thomas and vilified Anita Hill in his confirmation hearings for the Supreme Court.[39]

Donna Franklin, a professor of child welfare at the University of Southern California, suggests that black women may choose to identify with a black male defendant rather than a white female victim because racism has prevented black women from being in an economic position to pursue feminism. She states:

> The black woman's envy of white women was that they had a man taking care of them. Black women never had that luxury. We have been deprived of a provider by the system. We wish we could sit in the suburbs and write *The Feminine Mystique*. That's why black women and white women have always been apart. We can't move to the next level until we have those first needs met.[40]

Aside from these dramatic cultural differences, the second reason why race may have trumped gender as a perceptual prism had to do with the different evidence in this case that played into race-determined beliefs, as opposed to gender-determined beliefs. Some jurors may have recognized that the evidence of police misconduct was more directly relevant to doubts about Simpson's guilt or innocence than was the evidence of alleged abuse. Women may be more sensitive to domestic violence issues than men, but that does not mean they will easily be fooled into believing that domestic violence is predictive of spousal murder. Indeed, one scholar has suggested that they might have been able to resist such a ploy with fewer misgivings than men:

> The fact that these were women on the jury is very important, because they were able to assess the kind of card Marcia Clark was playing on them. . . . Is it just a leap of justice to say he finally killed? . . . I think this jury showed that although you had good reasons to think somebody may be pushed to kill if they had battered before, this is not enough to prove they actually did. I think the jury showed great ability to distance themselves from any personal prejudice.[41]

Even this recognition, however, may have been influenced by the relative importance of race and gender in the jurors' world-views.

But it was not only African-Americans

for whom "race trumped gender." Many white journalists saw it the race way. Jessica Seigel of the *Chicago Tribune* said that the Simpson story is "only about race. . . . If it were Joe Namath who had killed his wife, do you think we'd be making such a fuss?"[42] And Jeffrey Toobin of *The New Yorker* agreed: "To me, the reason anyone will care about this case five years, 10 years from now is because of what it illuminates about race in America."[43] Many women thought that spousal abuse "should be the central issue in the case," but that was because it is *their* agenda issue.[44] "But once the prosecution decided that the abuse issue didn't seem to be resonating with jurors, they quickly abandoned it [and] it quickly slid off the radar screens of the nation's news media," to the "outrage" of some feminists.[45]

No criminal defense lawyer can ignore this kind of data in making judgments about how to consider the prosecution's case and present the defense case. These data certainly corroborated our own gut views that we should downplay the domestic abuse evidence and focus our attack on the credibility of police officers like Fuhrman and Vannatter and the

competence and biases of the police forensic officials. If we had drawn an all-white
Simi Valley–type jury, we would have had
to reconsider our planned presentation.
Defense lawyers play the cards they are
dealt. They are rarely in a position to deal
the cards, either from the top or the bot-
tom of the deck.

In this case, we made scientific and
credibility challenges based on the evidence Judge Ito allowed us to use, which
was far less than was available. In his
closing argument, Johnnie Cochran made
the following plea:

> Stop this cover-up. . . . [B]oth prosecu-
> tors have now agreed that . . . there's
> a lying, perjuring, genocidal racist
> and he's testified willfully false in this
> case on a number of scores. . . . You are
> empowered to say we're not going to
> take that anymore. . . . [W]hen a wit-
> ness lies in a material part of his tes-
> timony, you can wipe out all of his
> testimony as a judge of the facts. . . .
> You're the ones who send the mes-
> sage.[46]

He also made a highly controversial reference to Adolf Hitler:

There was another man not too long ago in the world who had these same views, who wanted to burn people, who had racist views and ultimately had power over people in his country. People didn't care. People said he is just crazy. He is just a half-baked painter. They didn't do anything about it. This man, this scourge, became one of the worst people in the history of this world. Adolf Hitler, because people didn't care or didn't try to stop him. He had the power over his racism and his anti-religion. Nobody wanted to stop him and it ended up in World War II. And so Fuhrman, Fuhrman wants to take all black people now and burn them or bomb them. That is genocidal racism.[47]

Many critics — including defense team member Robert Shapiro — called this playing the race card. Judge Ito permitted Cochran to make the argument, over an objection by the prosecution.

I heard Cochran's argument for the first time when it was delivered. Although I participated in the preparation of the closing arguments, my role was limited to the evidentiary issues and the questions to be asked of Marcia Clark in anticipation of her "last word" rebuttal summation. I was not privy to the rhetorical flourishes Cochran would be making. Nor did I know in advance about Cochran's reference to Hitler. Although I'm not sure I would have made the argument myself, I was not offended by it. This is what I wrote in an article shortly after the verdict:

> There is, of course, no comparison between the incomparable evil inflicted by Hitler on millions of innocent Jews and the shakedowns, beatings, false arrests, perjury, swastika-paintings and evidence-planting allegedly done by Mr. Fuhrman. But Mr. Cochran did not suggest any such comparison, and his critics should have read what he actually said, rather than the media's characterization. What he did argue was that there is a similarity of "views" between Hitler and Mr. Fuhrman, and he is right. Mr. Fuhrman has advocated genocide — the mass burning, shooting and bombing of blacks, especially those involved in interracial marriages. Mr. Cochran also

reminded his listeners that we ignore people with such racist views at our peril, especially when they wear uniforms, badges and guns. . . . In fact, Mr. Cochran explicitly differentiated Hitler from Mr. Fuhrman, pointing out that Hitler "ultimately had power" and was able to carry out his racism. We must, of course, be careful in making analogies to the Holocaust or to Hitler. But we should not shy away from reminding the world that we ignore institutional racism of the sort long condoned by the Los Angeles Police Department at our collective peril. Mr. Cochran was absolutely on-target when he warned his listeners that when people don't care about racism and don't try to stop it, it can get out of control.[48]

Nevertheless, when I heard Cochran deliver those controversial words, I became concerned — not for moral reasons, but for tactical ones. My first reaction was the famous remark attributed to Talleyrand: "It is worse than a crime, it is a blunder." I feared that Cochran's statement could be racially divisive, thus increasing the chances for a hung jury. Indeed, after the verdict, one white juror expressed criticism of Cochran's closing argument on precisely those grounds. "It made me angry and disgusted. It felt like he was playing to emotions, and it bothered me, that he couldn't just stick to the facts."[49] When asked whether she believed Cochran was directing this argument to the black jurors, this juror replied: "It could be, because it couldn't have been directed at me. . . . I almost laughed a couple of times. It seemed like he was just over-dramatizing in some kind of hell-fire and damnation, preacher-type approach." Another juror — Hispanic — said that in listening to Cochran's closing he felt as if "I was in church."[50] No one will ever know for sure whether Cochran's rhetoric had a positive impact — conscious or subconscious — on the jurors. In the end, all the jurors who were interviewed focused on the evidence rather than the rhetoric, and most of them liked Cochran and trusted him.

Immediately after the swift verdict, Marcia Clark provided a simpleminded racial explanation that was echoed by many commentators and observers: "Liberals don't want to admit it, but a majority black jury won't convict in a case like this.

They won't bring justice."* Vincent Bugliosi, who prosecuted the Charles Manson gang, gave a similar assessment: "I've never seen a more obvious case of guilt. . . . Yet this jury apparently gave no weight to the mountain of incriminating evidence and instead bought into the defense argument that this was a case about race."[51] Apparently this view is widely shared in some quarters:

> Since the Simpson verdict was announced, more than a few people seem to think that the jury system needs to be revamped, that black people cannot discern fact from fiction and that a predominantly black jury will acquit a black defendant regardless of the facts.
> The prosecution's defenders say the race issue blinded the jurors to the evidence.

*Nor was Marcia Clark the only white woman to indulge in such bigotry. The head of the Los Angeles Chapter of the National Organization of Women, Tammy Bruce, was publicly censured by the national organization for racist statements about the Simpson case. The national president of NOW has told Bruce to apologize for having "made statements that clearly violate NOW's commitment to stopping racism." *The New York Times*, Dec. 11, 1995, p. A15.

Incited by Johnnie Cochran — good lawyer, bad citizen — to turn the trial into a political caucus, the jurors did that instead of doing their banal duty of rendering a just verdict concerning two extremely violent deaths. The jurors abused their position in order to send a message about racism, police corruption or whatever.[52]

The extremity of some of these simpleminded views has produced equally extreme and simpleminded claims from some that race played no role in this case.[53] The truth is more complex and multilayered. Though we will never be able to get into the minds of the jurors — even those who give (understandably self-justifying) accounts of their votes — it is clear that race alone cannot account for this verdict, especially since it was joined by three nonblacks, one of whom had previously turned around a jury that had originally voted eleven to one for acquittal. This is not to say that the verdict necessarily would have been the same if the case had been presented to an all-white or predominantly white jury. Race matters, in all kinds of subtle and overt ways.

For example, one middle-class black juror said that he experienced racism directly for the first time while on this jury, at the hands of court deputies. This experience "colored his view" of some of the police testimony. Although he thinks Simpson may have committed the murders, he is convinced that the police may have "attempted to frame a murderer." This juror may have become open to considering this possibility as a result of his treatment by deputies in this very case. If this is true, it certainly illustrates the unpredictable ways in which race can influence a juror. (Interestingly, the defense team was hearing reports of possible racism by deputies, and we were of two minds about how to react: On the one hand, no one wanted to tolerate any form of discrimination, but on the other hand, we suspected that any perceived racism on the part of uniformed deputies might redound to the disadvantage of the prosecution. As defense attorneys, we had to place the interests of our client first.)

It is precisely because race, gender, religion, class, age, and other such factors do matter that the Constitution demands that juries not be selected on the basis of discriminatory criteria. Sometimes nondiscriminatory criteria produce juries with disproportionate numbers of whites; at other times they produce juries with disproportionate numbers of blacks. In this case, the defense had precious little to do with the racial or gender composition of the jury. The prosecution, the judge, and the jury commissioner had far more influence on the makeup of the final panel.

Johnnie Cochran was picked to head the trial team before the racial makeup of the jury was known, although after it was known that the trial would be in downtown Los Angeles. Would Cochran have been picked if the trial was to be held in Santa Monica or Simi Valley? I think so, but I don't know for certain. Would Christopher Darden have been selected by the prosecution for a Santa Monica or Simi Valley trial? I don't know. Would Marcia Clark have been given the nod if one of the victims had not been a woman? No one will ever know.

What I do know is that from the beginning of time, trial lawyers have been selected with an eye on the jury. Fast-talking New York Jewish lawyers are not often selected to try cases in rural Texas.[54] Nor are slow-talking Texans often picked to try cases in the Bronx.[55] When I suggested Barry Scheck and Peter Neufeld play a greater role in the court-room, there was some concern about their accents, styles, and place of origin. Indeed, it soon became clear that Judge Ito had a problem with these New Yorkers: They talked too loud and too fast, and were too aggressive for his tastes. These are the facts of life in the world of trial law.

So, too, with regard to race and gender. Some black jurors may tend to listen more carefully to a black lawyer, just as some Jewish jurors may identify more closely with a Jewish lawyer. We certainly hoped and expected that Cochran's race would be a plus with some black jurors, just as the prosecutor hoped that Darden's race and Clark's gender would be a plus.

We certainly also hoped and expected that some of the black jurors would be open to the possibility that white police officers might lie about a black defendant. *We* believed that Vannatter and Fuhrman were not telling the truth. We hoped the jury would agree with us. We were pleased that we had a largely black jury, which might be more open to arguments about police perjury, evidence tampering, and so on — arguments we believed were correct. If that is playing the race card, then the race card *should* be played — because the fact is that police do routinely lie and do sometimes tamper with evidence, and it is good that juries include people whose life experiences make them receptive to these possibilities.

It is possible, of course, that a largely black jury could be wrong in a particular case and find police perjury where none occurred. It is equally possible that a largely white jury could also be wrong in a particular case and find no police perjury where it did occur. Which is the worse type of error? I submit that under our system of justice, it is far better for a jury to err on the side of finding perjury where it did not occur than in failing to find it where it did occur. This is precisely how one juror — a white woman — put it after the verdict. In describing why she voted for acquittal even though she was uncertain whether the police had tampered with evidence, Anise Aschenbach said: "If we made a mistake, I would rather it be a mistake on the side of a person's innocence than the other way."[56] This is the correct approach under our law because of the strong presumption of innocence, based on the judgment that it is better that ten guilty defendants go free than that one innocent be wrongly condemned. I believe it is also good policy, because most *judges* refuse to find perjury by the police even when it is obvious to everyone. The jury is our only realistic protection against police perjury, and if black jurors are more likely than whites to be open to finding police perjury, then that is a racial "bias" that promotes justice.

Indeed, it is fair to ask why so much more criticism has been directed against black jurors (and blacks in general) for "closing their minds" to the possibility that Simpson might be guilty, than against whites for closing *their* minds to the possibility that the police might have planted evidence against him. Lorraine Adams, a white reporter for *The Washington Post*, found that African-Americans were much more open-minded about the case than were whites. "The whites . . . are more implacable and [are] hearing less. . . . I find an unwillingness on the part of whites to hear, to actually listen and absorb and give credit to the black experience [with] the criminal justice system." Adams was especially critical of the white media, whose reporting in any "conspiracy" claim "always . . . says it's implausible." She found blacks "much more able to come up with reasons why [Simpson] could be guilty."[57] This observation led *Los Angeles Times* reporter Andrea Ford to ask why the media did not do stories "trying to explain why whites were so overwhelmingly certain of his guilt? Why were blacks, rather than whites, cast as the people whose position needed explaining?"[58]

In fact, the black suspicion of police — even if sometimes exaggerated — is generally more accurate than the white trust of police, which is also exaggerated. According to a *Los Angeles Times* poll, 67 percent of whites believe that "false testimony" by police is "uncommon," while only 21 percent of blacks believe it is uncommon.[59] Notwithstanding the vagueness of the operative terms, the empirical evidence suggests that the black respondents' position is closer to the truth.

Ford continued: "There's an underlying tone of, 'These [black] people are irrational. They're ignoring the evidence.' Well, what was so rational about those white people in these early polls deciding [Simpson] was guilty before they learned a scintilla of evidence? I have seen no stories on that."[60] Several white journalists were "equally outraged" at the implicit assumption that black open-mindedness was more "rational" than white closed-mindedness.[61]

If we consider the matter in a larger perspective, we can all agree, I hope, that racially diverse juries — in particular cases and in the range of cases — are essential for justice in America. For generations, there were no blacks on juries, even on juries that were trying black defendants. Those all-white juries made many mistakes, because they viewed the evidence through the prism of their white life experiences. All-black juries would make similar mistakes. In many parts of the country, even today, juries are still predominantly white, with only a few blacks. These juries, too, make mistakes based on a dominant white bias (although we hope that this bias is ameliorated somewhat by the presence of even a small number of blacks). We rarely hear complaints from the majority community or media about these mistakes.

Those who believe that *this* predominantly black jury may have made a mistake because of its dominant black bias, and that this bias was not ameliorated by the presence of three nonblacks on the jury, should consider that possible mistake in the context of our hundreds of years of jury mistakes on the other side. This is not an argument for some kind of "affirmative action" in jury trials. It is an attempt to explain that some degree of bias in assessing the evidence, based on race and gender, is inherent in the jury system. Sometimes the bias falls on one side. Sometimes it falls on the other. Yet the criticism of *this* verdict, on the ground of racial bias, has been louder, angrier, and more sustained than in any other case, with the possible exception of the first Rodney King verdict. Moreover, words were used to describe the Simpson verdict that have not been used to criticize other verdicts. Characterizing the Simpson jury as "dominated and controlled by highly emotional, racist blacks" and the verdict as a "racially motivated and racist verdict," "charade," "simply unbelievable," and "one of the biggest travesties in the history of American jurisprudence," suggest something beyond mere disagreement.[62] They suggest a double standard in evaluating the "erroneous" verdicts of predominantly white and black juries.

Several weeks after the verdict, Christopher Darden offered an assessment of the Simpson verdict dramatically different from the one offered by Marcia Clark. He was not prepared to characterize the verdict as "race-based," since, in his view, "a whole lot of other things" went into it. Paramount among those factors, he said, was the sorry history of the Los Angeles Police Department's abuses, which made the predominantly black jury more likely to acquit Simpson when considering the standard of reasonable doubt. If a juror's "experience has always been negative, if it involves contact with the police and courts, then what kind of a jury verdict can we expect?" Darden asked. He then reported that virtually any African-American man, himself included, could tell a personal story of injustice at the hands of the police. Darden thus confirmed the soundness of the defense approach of challenging the credibility of certain Los Angeles police officers in the expectation that the Simpson jury would be more open to such challenges than would be jurors to whom police abuses are a distant abstraction. As to those — including, presumably, some of his fellow prosecutors — who characterize this verdict as entirely race-based, Darden remarked that "It is easy to wave that flag."[63]

The jurors in this case — three quarters of whom were black women — viewed the case more through the prism of race than through that of gender because on its facts, it turned more on race-related than on gender-related life experiences. Even for the sole white woman on the jury, this case turned more on the racial bias of the police than on the spousal abuse of the defendant.

VI

Why Was There Such a Great Disparity Between the Public Perception and the Jury Verdict?

Columnist George Will spoke for many Americans when he said, following the verdict, that "Life is full of close calls, but the question of O.J. Simpson's guilt was not one of them. [Simpson got] away with murder."[1] The public perception that O.J. Simpson did it is very much at odds with the jury's verdict. This remains true even after one discounts the differences between the questions being answered by the two "fact-finders": the public's "Did he do it?" and the jury's "Did the prosecution prove its case beyond a reasonable doubt?" I am aware of no well-designed public opinion poll calculated to get at the public's perception of whether the prosecution proved its case beyond a reasonable doubt. But from what I have seen, heard, and read, I would expect that a large proportion of the public — certainly of the white public — not only believes that Simpson committed the murders, but also that the prosecution proved beyond a reasonable doubt that he did so. Part of the reason for this is that many in the public do not understand the important difference between these questions. Others do, but either pretend not to or else disapprove of what they regard as a legal technicality (or, as one of my correspondents put it, "the legal mantra of reasonable doubt"). But even many who understand and endorse the demanding legal standard believe it was clearly met in this case. I think that is incorrect, as I tried to show in Chapter IV. In this chapter I pose a different question: Why this great disparity?

One answer, and the one employed by critics of the jury, is that since this jury comprised nine blacks, it reflected the feelings of the black community that Simpson did not do it, or that even if he did, he should not be convicted by the white establishment. But what about the nonblack jurors? Did they just follow the black jurors? It certainly appears unlikely that Anise Aschenbach would be swayed by racial solidarity. Indeed, she was offended by Johnnie Cochran's closing rhetoric. But even what little we know of the jurors makes that reductionist scenario unlikely. Is there, then, an alternative explanation for the wide disparity between the public perception, especially in the white community, and the jury verdict?

I am aware of no scientifically valid polls or other studies that distinguish attitudes on the basis of how much of the actual trial someone saw and how much of the information was filtered through secondary sources such as reporters, analysts, talk show hosts, and friends. I do know, from my own observations, that many people — including some "experts" who did not watch the trial — were significantly mistaken about the actual evidence before the jury and the arguments actually made by the defense.

Consider, for example, the most dramatic moment of the trial, when prosecutor Christopher Darden asked Simpson to try on the gloves. I happened to be in the courtroom that day, sitting only a few feet away from where Simpson tried on the gloves. I saw every second of the drama. It was crystal clear to everyone within close view that the gloves simply did not fit. Perhaps the prosecutor would offer an explanation as to *why* they didn't fit. But the fact is they just didn't fit. Listen to Linda Deutch, a respected Associated Press correspondent, who sat in the front row. She was asked after the trial what were the turning points: "I thought really pivotal was the day of the gloves, the day O.J. Simpson tried on the gloves in court and they did not fit. It was clear they didn't fit. I was sitting right behind him. . . ."[2] The jurors, who also had a close-up view, apparently agreed they didn't fit. Yet for the millions of Americans who read about this pivotal incident in *The New York Times* — the newspaper of record — and the many other papers that carried the story by *Times* reporter Kenneth Noble, the incident appeared to be completely different.

"Gloves Fit Snugly on Simpson," read the headline in one newspaper carrying the story.[3] "Trying On Bloody Gloves, Simpson Finds Them Tight," read another.[4] The story purported to describe how "after a few moments in which the gloves *appeared* too small for his hands, which were already clad in latex-style gloves, he squeezed the leather ones on. They appeared snug and *the fingers had room to spare* at the top." Noble then quoted one "expert," law Professor Laurie Levenson, who said, "In my opinion, they were snug, but they were on his hand."[5]

This was simply not the same incident as the one I, Linda Deutch, and — most importantly — the jurors saw. But it is not surprising that *New York Times* readers who had not seen the glove demonstration either live or on television news might have a distinctly different impression of this critical event than did the jurors.

The prosecutors did, of course, try to explain away what they knew the jury had seen — namely, that the gloves did not fit. There was much speculation about the latex gloves mentioned in *The New York Times*. I have firsthand information about this issue. During the recess following the glove demonstration, I went into Simpson's holding cell with him, while the other lawyers talked to reporters about what had just happened. I took the gloves in with me and asked Simpson to try them on without the latex gloves, because I anticipated that the prosecution would ask him to do exactly that. He tried them on in the cell and they did not fit any better. The prosecutors obviously tried the same experiment and came to the same conclusion, because they never asked Simpson to try on the leather gloves without the latex undergloves. Yet — because of pundits who speculated without experimenting — the perception persists that the gloves would have fit had they been tried on without the latex gloves.

People really do listen to experts, and these experts have a responsibility to know the facts before they offer their expert opinions. Consider, for example, Professor John Langbein of Yale Law School, who appeared on the *MacNeil/Lehrer NewsHour* on October 4, 1995, and criticized juror Brenda Moran for not "bother[ing] to tell us what her answer was to the *very powerful expert evidence* about why that glove, in fact, didn't fit." However, the only expert scientific evidence regarding the supposed glove shrinkage came from a *defense* witness, Professor Herbert MacDonnell, who performed extensive experiments on blood-soaked gloves and found that they did not shrink. Professor MacDonnell told the jury on September 18, 1995, about these experiments, in which he smeared blood over two gloves identical to those in this case and dried them under the heat and humidity conditions of June 12, 1994.[6] The prosecution's expert, Richard Rubin, was not an expert in whether blood causes gloves to shrink. He performed no experiments. And even Rubin testified that a small amount of blood — such as the amount found on the gloves here — would *not* cause significant glove shrinkage.[7] If exposure to rain and snow had caused the shrinkage, then the gloves would have shrunk before the night of the murder and would not have fit Simpson on that night.

Professor Langbein's rhetorical question suggests that he was unaware of Professor MacDonnell's testimony, unlike the members of the jury, who heard it. Langbein also gave his view that Simpson's guilt was an "easy call" in part because of "the evidence of *blood all over his bedroom*." In fact, there was no blood at all in Simpson's bedroom, with the exception of the microscopic stains on the socks, which the jury believed might have been tampered with. Viewers who listened to Professor Langbein were thus significantly misled by his lack of knowledge coupled with his apparent certainty and expertise. It is a dangerous combination, conducive to widening the perceptual gap between jurors who were actually there and outsiders who relied on commentators like Professor Langbein.

Talk show hosts also misled the public. For example, Larry Elder of Los Angeles' KABC radio insisted that when Mark Fuhrman was called by Nicole Brown back in 1985, he found O.J. Simpson "beating the crap out of her." This "fact" became the foundation for an entire line of argument "proving" that Fuhrman had no animus against Simpson, because if he did, he could easily have arrested Simpson back in 1985 for assault. But Elder was, of course, totally wrong. When Fuhrman arrived, he saw that O.J. Simpson had broken the window of *his own* car and had never touched Nicole Brown. Fuhrman had no legal ground on which he could have arrested Simpson, so Elder's entire argument crumbles. Yet he repeated it, and his listeners probably believed it.

Another, even more influential example of misleading information came from George Will, who went so far as to tell his readers that "If 90 percent of the evidence against [Simpson] had been excluded — indeed, if the defense had been allowed to decide which 90 percent would be excluded — the remaining 10 percent would have sufficed."[8]

Perhaps because he is not a trial lawyer, Will fails to understand that the strength of a case is not measured by the quantity of the evidence alone. Of course, the *quantity* of the prosecution's evidence would have "sufficed" — if that evidence was *qualitatively* acceptable, if police such as Fuhrman and Vannatter had not tampered with it. If *all* the evidence were corrupted, it would not, of course, matter how much there was. For example, in the 1970s I litigated numerous cases on behalf of dissidents in the Soviet Union. Everyone — especially George Will — recognized that the KGB often fabricated evidence. For example, the KGB concocted false documents purporting to prove that Anatoly Scharansky was an American spy. No one really believed this evidence. Would George Will suddenly have concluded that Scharansky was indeed guilty if the KGB had come up with even more documentary evidence of his "guilt"? Of course not. A police agency capable of forging one document is capable of forging many. Indeed, it has now been acknowledged that the KGB had an entire sector devoted to forging documents.

I am not comparing the Los Angeles Police Department to the KGB, nor am I arguing that all the evidence in the O.J. Simpson case was in fact corrupted. I am suggesting that if some of the evidence was tampered with — and the argument with respect to the socks is quite compelling — then the jury would be obliged to regard with suspicion all the evidence to which the corrupt police officers had access. That suspicion might reasonably lead them to discount some more of the prosecution's evidence, without which the circumstantial case would be less than convincing.

The most "incriminating" blood evidence was the most likely to have been tampered with: the blood on the glove, the socks, the gate, and the Bronco. And the blood least likely to have been tampered with — Simpson's degraded and discolored blood at the crime scene, and the blood drops on his own property — was the least incriminating and the most consistent with an innocent explanation. Much of the other evidence — the hair, fibers, shoe prints, and so on — was also consistent with innocence. The strength of the prosecution's case was in the *combination* of all these individually ambiguous items. Thus, any 10 percent — even if it were uncorrupted — would not have "sufficed" under the standard of proof beyond a reasonable doubt. The only exceptions are the Rockingham glove and the socks, but they have "reasonable doubt" written all over them. Indeed, if I had to follow the Will scenario and pick the 10 percent of the evidence to present to the jury, I would choose the most apparently incriminating evidence — the socks, the glove, and the back gate — precisely because that evidence was most likely to have been corrupted. Without that evidence, no other 10 percent — or 20 percent or 30 percent — would be enough to meet the standard of "guilt beyond a reasonable doubt."

I wonder if Will believes that the four policemen who said they did not suspect Simpson when they entered his property were telling the truth. If not, they were part of a police conspiracy to lie and to cover up illegal conduct. I wonder if Will is certain that the socks were not tampered with, and if so, how he deals with the series of unexplained coincidences I describe in Chapter IV. Or does he believe that the police tried to "frame" a guilty man, and if so would he have voted for a conviction? Or has he simply failed to consider these factors in a systematic way? I believe that George Will's failure to consider these scenarios, and his uninformed certainty that any 10 percent of the prosecutor's evidence proves Simpson's guilt beyond a reasonable doubt, lead him toward what he seems to admit are his "partially" racist assumptions. This is how he himself puts it:

> There was condescension, *colored by racism,* in some of the assumptions that the jurors would be incompetent jurors and bad citizens — that they would be putty in the hands of defense attorneys harping on race, that they would be intellectually incapable of following an evidentiary argument, or, worse, they would lack the civic conscience to do so. But *those assumptions seem partially validated* by the jury's refusal even to deliberate.[9]

To argue that "condescension, colored by racism" has been "partially validated" is to acknowledge a kind of bias unacceptable in American society. Too many Americans seem prepared to view the evidence in this case through the prism of such racial bias against black jurors, especially when that view is confirmed by so respected a journalist as George Will. It is interesting to contrast Will's easy willingness to assume that the Simpson jury's verdict was based on racial factors with his adamant unwillingness to believe that death penalty verdicts imposed by predominantly white juries are based on racial factors. In 1987, the Supreme Court had before it a case challenging the administration of capital punishment in Georgia, on the ground that Georgia juries are four times more likely to impose the death penalty on blacks who kill whites than on whites who kill blacks. Will railed against those who concluded — on the basis of extensive statistics — that race was a factor in these decisions. He characterized the data as "a statistical *discrepancy* that *coincided* with race" and produced every possible rationalization to "demonstrate" that the predominantly white Georgia juries considered everything but race.[10] But on the basis of *no* data, statistical or otherwise, Will is sure that the Simpson jury's decision was based on race. Is this not racial bias?

I dwell on Will's views of the case because he is, indeed, influential and representative of a bias revealed by other commentators. Without any such bias or predisposition, the evidence looks quite different from the way Will described it. It is interesting to compare the strength of the defense's circumstantial case that blood was planted on the socks, for example, with the strength of the prosecution's overall circumstantial case that Simpson killed the two victims. Can it really be said that the defense's case for blood having been planted on the socks — Vannatter walking around with Simpson's blood, the videotape of the bedroom, the presence of EDTA, the blood-splatter pattern, and so on — is significantly less compelling than the prosecution's case for guilt? Yet most of the commentators who have described the prosecutor's case as "open-and-shut" have characterized the defense's case that evidence was planted as "speculative" or "unfounded." In fact, neither side's case is open-and-shut; both have evidentiary foundations and speculative elements. But the prosecution bears the burden of proving the defendant's guilt, while the defendant need only raise reasonable doubts about whether blood was planted on the socks.

It is fascinating how the intelligent human mind analyzes the same facts so differently on the basis of a prior assumption of guilt or innocence. The very same people who could not conceive of the possibility that Fuhrman might have planted the glove — because it would be too risky to do so — were entirely prepared to accept the possibility that Simpson returned from Chicago with the murder weapon and bloody clothing in his luggage, which his friend and lawyer Robert Kardashian then took home. For this to have happened, Simpson would have had to engage in the following actions and thought processes. He would have had to take the knife and clothing through airport security from Los Angeles to Chicago, knowing that the bodies might be found well before the plane landed in Chicago and that police might be waiting for him, and his luggage, at O'Hare Airport. Once in Chicago, where he learned of the discovery of the bodies and agreed to return home immediately, he would then have decided to take the knife and clothing back to Los Angeles — and again, through airport security, which by this time might have been alerted by Los Angeles police to conduct a search. Moreover, Simpson would know that Los Angeles police might be waiting for him at the airport, very possibly with a search warrant or arrest warrant. In fact, the police did have the opportunity to seize all of Simpson's luggage but instead allowed Mr. Kardashian to take it home. It is precisely this luggage that would have contained the knife and bloody clothing.

According to this scenario, Simpson was saved from certain detection by serendipity: The police allowed these items to go home with Simpson's "co-conspirator." Moreover, the prosecution knew that Kardashian had the luggage for several months before it even attempted to question him about its contents.

As absurd as the traveling-evidence theory is, it continues to be offered even today by otherwise quite intelligent people, blinded by their conviction that Simpson must be guilty, and frustrated by their inability to figure out how he got rid of the weapon and clothing. These same intelligent people refuse to consider the possibility that the police officer who dictated the Fuhrman tapes may have been capable of planting the glove.

A number of other influential myths were perpetrated by media pundits. One of the most pernicious and widespread was that, in order to prevail, the defense had to prove a massive conspiracy involving the entire Los Angeles Police Department, the FBI, and the private laboratories that tested the blood samples. This theory is a variation on the Will theme, since it assumes that the prosecution's case was so strong that if any portion of it was uncorrupted, the evidence of guilt would still be overwhelming. It would follow from that assumption that the defense must be claiming that all the evidence had been corrupted. And for all the evidence to have been corrupted would have required a broad-based, pervasive conspiracy and cover-up. Commentator after commentator asked rhetorically how the Los Angeles Police Department could be smart enough to pull off so widespread a frame-up, yet stupid enough to botch the investigation the way it did. As one pundit put it: "They can't be *both* James Bond *and* the Keystone Kops." Even comedians — Robert Klein, for one — had a ball mocking this defense argument. A columnist for the *Des Moines Register* mocked the defense argument in characteristic style:

When in doubt plead conspiracy. When in double doubt, plead conspiracy and argue that the other side is also incompetent. In other words, the police are smart enough to carry out a complex plot to frame Simpson, but dumb enough to treat the blood samples like so many condiment packets from the drive-through window at McDonald's. Pleading conspiracy and incompetence at the same time is like grumping about a lousy meal, then complaining about the small portions.[11]

The *St. Petersburg Times* had "Defense Attorneys Accusing the Los Angeles Police of a Department-wide Conspiracy to Frame Simpson."[12] The *Atlanta Constitution* called it "the wide conspiracy needed to plant the mountain of evidence against Simpson."[13] Even *The New York Times* characterized the defense claim — in a news report — as "broad or wide-ranging conspiracy."[14]

The only problem with all these stories is that the defense never argued that there was a widespread conspiracy. The jury understood precisely what the defense was, in fact, claiming, and several of the jurors said, after the verdict, that they agreed with our far narrower and more fact-based argument. We charged a handful of Los Angeles police officers with conspiring to lie about why they went to Simpson's house and entered his property without a warrant. The jury — and many experienced lawyers — agreed with us on *that* conspiracy. Having established its likelihood, we then raised questions about the actions of an even smaller number of bad cops — Vannatter and Fuhrman — who could easily have sprinkled Simpson's blood, which Vannatter had been carrying around for three hours, on the socks, the glove, and the back gate. That was the conspiracy. And if the jurors believed that this conspiracy may have occurred, then they could reasonably distrust the rest of the evidence, without the need to include many others in any conspiracy or cover-up. Moreover, if the defense was right, the conspirators were never James Bonds. After all, they did get caught. They were the Keystone Kops, but with malice aforethought.

Finally, there is no inconsistency between negligence and corruption. Negligence creates the *opportunity* for corruption. Had the LAPD been scrupulous in its evidence collection — had it played by the book — Vannatter would never have had the opportunity to walk around with Simpson's blood for three hours. Nor would Fuhrman — who was supposed to be off the case — have had the opportunity to "find" the glove. If the criminalists had clearly established whether the blood was on the socks and the back gate on the day of the murders, there would have been no opportunity for anyone to plant it or to claim it was planted. If Thano Peratis had kept a record of precisely how much blood he took from Simpson, there would have been no opportunity for dispute over whether Vannatter sprinkled the blood on the socks and gate.

Another myth relating to the blood evidence was that the DNA alone proved that Simpson did it, and that in order to secure an acquittal, the defense would have to disprove the validity of DNA. But the processes by which the jurors arrived at the reasonable doubts, outlined in Chapter IV, all presuppose the *accuracy* of the DNA analysis and assume that all the blood identified as Simpson's did, in fact, come from him and that all the blood identified as Goldman's and Brown's came from them. If any jurors experienced doubts about the DNA — about either the science itself or, more likely, the application of the science under the unprofessional conditions of this case — those doubts would have been above and beyond the reasonable doubts previously outlined. Put another way, even if the jurors believed that all the blood was properly typed and identified, they might still have reasonably suspected that the most incriminating of the blood drops — those found on the socks, the glove, the back gate and the Bronco — might have been planted.

Some myths die hard. At the very beginning of the case, the prosecution alleged that the murders were committed by a knife purchased by Simpson at a particular cutlery store shortly before the murders took place. They even introduced the owner of the store at the preliminary hearing to testify as to the purchase. Then the defense found something in Simpson's home that, pursuant to California practice, was secured by a judge, placed in an envelope, and given to the court. Everyone speculated about the contents of this mystery envelope. I will never forget an encounter I had with a TV reporter shortly after the "envelope" story made headline news. My daughter and I were at Martha's Vineyard airport; she asked whether she could have some M & Ms from a vending machine that sold loose handfuls. I told her she could get the M & Ms but would have to wait until after dinner to eat them. I got an envelope from USAir and put the loose M & Ms in it. A reporter then approached and asked me, "What's in the envelope?" I replied, "I'm going to tell you." Expecting a scoop, she turned on the camera only to hear that the envelope contained M & Ms. I even showed her the contents. She said, "Not that envelope — the one in the O.J. case." I replied, "Oh, *that* one! I can't disclose *its* contents." To this day, there is still speculation as to what was in *that* envelope, with most pundits concluding that it was the knife Simpson bought before the murders — and that it had never been used. While I cannot confirm this, neither will I deny it.

Some of the media myths were perpetrated by the prosecutors. Consider this one, which Simpson himself corrected on the day after the verdict. A woman called the Larry King show on October 4, 1995, to ask about the prosecution's claim that the limousine driver had seen a six-foot-tall African-American walking quickly from the driveway toward the house, and that this black man must have been Simpson returning from an attempt to hide the bloody glove. There had been all kinds of speculation about the incriminating nature of this dark, shadowy figure. Simpson solved the mystery with his own phone call to the show. "It was me," he said. "I was walking out of my front door, dropping my bags, and going back in."

But what about the driver's testimony that the man was coming *from* the driveway? There was no such testimony. During her closing, Marcia Clark had tried to stretch the driver's testimony to reach the driveway, but she was cut off, because that is not what Park saw. He saw precisely what Simpson said happened. In fact, he illustrated where the figure was by pointing to a spot on a picture of the area. The man had been nowhere near the driveway. Yet the myth persisted in the media until Simpson was able to clear it up on television, as Cochran had earlier done in the courtroom. It persists to this day, even in court papers filed by the Browns and Goldmans in their civil suit, but it is false. Thus, a suspiciously incriminating scenario was easily explained in an entirely innocent manner, but not before many members of the public included it in their list of proofs positive that Simpson must be guilty.

An important reason, therefore, why much of the public has a different view of the facts than did the jurors is that there were two radically different trials: the one before the jury, and one before the public. (Actually, there were *three* different trials — the third was in the predominantly black press, much of which favored Simpson. But I am focusing on the mainstream press, because the question I am trying to answer is why there is such a great disparity between white public perception and the jury verdict.) Some observers saw both the jury trial and the media trial. Some saw only the media trial; the jurors saw only the jury trial. On the issue of spousal abuse, there were certainly two very different trials. The public saw and heard many unproved allegations of abuse; the jury heard only one admitted instance of physical violence, and a small number of other disputed instances of rude, insensitive, and cruel behavior.

This is certainly not the first case in which the public has had different information than the jury. In the William Kennedy Smith case, the public knew far more about the background and prior histories of both the defendant and the accuser. The same was true of the von Bülow case and many others. At least two aspects of the Simpson case were, however, atypical. The first was the risky decision made by the defense early on to challenge the secret grand jury proceedings and have the prosecution's case presented publicly at a preliminary hearing. This decision helped the case before the jury, but at the cost of hurting the case in the court of public opinion, and may have contributed to the enormous disparity between the public perception and the jury verdict.

Another atypical factor was that in the Simpson case, more than in any other in history, the voices of the victims were heard loudly, clearly, and frequently in the media. But they were not heard so clearly in the courtroom. Historically, the American criminal trial has involved an adversarial contest between two parties — the prosecution and the defense. Although the prosecution generally purports to speak for the victims, especially if they are dead, the prosecution's actual client is the state, not the victim or victims. Notwithstanding this clear legal rule distinguishing the interests of the state from those of the victim, the families of victims generally rely on the prosecution to speak for them. That is often a great mistake, since the practical interest of the prosecution may be different from those of the victims' families.

In the Simpson case, the families of the victims, especially the Goldman family, spoke for themselves — outside the courtroom. They did, of course, fully cooperate with the prosecutors as well. But their voices were also heard independently. They held frequent press conferences; their lawyers regularly appeared on television shows; they sat in court nearly every day; and they filed lawsuits against the defendant. In this respect, the Simpson trial before the court of public opinion was conducted more like a French trial than like a typical American trial. In France, victims and their families play a legal role in the criminal prosecution. In the Simpson case, while the victims' families may not have played a formal legal role in the courtroom, they were omnipresent outside the courtroom.

Moreover, an entire television industry has been built around victims. In the Simpson case, Geraldo Rivera became the television voice and picture for the victims. His entire show, viewed by millions every night, presented the case through the victims' perspective. Although he made admirable efforts to present differing viewpoints, Rivera himself openly sided with the victims and gave voice to their perspective. People who regularly received their information about the case from Rivera received it through someone who assumed Simpson's guilt. Other shows, although to a lesser degree, did the same thing. No show, no pundit, no newspaper — certainly none catering to the largely white audience that strongly believed Simpson guilty — presented a perspective opposed to Rivera's. This could not help but to widen the gulf between white public perception and the verdict of the jury.

The defense was, of course, aware of this gulf, and we were concerned by it for several reasons. In the event of an acquittal, we knew that our client would return to a world in which many would treat him as guilty. In the event of a conviction, we would face appellate courts with a predisposition to find any errors "harmless" because of the "defendant's obvious guilt," as courts often put it. In the event of a hung jury, we would face the daunting prospect of finding several dozen people who could still apply the presumption of innocence. Accordingly, we did not remain silent during the course of the trial. We defended our client both in the court of law and in the court of public opinion.

I am often asked, in an accusatory tone, why I defend my clients in the media. First, I do not deny that this is what I do. Some lawyers adamantly refuse to speak to the press, reserving their arguments for the courts. Others leak information to the press and then publicly deny that they are the source. The law firm of Williams and Connolly — legendary lawyer Edward Bennett Williams's old firm — has a policy of not speaking to the press about its cases. When Williams was running the firm, speaking to the press was not necessary. He had direct access to publishers, editors, and top reporters, and he was a world-class leaker and spin master. Now some of his old firm's clients may well suffer from the rigid policy. They suffer because prosecutors almost always try their cases in the media, and if defense attorneys don't defend them in the media, they can lose ground not only in the court of public opinion, but in the court of law as well.

Most large prosecutorial offices have a

full-time public relations staff, hire media consultants for important cases, and have thick Rolodexes with the home phone numbers of friendly reporters to whom they provide a constant stream of confidential scoops. In a recent public discussion about the media and high-profile cases, my friend Linda Fairstein — the chief of the sex crimes division of the Manhattan District Attorney's Office — solemnly declared that she would be fired if she ever leaked information to the media. I responded with a chuckle, "Of course, *you* would be fired, because *your boss* wants to do all the leaking." Her boss, the legendary prosecutor Robert Morgenthau, has been accused of being one of the world's greatest leakers and media massagers. He is the master of the orchestrated media campaign, and his student Rudolph Giuliani parlayed his mastery of the media into the mayoralty of New York City.[15]

When it comes to the media, defense attorneys are rank amateurs compared to prosecutors, for one obvious reason: Prosecutors have constant access to a stream of secret information that the media want and that the prosecution wants the media to publish. But prosecutors don't want their fingerprints on the information, so they develop long-term confidential relationships with the most important media people in their jurisdiction. Few such recipients of this valuable prosecutorial information would ever burn a prosecutor, either by revealing the source or by giving the story a negative spin, for fear that the information might dry up. Defense lawyers, on the other hand, rarely have access to secret information; when they do, the information is usually of a sort they do not want to see published — for example, an admission by the defendant that he did it.

Moreover, any given defense attorney handles cases in which the media are interested only episodically, whereas the prosecutor's office — which is city-wide or county-wide — is a constant source of newsworthy stories. The media, therefore, need not be as solicitous of the defense as of the prosecution. In addition, most defendants don't even want their names in the paper. They would be happy with the British rule, which limits press coverage of ongoing cases and forbids either the prosecution or the defense from speaking to the media until after the verdict.

The prosecution, on the other hand, lives

by the media. Most district attorneys are elected. They need to keep their names before the public. Further, since most defendants are — as a statistical matter — guilty, the prosecution benefits by getting its story out there as soon as possible, in order to create an atmosphere favorable to conviction. Prosecutors also want potential witnesses, especially those close to the defendant, to realize that the defendant is going down, so that they will be inclined to abandon him and make a deal with the prosecution. (Rudolph Giuliani was quite open about sending this message in high-profile cases.) Finally, even if there are ethical or legal restrictions on prosecutors' leaks of information, they can always have the police do it for them. Prosecutorial and police leaks are an important part of the arsenal arrayed against defendants, and the defense lawyers who ignore this reality do so at great risk to their clients.

The *Los Angeles Times*, for example, in a postverdict review of the Simpson case, concluded that "Police prosecutors and sources close to them struck first in the media wars that immediately enveloped the O.J. Simpson murder case."[16] They engaged in a series of "orchestrated leaks" and disclosures, which culminated in the release of the 911 tape of the call made by Nicole Brown to the police. Stryker McGuire, the West Coast editor of *Newsweek* and a frequent recipient of those leaks, concluded that they were deliberately designed to shape public perception and influence legal strategy in order to overcome Simpson's perceived popularity.[17]

The defense team had no choice but to defend Simpson in the court of public opinion, since that was the forum in which the prosecution and police were deliberately beginning his trial. As U.S. Supreme Court Justice Anthony Kennedy recently put it:

> An attorney's duties do not begin inside the courtroom door. He or she cannot ignore the practical implications of a legal proceeding for the client. . . . [A]n attorney may take reasonable steps to defend a client's reputation and reduce the adverse consequences of indictment, especially in the face of a prosecution deemed unjust or commenced with improper motives. A defense attorney may pursue lawful strategies to ob-

tain dismissal of an indictment or reduction of charges, including an attempt to demonstrate in the court of public opinion that the client does not deserve to be tried.[18]

What a defense attorney "may" do, he *must* do, if it is necessary to defend his client. A zealous defense attorney has a professional obligation to take every legal and ethically permissible step that will serve the client's best interest — even if the attorney finds the step personally distasteful. Reasonable lawyers can and do disagree about whether speaking to the media may help or hurt a given client's cause. But once it is decided that doing so will help, the lawyer should not decline a client's request to be defended in the court of public opinion, unless such a defense would violate some ethical or legal rule.

One of the hardest decisions faced by a defense lawyer is whether to support or to oppose the televising of the trial. Sometimes that decision is made with no input from counsel, but often the court will ask the prosecutor and defense counsel to take a position on this issue. In doing so, defense lawyers should consider *only* the best interest of their clients, and never their own views about the televising of trials or what effect the added publicity may have on their own careers.

In the Simpson case, our opinion was requested, and I had to set aside my views as a civil libertarian that all trials should be televised. I also had to set aside my views as a teacher that only trials that will educate the public should be televised. Nor would I consider what impact television would have on the image of lawyers or on my own reputation. The only appropriate question was how televising the trial would affect Simpson's chances for a favorable outcome.

In every individual case, the answer will be different. Some defendants will benefit and others will lose from their trials being televised. I was influenced in my thinking by my recent experience as the appellate lawyer for Mike Tyson. His trial had not been televised and the world learned about the evidence through the reporters who covered the trial, most of whom had a distinctly anti-Tyson bias. Moreover, the trial judge, Patricia Gifford, made numerous rulings that she never would have gotten away with had the case been nationally televised. First, she allowed herself to be hand picked by the prosecution, rather than randomly selected, as occurs in every city in America except Indianapolis. She also excluded the testimony of three crucial eyewitnesses who would have proved that the alleged victim lied about her lack of sexual interest in Tyson.

Finally, in their closing arguments, the prosecutors told the jury things they never would have dared to say in front of a national audience. For example, they made the "dressed for sex" argument, suggesting to the jury that if the alleged victim had really wanted to have sex with Tyson, she would have worn her black see-through panties rather than her polka-dotted ones. Because the prosecutor gets the last word, the defense could not tell the jury that the see-through panties had been washed and were not yet dry when Tyson called. The prosecutor also implied that the victim was a virgin, when in fact she had previously engaged in voluntary sex with a high-school classmate — whom she had then falsely accused of raping her.[19]

I was convinced that Tyson had suffered because his trial was not televised, especially since his trial lawyer never spoke to the media, while the prosecutor talked nonstop to everyone. I did not want to see the same mistake made with O.J. Simpson. There was, of course, a downside to the televising of the Simpson case. But on balance, we all believed that the television camera would assure closer scrutiny of the prosecution's case and of the judge's rulings. As for talking to the media, we knew the prosecution and the police would be leaking their evidence in a steady stream, and we wanted the world to see and hear our side of the case as well.

As an appellate lawyer, I am in a somewhat different position than trial lawyers with respect to televising trials. Although the law requires appellate judges to decide the appeal on the cold record of the case and on the legal issues, I know that appellate judges are human beings who are influenced by the public perception of a trial's fairness and a defendant's guilt or innocence. I also know that appellate judges watch highly publicized trials and form impressions. By the time we had to decide whether to support or oppose television coverage of the Simpson trial, the public perception was decidedly against Simpson, particularly in the community from which most judges come. I knew we had a strong case, and I thought we had little to lose and much to gain by having that case presented to a television audience.

Television coverage hurt Simpson in the short run, since the prosecution got to put on its case twice before the defense ever called a witness. But the coverage helped Simpson considerably in the long run. I am convinced that those who watched most of the trial had a better sense of the weakness of the prosecution's case than those who followed it through the eyes and words of reporters. The many misconceptions about the prosecution's evidence, the defense's evidence and arguments, and the basic facts were only heightened by the generally mediocre and often opinionated commentary offered on the evening recaps from which millions of Americans obtained their "news." It was obvious that several of the frequent commentators — busy lawyers — rarely watched the day's proceedings; they were grossly inaccurate in describing and assessing what had occurred. It was often embarrassing to watch legal commentators speculating wildly about issues they knew little about. For the most part, the professional journalists — most of whom were nonlawyers — were far more perceptive than the lawyers in describing and analyzing the "action." There were, of course, some very astute legal analysts — such as many on CNN and Court TV, and a few on the major networks — but they were the exception to an otherwise sad rule.

Since the end of the case, there has been much debate about whether future trials should be televised. That is the wrong question. The right question is far broader: Should trials be covered by the media the way they are covered in this country, or should we introduce a system more like that governing trial coverage in Great Britain, Canada, and some other countries, where lawyers may not speak to the media and where the media are severely restricted in what they can report about an ongoing case?

Once it is decided that lawyers — prosecutors and defense attorneys — may try their cases on the courthouse steps and on *Nightline*, then it is foolish not to allow television cameras into the courtroom. The television camera assures greater accuracy, less bias, and more direct observation of the trial. To be sure, there are some small additional costs — lawyers may play to the camera, and perhaps the televising causes some delays. But most of the real costs erroneously attributed to the televising of trials are more correctly attributable to the trying of cases in the media. The television camera is far more disturbing on the courthouse steps than it is in the courtroom itself. Nearly everything bad that the camera can do in the courtroom can be made worse on the courthouse steps.

Imagine what would have occurred in the Simpson case if everything else had been kept constant, but the television camera was removed from inside the courtroom. The "circus" atmosphere would have intensified. The only television footage available to the public would have shown lawyers scrambling to get their sound bites on the air. The relatively dignified and substantive courtroom proceedings would never have been seen. The case would still have been tried in the press, but without the benefit of rules of evidence. It would have been a free-for-all, with far too much inference in the hands of reporters, lawyers, spin doctors, and pundits. No one, except for a few dozen reporters and a handful of courtroom observers, would have seen for himself or herself whether or not the gloves actually fit. Television in the courtroom helped to keep everyone more honest.

It makes little sense, in my view, to censor the *only* unbiased, direct, and entirely truthful reporter of the trial — the courtroom television camera — while still allowing extensive coverage by more biased, partisan, and inaccurate human reporters. Our Constitution would not permit us to adopt the British system, which is tantamount to censorship; nor would its adoption be wise as a matter of policy. Watergate, Whitewater, and many other scandals would never have been exposed under the English rules. We must learn to live with the kind of television coverage of trials that the Simpson case exemplified and perhaps took to an extreme. But we must become better at it, so that Americans who watch the court proceedings and those who read about them do not experience *different* trials, as they did in the Simpson case. We must try to narrow the gulf between verdicts by jurors and verdicts by the court of public opinion, or else we risk losing public confidence in the administration of justice.

VII

Can Money Buy an Acquittal?

Among the criticisms of the legal system most frequently voiced after the Simpson verdict is that money determines the outcome of cases. In fact, an important kernel of truth is contained in this criticism, but it must be placed in its proper perspective.

There are several possible reference points against which the amount of money spent by the Simpson defense can be compared. The first, and the one most often mentioned, is the contrast with other, less affluent defendants. Simpson spent many times more than the typical defendant, even a defendant in a capital case. Indeed, most defendants facing the ultimate punishment are indigent, and many states enforce strict limits on the amount of compensation their court-appointed lawyers can receive. This does not mean that their appointed lawyers cannot spend as much as they choose, but the money will have to come from their own pockets. I know this from personal experience, because I litigated a death penalty case on behalf of two brothers for more than ten years, and spent tens of thousands of dollars of my own money on their defense.[1] Ultimately, the death sentence was reversed, but not without thousands of hours of uncompensated time spent by a team of excellent volunteer lawyers and students.

Few death row inmates have access to lawyers willing to spend their own time and money to save their lives. Most are relegated to a single, inexperienced lawyer, who has no budget for investigation and a cap of several thousand dollars for the entire case, including appeals. In one case now pending review, a death row inmate — who many observers believe may be innocent — was represented by an inexperienced lawyer who spent less than twenty hours preparing the case and did not even cross-examine the major prosecution witness, who may well have been the real killer.[2] Contrast this with the efforts made by Simpson's legal team and the cost of his defense.

This disparity is not fair. But the victim of the unfairness is the indigent defendant who is denied the resources to challenge the prosecution's case against him. The remedy is not to bring affluent defendants like O.J. Simpson down to the level of indigent defendants by placing a cap on what they can spend, as some have proposed. Indigent defendants would not benefit from such a cap. Indeed, they, too, would be hurt, since the money affluent defendants spend often helps *all* defendants. For example, the challenges directed by the Simpson defense team against the ineptitude of the Los Angeles forensic labs will assist indigent defendants in making similar challenges. That is why lawyers who defend the indigent are not calling for a cap on spending by wealthy defendants. Indeed, they are calling for an increase in the resources allocated for the defense of the indigent — an increase hypocritically opposed by many who are most vocal about the "disparity" reflected by the Simpson case.

A second basis of comparison can be found between the resources available to affluent defendants like Simpson and the resources available to the prosecution. Here, there is even greater disparity. The prosecution *always* has more resources than the defense, even when the defendant is an O.J. Simpson, a Michael

Milken, a Leona Helmsley, or a Mike Tyson.

In the Simpson case the prosecution spent more, in absolute terms, than the defense. The defense had about a dozen lawyers, while the prosecution used nearly four dozen. In a recent internal memorandum written by an assistant district attorney, it was disclosed that no trial in the history of the Los Angeles District Attorney's Office "has enveloped and consumed the passions of the members of our staff more than *People v. Simpson.*" Despite the fact that the Los Angeles prosecutor's office has approximately a thousand lawyers, the Fuhrman case was sent to the State Attorney General's Office for a decision whether to prosecute because virtually everyone in the local office had some involvement — direct, indirect, or vicarious — in the Simpson prosecution. Moreover, the defense had only a handful of investigators, while the prosecution had access to the entire Los Angeles Police Department, the FBI, the Chicago Police Department, and even Interpol — tens of thousands of officers.

Beyond these material resources, the prosecution had the power to threaten some witnesses and grant immunity to others; and it had the entire sovereignty of the State of California — including its tax base — behind it. The prosecution almost always has the judge, who is typically a former prosecutor, on its side. No defendant, regardless of personal wealth, can compete with a government, its police, its prosecutors, and its judges. Finally, the prosecution represents "the people" — an imposing symbolic advantage. In the next chapter, I will explore other important differences between the prosecution and the defense — differences that create prosecutorial advantages for which no amount of money can ever compensate.

The real complaint, implicit in much of the current criticism of the resources available to O.J. Simpson's defense, is that he was one of those rare defendants who could challenge the prosecution's case on a relatively level playing field. Most people naturally root for the prosecution and want it to win, as it almost always does. Anything that assists a defendant in challenging the prosecution is unpopular. Anything bearing the label "prosecution," "victim," or "district attorney" is popular. It is no accident that being a district attorney is a stepping-stone to higher political office. President Clinton, like a significant percentage of U.S. senators, representatives, governors, and mayors, is a former prosecutor. Name a former defense attorney in higher office today. The same is true of the bench, which has many former prosecutors (such as Lance Ito), but few former defense attorneys.

For our adversary system of justice to work, it requires a relatively level playing field, on which defendants can adequately challenge the prosecution's case. Without challenge, police and prosecutors become lazy and even corrupt. They become too used to winning, even in questionable cases. It is imperative, therefore, for the criminal justice system to provide more resources to indigent defendants. Had Simpson been yet another indigent defendant denied the resources needed to challenge the prosecutor's forensic case, he might well have remained in prison. His lawyers, like most defense attorneys, would have had no choice but to accept the prosecution's forensic evidence. Nor would they have been able to travel to North Carolina to litigate and appeal the ruling regarding the Fuhrman tapes. That would have been unfair. Even prosecutor Christopher Darden recognized this when he said that one of the reasons he decided to become involved in the Simpson case was because it was one of the few cases fought on a relatively level playing field, with adequate resources on both sides.[3]

Yet some still complain that Simpson "bought" his acquittal. But consider this: If Simpson had been sick, no one would have complained if he spent his money on the best medical care available, including a team of experienced specialists. The fact that he was getting better medical care than an indigent patient would have been accepted as part of our free-market system. Efforts would be made to elevate the level of medical care available to poor patients, but few would suggest bringing wealthy patients down to the level of medical care available to the poorest of patients. But if the same wealthy person spends his money to defend himself, he is accused of distorting the system.

Yes, there is something very wrong with a system under which the wealthy can obtain better legal help — or better medical care — than the poor. But again, the remedy for this unfairness is not to deny the wealthy the opportunity to challenge the even more formidable resources of the state. It is to provide additional resources to indigent defendants, so that they, too, can try to keep the prosecution honest.

A recent study of the U.S. justice system concluded that money can have a decisive impact on jury verdicts — but in a way different from that suggested by the conventional wisdom. "This much is certain: money buys research [by which the writer means "investigation"]; research digs up facts, and facts can overpower jurors."[4] This same study concluded that the courtroom skills of high-priced lawyers are less important than their investigative talent and resources: "The importance of the lawyer's golden tongue is probably overrated; it is the witnesses that the lawyer presents before the jury who do the most persuasive talking. The lawyer's most decisive role is therefore in building a solid case."

Moreover, all the money in the world cannot change the verdict in a clear case. Many wealthy defendants lose, despite the expenditure of large fortunes: Michael Milken's wealth did not keep him out of prison, nor did Leona Helmsley's; Patricia Hearst's family resources probably inclined the courts to lean over backward to assure that she was not benefitting from any favoritism. However, it is true that

271

no wealthy people are ever executed. Since Clarence Darrow saved Leopold and Loeb from the electric chair, the death penalty has been reserved essentially for the poor. That is a separate scandal, but it does not prove that money alone can buy an acquittal for the guilty rich.

It is not true, although it is often asserted, that any criminal case necessarily has some weaknesses that can be exploited by a high-priced lawyer with unlimited investigative resources. The slogan that an old Texas lawyer reputedly had on his office door, "Reasonable doubt for an unreasonable price," was puffery. No amount of money can buy reasonable doubt in an open-and-shut case. In a close case, however, the investigative and other resources that money can buy may well make the difference between conviction and acquittal.

The Simpson case illustrates the perceptiveness and accuracy of these conclusions. Simpson's wealth allowed his lawyers to retain the world's leading forensic experts and to challenge virtually every aspect of the state's forensic case. It also allowed him to retain legal specialists — such as Barry Scheck, Peter Neufeld, and Robert Blasier — knowledgeable enough to make the best use of these experts and to task them immediately. Juror comments also confirm the conclusion that it is "the witnesses" more than "the lawyer's golden tongue" that may make the difference in a close case.[5]

Money, of course, is not always used effectively, even if it is available to the defense. In the Claus von Bülow case, for example, the defense lawyers at the first trial were simply not prepared to challenge the state's forensic case. In a dreadful mistake that almost cost von Bülow his liberty, his original trial lawyers "stipulated" that the substance found inside a needle discovered in the infamous "black bag" was insulin. In a recent interview, the lawyer acknowledged that he was asleep at the wheel:

> Asked recently why the defense originally agreed that there was insulin in the needle, John F. Sheehan, a member of the defense team who now sits on the Rhode Island Superior Court, said, "I didn't know what I was doing. I never should have stipulated to that because there wasn't insulin on the inside of that needle. I don't think we prepared our case that well. We didn't

273

have sufficient medical evidence to rebut theirs. And then we later found that evidence."[6]

Judge Sheehan is wrong in saying "we later found" the medical evidence that rebutted the prosecution's case. When my team took over the case, we started from scratch, reexamining every piece of forensic evidence presented by the prosecution — and doing so paid off. We retained first-quality experts and were able to destroy the prosecution's forensic case on appeal and at the second trial. It cost us hundreds of thousands of dollars to bring out the truth, but it was money well spent. Had von Bülow lacked the resources necessary to conduct this renewed investigation, the result in his second trial might have been the same as in his first, where an ill-prepared defense team, which had the resources to challenge the forensic evidence, chose instead to "stipulate" to a critical incriminating fact that turned out to be false.

In the Simpson case, we stipulated to almost nothing and challenged nearly everything. We independently investigated and reinvestigated every conclusion reached by prosecution witnesses. By the end of the case, we probably knew more about the Los Angeles Police Department forensic labs than the people who ran them. In conducting these extensive investigations, we did what prosecutors often do and what defendants rarely do: We left no stone unturned. When prosecutors are thorough in their search for incriminating evidence, they are praised for ferreting out the facts. Yet when defense attorneys are equally thorough in their search for exculpatory evidence, they are condemned for trying to "buy" an acquittal. The defense can "buy" an acquittal only if the other side — the police and prosecutors — give it openings to exploit and if the facts are ambiguous enough to bear an interpretation consistent with innocence. In the Simpson case, money mattered, just as the absence of money matters in the thousands of cases in which defendants are denied a fair opportunity to challenge the prosecution's evidence because they lack the resources to mount such a challenge.

The time has come to provide all defendants, especially those facing execution or long prison terms, with resources sufficient to challenge prosecution cases. This is not to propose that every indigent defendant have a team of twelve defense lawyers, three investigators, and six forensic experts appointed to assist him. But all indigent defendants — indeed, even working-class defendants — who have a large team of prosecutors, police, and experts arrayed against them should be afforded a reasonably comparable defense team. Those who believe that the criminal trial should focus more on finding truth and less on promoting other values should support such reforms, since an unchallenged prosecution is less likely to produce truth in the long run than a prosecution zealously challenged by a defense with the resources necessary to create a level playing field. If justice is to keep her scales in balance, the defense must have resources equal to those of the prosecution.

In the Simpson case, the defendant had the resources necessary to challenge every aspect of the prosecution's case. Had he not had these resources — or the celebrity that enabled him to obtain them by writing a book and selling autographs — he might not have won the case. In this sense, his money helped him secure an acquittal, just as it might have helped him secure a full recovery from a treatable disease. But money cannot cure an incurable disease. Nor can it buy an acquittal for a defendant whose guilt is clear and certain.

VIII

Are Prosecutors and Defense Attorneys Advocates Only for Their Clients, or Also for Justice?

The role of defense lawyers and prosecutors in criminal cases is misunderstood by much of the public, including the well-informed public. Even many lawyers have little real understanding of what advocates are expected to do in a hotly contested criminal trial.

Several weeks after the Simpson verdict, my wife and I were walking down Madison Avenue in New York when a well-dressed woman approached us and said, "I used to love you so much, and now I'm so disappointed in you — and my husband would use even stronger words." She explained, "You used to defend Jews like Scharansky and Pollard.* Now you

*Natan Scharansky was a Jewish dissident who was falsely accused by the Soviet Union of spying for the United States. Jonathan Pollard, an American Jew, pleaded guilty to spying for Israel.

defend Jew-killers like O.J." I replied that she was wrong ever to have loved me because she probably didn't understand what I do. A few blocks farther along, a black man hugged me and said, "Great job. I love what you do." I told him not to love what I do or else he would soon be disappointed.

These two encounters — and the hundreds like them I have experienced over the years, especially since the Simpson verdict — underline the public reaction to defense lawyers. When we represent defendants they like, the public loves us. When we represent defendants they dislike, the public hates us. For some criminal lawyers, this poses no problem, since they choose clients on the basis of their popularity. These lawyers would never dream of representing any client who is disliked by the public. I know several such lawyers, some of whom consult with public relations experts before they take on a controversial client.

Other criminal lawyers select their clients on the basis of causes or constituencies. They will represent defendants who may be disliked by the *general* public, as long as their *particular* constituents approve of the defendant. Many feminist lawyers will defend any woman who has killed or maimed a man, regardless of the circumstances, because they know they can count on support from certain feminist groups. William Kunstler, a political lawyer, often represented clients who were unpopular with the general public; but they were always popular with Kunstler's particular left-wing constituency. There are right-wing analogues to Kunstler.

Criminal lawyers who are true civil libertarians have no constituency. Many lawyers who claim to be civil libertarians are merely *using* principles of civil liberties to further their political ends. During the period when the left was persecuted by antilabor forces, McCarthyites and anti-immigration zealots, many on the left became civil libertarians. More recently, when civil liberties were employed against some of the left's own agendas — such as racial quotas, university speech codes, and "political correctness" — some began to see civil libertarians as the enemies of the left. At about the same time, a few conservatives took on the mantle of civil liberties to challenge these same agendas. Many African-Americans who champion free speech when Louis Farrakhan is censored by some university call for censorship of white racist speakers. Many Jews who supported freedom of speech for Meir Kahane were appalled when the ACLU defended the right of neo-Nazis to march in Skokie. Fair-weather civil libertarians are often "disappointed" by civil libertarians who defend the rights of the individual without regard to politics, gender, race, or other agenda concerns.

The verdict in the Simpson case resulted in an outpouring of "disappointment" unlike that in any other case during my thirty-two-year career as a lawyer. Many people took the acquittal personally, as if they themselves had been denied justice by what they perceived as an illegitimate result. My hate mail, which used to be limited to crackpot anti-Semites railing against my Jewishness, suddenly became more mainstream, although certainly no less vitriolic. Indeed, some of the most virulent, hateful and bigoted letters came from Jews who said they used to love me, but now hate me. Most of them focused on one of three themes. The first is typical of all my hate mail: How can you represent someone who I think is guilty? A few representative examples:

In the past, I have purchased your books, have listened to you on talk radio and have admired you for your intelligence and your commitment to individual and civil rights. . . . It is evident your philosophy was applied to the Simpson trial. Winning at any cost without any concern for our right to be protected from murderers is immoral, abominable and self-serving. Everyone is entitled to a defense which should be based on truth not on lies made up by those of your ilk. The time has come for reasonable persons to change the statutes dealing with conducting a client's defense. . . . When OJ Simpson murders again, the blood is on your hands and that of your defense colleagues.

I am writing this letter with tremendous pain in my heart. I can't believe that my idol could turn on me like you have. . . . From the first time I read any of your works, I became a true believer in what I thought you stood for. I always believed you were the torch bearer for all our Jewish causes and our protector from all the anti-Semites that are out to hurt us. . . .

[W]ith your decision to join the Simpson defense team you took that trust and threw it in the garbage. . . . Is winning the only important thing to you, what about our brother Ronald who was butchered by your client, where does he win. How about our community, when do we finally win. Shame, shame, shame.

I am sending you my copy of *Chutzpah*. . . . I found *Chutzpah* inspiring. . . . Many of us have some understanding of the so-called legal justice system and we do not expect perfection. However, especially you may be held to a higher moral standard. I would demand that you not participate in an exercise cunningly designed to distort what you are certain is the truth resulting in freeing a person guilty of a most serious crime. . . . Do not bother to tell me about the lawyer's duty. You are not compelled to accept a case. Let lesser lawyers ignore morality and defend the clearly guilty. . . . Now I associate you with Simpson's guilt.

I am writing this letter to voice my

utmost disgust with your actions in assisting O.J. Simpson in being acquitted. The fact that you could defend a man who clearly mercilessly butchered two innocent people was truly sickening. There was a time when I looked up to you as a person who represented what was good in America. I now see you as the perpetrator of the worst form of evil.

I am used to this kind of mail. I have gotten precisely the same kind of criticism from anti-Semites and anti-Zionists for representing Jonathan Pollard, Rabbi Meir Kahane, members of the Jewish Defense League, Rabbi Bernard Bergman,* and other Jews. I received similar mail about Claus von Bülow, Mike Tyson, Michael Milken, and Leona Helmsley. The only difference is that, in effect, the letters from Jews about the Simpson case charged me with disloyalty for siding with a black defendant rather than a Jewish victim. This genre of criticism stems simply from a refusal to understand the role of defense counsel in our adversary sys-

*Bernard Bergman was a nursing-home operator in New York who went to prison for fraud.

tem of justice. My responsibility as a criminal defense lawyer is not to judge whether my client is innocent or guilty. Generally, I don't know. My job is to advocate zealously, within the rules. That is what I did in the Simpson case and I am proud of my work.

The second theme is particularly disturbing, coming as it does predominantly from Jewish letter-writers. It articulates a stereotype about Jews that usually comes from bigoted non-Jews: that all Jews care about is money. The word "greed" appeared over and over again, but this time from the mouths of Jews. Some examples:

> I cannot even fathom how you can have the beitzim [balls] to even think of walking into a shul, to defend your disgusting greed for money. . . .

> As a Holocaust survivor, I am ashamed you are a Jew. You never met a $ you did not like. You fulfill the stereotype of a Jew, and I declare you: not Jewish. You showed your greediness — your chutzpah — when you went to California to plead for another greedy — not a black man — but a

nigger who like all black men use drugs and all cheat on their wives. Be a Jew. Go to the defense of Jews.

The buck uber alle$$. You may become anathema to us Jews, but what the hell, justice must always pay second fiddle to $$$$$$.

Your role in the O.J. Simpson case showed a clear picture of a lawyer who will sell his own mother — if the price is right. . . . I am a Holocaust survivor and very often I think about the Judenrat in my native Lodz ghetto or for that matter in other ghettos. . . . You remind me of them, but your price is in dollars and cents.

Perhaps Harvard should change its noble insignia to read VERITA$.

I never take cases because of the fee, and half of my cases are pro bono. In fact, my fee in the Simpson case was relatively small, but when critics don't like which side a lawyer is on, they often focus on the fee.

The third — and most disturbing — theme revolved around the actions of my co-counsel Johnnie Cochran in "comparing" Detective Mark Fuhrman to Adolf Hitler, in surrounding himself with Nation of Islam bodyguards after receiving death threats in the courtroom, and in "playing the race card." Here are some examples:

How can you and the other Jewish attorneys be associated with an anti-Semitic [sic] like Johnnie Cochran? Who is a pal of Farrakhan, the most anti-Semitic person in the United States, who also happens to be Cochran's personal body guard?

You have let down your fellow Jews who have loved, honored, supported and admired you, until you aligned yourself now with a racist attorney who has engaged a racist, anti-Semitic Nation of Islam group to defend him.

Due to your recent participation in the trivialization of the Holocaust, I am no longer interested in your discussions of Jewish ethos and ethics.

I find it impossible to believe that the

same man who wrote *Chutzpah* linked arms with and acted so deferentially to a man who was guarded by members of the Nation of Islam and who is supporting those self-avowed anti-Semites in the march in D.C.

I am sick at heart to write this: I am compelled by conscience to repudiate you as a fellow Jew. You made me proud when you wrote *Chutzpah* and paraded your Jewishness so boldly, but you now embrace a blatant murderer and his champions and even justify that chief champion's invocation of Hitler to justify his utterly unabashed demagogic appeal in defense of a client. How can you so turn your back on six million of our brothers and sisters?

Some years back I wrote you a love letter of sorts after reading your book *Chutzpah*. I was so delighted with you and with what you stood for — pride in your heritage and the energy to fight for true justice. . . . Now I am writing again this time it is a hate letter of sorts. After watching you during the Simpson trial I am disgusted

with you and with what you stand for
— free a guilty (black) *rich* man at all
costs: smear the police, lie to the public,
bring Hitler back from hell to work as
a witness on the killer's defense.

It is remarkable how many of the letter-
writers completely misinterpret the message of Chutzpah as a tribal plea for
parochial Jewish rights, rather than for
universal human rights from which Jews
must not be excluded. More to the point
here, the Jewish outrage at a black man's
referring to Hitler seemed a bit overdone,
especially since many Jews seem to make
far more outrageous Hitler comparisons
with far less criticism. Ben-Gurion compared Begin to Hitler. The former director
of the Anti-Defamation League called Farrakhan a "black Hitler." Others who have
recently been compared to Hitler include
the Russian right-wing politician
Vladimir Zhirinovsky, Yassir Arafat,
Ariel Sharon, Saddam Hussein, and talk
show host Gordon Liddy. Most painfully
in light of subsequent events, several ex-
tremist American and Israeli rabbis had
compared the late prime minister Yitzhak
Rabin to Hitler, and before the assassination there had been little criticism from

the people who condemned Cochran. Indeed, one rabbi who criticized Cochran had himself compared Rabin to Hitler. But the criticism against Cochran was loud, sustained, and broadly based, including a highly publicized broadside from the executive director of the Anti-Defamation League.[1]

Yet the fact is that Johnnie Cochran did not compare Mark Fuhrman to Hitler. He compared, and decried, their racist views. According to the *Los Angeles Times*, Cochran's statement was inspired by a conversation that he had with a Jewish lawyer named Charles Lindner:

> "When Johnnie and I started talking about Fuhrman, I brought up my mother's experiences in Munich. . . ." Lindner, the former president of the Criminal Courts Bar Association, said. . . . "Her entire family was killed in the gas chambers by a house painter who was crazy and no one took him seriously until it was too late."

Lindner recounted his family history to Cochran in an effort, he said, "to get Johnnie into the frame of mind to talk about Mark Fuhrman as the personification of evil." The newspaper quoted Lindner as going on to say: "I was the stimulus for Johnnie's comments. And for those who say that Hitler is proprietary to the Jews, he isn't. What we were trying to convey . . . is that we shouldn't allow men like this — either Hitler or Fuhrman — to have control over people's lives."[2]

Cochran was absolutely on target in warning his listeners that when people don't care about racism and don't try to stop it, it can get out of control. I have heard similar statements made by prominent Jews on many occasions. Imagine if Fuhrman had said about Jews what he said about blacks if he had said "The only good Jew is a dead Jew" or "Jews should be rounded up and burned" and "turned into fertilizer." Would anyone object if a Jewish lawyer had said that these were the "same views" expressed by Hitler? I doubt it. Nor would Jews object were a fellow Jew to express concern that if we ignored such views, they could escalate into actions.

The universal message of the Holocaust was perhaps best captured by the German minister Martin Niemoller, who said: "The Nazis came for the Communists and I didn't speak up because I was not a

Communist. Then they came for the Jews and I didn't speak up because I was not a Jew. Then they came for the trade unionists and I didn't speak up because I was not a trade unionist. Then they came for the Catholics and I was a Protestant so I didn't speak up. Then they came for me . . . By that time there was no one to speak up for anyone."[3] No one should object when an African-American expresses concern that by ignoring genocidal talk against blacks by a police officer, we may be inviting genocidal action against others as well.

The other criticism directed at Cochran was that he used Nation of Islam guards to protect himself from death threats. Although Cochran assured me that he used these bodyguards only as an emergency stopgap and that he intended no message, I believed it was a mistake — and I told him that. He agreed and told me that he would no longer use them. Nor has O.J. Simpson employed Nation of Islam bodyguards. And neither Simpson nor Cochran attended the Farrakhan-sponsored Million Man March on Washington. In fact, Cochran specifically condemned Farrakhan's message of hate. By recognizing the difference between a friend with whom I had a disagreement (Johnnie Cochran) and an enemy with whom I could not reason (Louis Farrakhan), I was able to have some influence on the friend.

Finally, there was vehement criticism of the defense for "playing the race card." The term itself — as Henry Louis Gates, Jr., tells us — is "a barrier to inter-racial comprehension" which "infuriates many blacks."[4] Race was irretrievably introduced into the trial when Marcia Clark embraced Mark Fuhrman *after* being told of his racism. She had to know that Fuhrman was lying when he denied using racist epithets. So did dozens of other prosecutors, police, and friends of Fuhrman, who all sat silently by and allowed the lie to go uncorrected until the tapes were discovered. The so-called race card was dealt by the prosecution and trumped by the defense, as the defense was obliged to do.

As the respected judge Leon Higginbotham put it: "If the defendant had been Jewish and the police officer had a long history of expressed anti-Semitism and having planted evidence against innocent persons who were Jewish, I can't believe that anyone would have been saying that defense counsel was playing the anti-

Semitism card."[5] Would anyone feel that the Jewish defendant had been adequately defended if the bias of that anti-Semitic witness had not been exposed?

There were many non-Jewish hate letters as well, although none of them claimed to be disappointed in me:

> When I first found out about Mark Fuhrman making remarks, "that he wanted all the niggers burned," I was appalled. I thought that he was the most rotten, horrible, terrible, despicable excuse for a human being that ever lived. . . . Then the verdict came in, "Not Guilty" for O.J. Simpson, and I immediately changed my mind. I now think that what Fuhrman said is the best idea anyone in the world has had since Adolph Hitler.

> I've been watching your performance on TV. Your Nigger looking hair makes me think you are a nigger lover. You know that jury that turned the Bastard free is a low class, low educated bunch of NIGGERS. . . . What you need for your role in this case is a knife slid across your Neck like Ron Goldman got from OJ the

Master Nigger. Nicole asked for what she got.

Other, more reasonable letters focused on the "sleazy" tactics employed by the defense to "get your guilty client off." One letter contained a *New Yorker* cartoon, which spoke for many Americans. It shows a prisoner complaining to his cellmate: "I had a pretty sleazy lawyer, but evidently not sleazy enough." This was a common theme, as reflected in the following letter:

> Rats escape through the tiniest cracks and your kind devise every means. In your view "Justice" is a chess game — nothing more. Same as Monopoly. Justice has been flushed down the toilet bowl and you know it. The whole trial was a complete waste. Ito kept the jury in the dark time and time again. Not only do *you* stink to high heaven so do your cohorts. *Pooh*. You do not serve Justice!

The most common complaint about lawyers — especially criminal defense lawyers — is that they distort the truth, and there is some sense in that accusation.

But as I explained in Chapter II, a criminal trial is anything but a pure search for truth. When defense attorneys represent guilty clients — as most do, most of the time — their responsibility is to try, by all fair and ethical means, to *prevent* the truth about their client's guilt from emerging. Failure to do so — failure or unwillingness to object to the truth on the ground that it was improperly obtained — is malpractice, which could get a defense lawyer disbarred and earn his client a new trial, at which he would be represented by a zealous defense lawyer willing and able to try to stop the truth from being proved.

Like it or not — and I like it — that is what our Constitution and our legal system require of defense counsel. Our legal system also permits the prosecutor to try to prevent certain truths from being proved, if the defense tries to prove them through hearsay or other improper evidence. But our legal system insists that the truth be suppressed exclusively by lawful and ethical means. A "sleazy" lawyer — at least according to the Code of Professional Responsibility — is one who tries to prevent the truth from emerging by unethical or illegal means. A sleazy lawyer is also one who generally behaves in a manner inconsistent with the proper role of the professional advocate.

In the Simpson case, as in any long and hotly contested case, neither side behaved perfectly. (Nor did any of the other participants, ranging from the judge to the media.) The prosecution and the defense worked long hours, under the pressure of unprecedented publicity and scrutiny. It is fair to say that both sides made mistakes, lost tempers, indulged in pettiness, and went right up to — and perhaps, in some instances, over — various legal and ethical lines. It is tempting to Monday morning quarterback, as many commentators did. It is easy to focus on the mistakes and ignore the good lawyering. Each of the major lawyers had their great moments, and many of them had some very bad moments. I certainly miscalculated the effect that my statement about police perjury would have, and if I could do it over again, I would have waited until the trial was over to say what I did about the pervasiveness of this problem. Virtually every defense lawyer I have spoken to regrets at least one statement, question, argument, or decision he or she made during the case. I am certain the same is true of the prosecutors.

Having cautioned about the dangers of after-the-fact criticism, I am now going to engage in some — not to praise the defense or gratuitously denigrate the prosecution, but to make what I believe is an important point. The media and the public tend to evaluate the performance of advocates (and other participants in the legal process) not so much by reference to the objective professional quality of their work, but far more by whether they are on the same side as the advocate. Most Americans were on the side of the prosecution in this case and concluded, therefore, that the prosecutors did a better job than the defense lawyers. Yet a fair assessment of the record will show that by every measure of legal ethics, professional etiquette, and fair and effective advocacy, the prosecution did far worse than the defense. Moreover, the ethical and professional derelictions of the prosecution contributed significantly to their losing the case.

The prosecution leaked more information, spoke to the media more often, and generally tried its case in the press far more extensively than the defense. And it began doing so even before the defense team was assembled. Many of the leaks turned out to be false. More important, the prosecution badly hurt its own court case by providing the defense with the ammunition it needed to get the grand jury proceedings dismissed on the ground of pretrial publicity. At the subsequent preliminary hearing, the prosecution was forced to present its case prematurely, which worked to the benefit of the defense.

At the trial itself, the prosecutors called several witnesses who they had to suspect, at the very least, were not telling the truth, whereas the defense decided not to use several witnesses whose credibility was called into question after Johnnie Cochran told the jury he would use them. Two of the witnesses called by the prosecutors — Detectives Vannatter and Fuhrman — may well have cost them any chance they had of winning this case or even getting a hung jury. I have already focused on Vannatter. Now for Fuhrman.

An internal memorandum by the head deputy of the Special Investigations Division of the Los Angeles District Attorney's Office reveals that the consensus in that office is that "Fuhrman's conduct is . . . the principal reason why the case was lost." If that is true, then Marcia Clark is the principal *person* who lost the case. It was she who, as chief trial counsel, decided to call Fuhrman as a trial witness. Her defenders argue that since she could not have known about the tapes, her decision to call Fuhrman was both ethically permissible and tactically wise. But let us consider what she did know at the time she not only called Fuhrman as a witness but came as close as she could to embracing him and vouching for his credibility in front of the jury.

Remember that Clark went out of her way to get Fuhrman to deny the accusations of racism. This is how she began her examination, with an uncharacteristically warm smile on her face:

Q: Detective Fuhrman, can you tell us how you feel about testifying today?
A: Nervous.
Q: Okay.
A: Reluctant.
Q: Can you tell us why?
A: Throughout — since June 13, it seems that I have seen a lot of the evidence ignored and a lot of personal issues come to the forecourt. I think that is too bad.

Q: Okay. Heard a lot about yourself in the press, have you?

A: Daily.

Q: In light of that fact, sir, you have indicated that you feel nervous about testifying. Have you gone over your testimony in the presence of several district attorneys in order to prepare yourself for court and the allegations that you may hear from the defense?

A: Yes.

Q: And in the course of that particular examination, sir, was the topic of your testimony concerning the work you did in this case, the actual visitation to Bundy and Rockingham, was that discussed?

A: No.

Q: It dealt with side issues, sir?

A: Yes, it was.

. . . .

Q: Now, back in 1985 and 1986, sir, can you tell us whether you knew someone or met someone by the name of Kathleen Bell?

A: Yes, I can tell you. I did not.

Q: But you do recognize the name, don't you, sir?

A: Yes.

Q: When was the first time that you

heard that name?

A: It was in '94, I believe in the fall of '94. I don't know exactly what month.

Q: And how was it that you heard her name in connection with what?

A: In connection with allegations of statements I made to her at a date some time in '85 or '86.

Q: And where did you hear those allegations, sir?

A: In the news.

. . . .

Q: Do you remember meeting a woman named Kathleen Bell at that Marine Recruiting Office between 1985 and 1986?

A: No.

. . . .

Q: Did you see a woman who called herself Kathleen Bell [on the Larry King show]?

A: Yes.

Q: And did you recognize her?

A: No, I did not.

. . . .

Q: Did the conversation Kathleen Bell describes in this letter occur? [The letter is reproduced on pages 171–72.]

A: No, it did not.[6]

At the time Clark was coddling Fuhr-man in this way, this is what she knew about him, and what she also knew *the jury would never learn* until the trial was over.

In September 1981, Fuhrman had filed a claim seeking a disability pension from the Los Angeles Police Department. In the course of those proceedings, he explicitly used the "N" word in complaining to doctors that during the last six months of his service in the Marines, he "got tired of having a bunch of Mexicans and Niggers that should be in prison telling [him] they weren't going to do something." He also admitted to doctors that he was "preoccupied with violence" and had "bec[o]me uncontrollable with rage" as a result of "stress" at work. He said that his "behavior became abusive toward prisoners and others that would resist his arrest," that "he might kill somebody if he didn't get out of this type of occupation," and that "he feels enraged if he doesn't like somebody and would as soon slit the person's throat as talk to him." He liked the feeling of "put[ting] a shotgun to [someone's] head" if that person was "doin' something, acting cool, thinking no one sees him." He "bragged about violence he used in subduing suspects, including chokeholds, and said he would break their hands or face or arms or legs, if necessary"; he said he was "putting people in the hospital with broken hands, faces, arms and knees," and that "if [he] tried to choke somebody out, [he'd] try to kill them." It is obvious from the context that Fuhrman's rage is directed primarily at minorities. One physician presciently warned that Fuhrman's " 'overall production' [of arrests] was unbalanced because he was constantly trying to make the 'big arrest.' "[7]

This disability claim was denied sometime in 1983 on the ground that Fuhrman was "not truthful" and might be "malingering" in order to obtain a pension by false pretenses.[8] So anyone reading the file of this case — as Clark did — would have to conclude that Fuhrman was either a racist, or a liar, or both. This was less than two years before the beginning of the ten-year period concerning which Judge Ito had ruled it would be permissible to question Fuhrman about his racism. Marcia Clark knew, therefore, that the jury would not learn about what Fuhrman had told the doctors. Virtually everything Fuhrman eventually said on tape from 1985 through 1986, he had told the doctors just a few years earlier. He had even used the "N" word in a context that made it clear the epithet was part of his everyday vocabulary.

Clark had to know that the kind of racism and violence reflected in these interviews is not cured overnight. Moreover, she knew that numerous witnesses — many with no axes to grind — were prepared to testify that Fuhrman had made almost identical statements to them during the ten-year period. Most persuasive was Kathleen Bell, a woman who was reluctant to testify for the defense because she believed that Simpson was guilty. Bell had written the following letter to Johnnie Cochran:

Dear Mr. Cochran:

I'm writing to you in regards to a story I saw on the news last night. I thought it ridiculous that the Simpson defense team would even suggest that their *[sic]* might be racial motivation involved in the trial against Mr. Simpson. I then glanced up at the television and was quite shocked to see that Officer Ferman *[sic]* was a man that I had the misfortune of meeting. You may have received a message from your answering service last night that I called to say that Mr. Ferman may be more of a racist than you could even imagine.

Between 1985 and 1986 I worked as a real estate agent in Redondo Beach for Century 21 Bob Maher Realty (now out of business). At the time, my office was located above a Marine Recruiting center off of Pacific Coast Highway. On occasion I would stop in to say hello to the two marines working there. I saw Mr. Ferman there a couple of times. I remember him distinctly because of his height and build.

While speaking to the men I learned that Mr. Ferman was a police officer in Westwood, and I don't know if he was telling the truth, but he said that he had been in a special division of the Marines. I don't know how the subject was raised, but Officer Ferman said that when he sees a "Nigger" (as he called it) driving with a white woman, he would pull them over. I asked would he if he didn't have a reason, and he said that he would find one. I looked at the two marines to see if they knew he was joking, but it became obvious to me that he was very serious.

Officer Ferman went on to say that he would like nothing more than to see all "niggers" gathered together and killed. He said something about burning them or bombing them. I was too shaken to remember the exact words he used. However, I do remember that what he said was probably the most horrible thing I had ever heard someone say. What frightened me even more was that he was a police officer.

I am almost certain that I called the LAPD to complain about Officer Mark Ferman, yet I did not know his last name at the time. I would think that the LAPD has some record of this.

Now that I know Mr. Ferman was the investigating officer, I must suggest that you check into his background further. I am certainly not a fan of Mr. Simpson, but I would hate to see anyone harmed by Officer Ferman's extreme hatred. . . .

Sincerely,
Kathleen Bell[9]

Finally, in addition to Bell and the other witnesses, an assistant district attorney named Lucienne Coleman — a seventeen-year veteran of the Los Angeles District

Attorney's Office — had provided Clark with devastating information about Fuhrman from highly reliable *police* sources.

In the first two weeks of August 1994, Coleman, who had been a friend of Marcia Clark for "many years," approached her and informed her of a conversation with Los Angeles Police Department homicide detective Andy Purdy a month earlier. When Coleman remarked to Purdy "how ridiculous [it] was" for the Simpson defense to claim that "Fuhrman had planted the glove at Rockingham," Purdy responded that "these allegations were not ridiculous at all." Purdy went on to inform Coleman that he "had recently married a Jewish woman and Fuhrman had painted Purdy's locker with swastikas." Coleman further informed Clark that she had learned that "a black officer named Maxwell" had been at "a picnic or barbecue" and had heard Fuhrman "tell others that he had seen Nicole Simpson's 'boob job' and that it looked great." Other officers, according to Coleman, had heard Fuhrman make similar remarks about Nicole's breast augmentation. Coleman also informed Clark that she had "heard that Fuhrman walked around on week-ends [sic] wearing Nazi paraphernalia." According to Coleman, Clark exploded, saying: "This is just bullshit being put out by the defense!" Coleman responded that "she hadn't heard these allegations from the defense but, rather, from LAPD officers." When Coleman "suggested that the District Attorney's Office look into these allegations," Clark "angrily" stated that she was "tired of other D.A.'s trying to get involved in [her] case for their own self-aggrandizement."[10]

Marcia Clark thus knew pretty much everything about Fuhrman that would eventually come out on the tapes *before* she called him as a trial witness. What she didn't know was that there would *be* tapes to prove it. The substance of Fuhrman's racism — his use of the "N" word, his violent hatred of black men married to white women, his willingness to lie, and accusations that he had planted evidence — was all known to Clark. But she nevertheless called him as a witness because she thought the jury would disbelieve the disinterested eyewitnesses, whose testimony was corroborated by documents that the judge had kept from the jury. This decision, according to her own colleagues, may have lost her the case.

Again to the detriment of its case, the

prosecution — especially Marcia Clark — made repeated personal attacks on defense lawyers, using unprofessional language and hyperbole. Though Clark was careful not to engage in such conduct in front of the jury, many courtroom observers believe that her frequent outbursts seriously damaged her credibility with Judge Ito. I experienced Clark's courtroom antics personally the first time I argued before the judge. I was asked to argue a rather bland and technical motion, largely to create a record for appeal. The issue involved the proper standard to be used by Judge Ito in dismissing any further jurors, since we were now down to just two alternates. My argument took place the day after the prosecution asked Simpson to try on the gloves. I began as follows:

MR. DERSHOWITZ: Good morning.

Thank you very much, Your Honor, for accommodating my schedule. I will try to keep it very brief knowing that the jury is out this morning. We are very concerned about the possible specter of a mistrial hanging over this very lengthy trial. The defendant, O.J. Simpson, has the right to have his case decided by this jury and not some subsequent jury. Yesterday's incidents and events make it as clear as any events could ever make it why the prosecution would benefit if they had a second opportunity to try this case.

If the prosecution had a second opportunity, if they could do what we did when we were kids, we called a do-over, obviously they would try this case rather differently.

I doubt that we would see O.J. Simpson being asked to try on his gloves. I doubt that we would see Dennis Fung being called as a witness.

That is precisely why the double jeopardy clause, both under the United States Constitution and its more expansive view, under California law, gives the prosecution simply one shot, not another chance.[11]

After describing our "concern" that the prosecution may have been moving to strike jurors in an effort to secure a mistrial, I presented two motions. The first was that no further jurors be struck except for "manifest necessity"; the second was that, if there was to be a mistrial, the court should hold "an evidentiary hearing" on the reasons why jurors were struck. It was all very academic, presented in a low-key conversational tone, and quite boring.

Until Marcia Clark got up to respond. This is how she began — in a loud, shrill voice:

> Of all of the motions made by the defense, I find this one *the most offensive, groundless* and *baseless*.
>
> This was a motion filed deliberately for inflammatory effect. It has no law in its support. It has no facts in its support. This is a *scurrilous* attempt to inflame the community, if not the very jury itself.
>
> It may be constitutionally protected speech, Your Honor, but constitutionally protected does not mean *moral*, does not mean *ethical* and does not mean *truthful*.
>
> And the *groundless, baseless, inflammatory* allegations contained in this motion are the lowest tactics I have seen yet in this case [italics added].[12]

Had this been the only time Clark used such hyperbole and accusatory language, it would be fair to wonder whether it was deserved. But she used such language against every member of the defense team, nearly every day. As I sat down, Bob Shapiro whispered to me, "Welcome to the 'Marcia Hit Parade.' "

That evening, when I was interviewed by Larry King about Marcia Clark's vitriol, I suggested that the media put together a montage of "the best of Marcia Clark" shouting about how nearly every motion the defense filed was always the "lowest," the "most offensive," and the most unethical. The media did not take up my proposal, so I have put together a few of my favorites. They do not have the impact in print that they would on video, but they do convey some of the flavor of Marcia Clark crying wolf so often that nearly everyone in the courtroom — especially Judge Ito — simply stopped taking her seriously.

Referring to Attorney Carl Douglas:

I am *shocked*. I am *shocked*. I have never seen a defense attorney behave this way. I have *never* seen this happen. . . . I've *never* seen this, and I've *never* seen it in such a *blatant* form, in an effort to . . . sandbag the prosecution, to blindside us. . . . I find this *unbelievable* — what I have seen. And to hear this tape was just — I am speechless. . . . This is a sinister scheme. This is a conspiracy [italics added].[13]

Referring to Professor Gerald Uelmen:

It is *ridiculous*. It is *absurd*. Mr. Uelmen stands up and argues out of both sides of his mouth simultaneously. What a feat! . . . I mean, is that the *stupidest* move you've ever heard? Hi, Mom, you know, I'm gonna move some evidence now [italics added].[14]

Clark also accused Uelmen of making "hysterical proclamations" and "hypocritical ramblings that are impeached by their own actions."[15]

Clark, of course, cried sexism when her own rantings were characterized as "hysterical."[16]

Referring to Professor Barry Scheck:

Mr. Scheck posed a question that was *so unethical* and *so improper* that I think that the transcript should be sent to the state bar. . . . I find this not only appalling but I am ashamed, as an officer of the court, to see this kind of behavior. . . . [T]here is no lawyer with half a brain, with an I.Q. above 5 who would not have known that such a question is improper . . . highly *inappropriate, unethical,* and a deliberate effort to thwart justice and prejudice the right of the people to a fair trial [italics added].[17]

Referring to Robert Blasier:

I'm really *outraged* at the manner in which this defense has proceeded. It's a trial by ambush. . . . It's *ridiculous*.[18]

Referring to Peter Neufeld:

I could play the same nitpicky game they're playing and pick at every nitpicky violation, I demand sanctions and I demand they be put in jail and I demand they be held in contempt. I don't do that. I don't need to do that. I can just practice law. I can just try my case without playing these little games here. About nanny, nanny, nanny and neener, neener and who's got the last sanction? Who's going to pay money this time? This is *sickening*. You know what we've descended to in this case. . . . To make the mountain out of the molehill that this is, it's ridiculous. . . . I've *never* seen law practiced this way, with lawyers asking for monetary sanctions against the other side, *never*. . . . I am dismayed and I am embarrassed and I am ashamed of my profession when I see it practiced like this. . . . This is *ridiculous*. I mean, we have reached *the most far-out reaches* I have ever seen. I'm actually speechless, I can't believe what I'm hearing. . . . This is *absurd* [italics added].[19]

Referring to a small glove, Clark said with a smirk, "Small size — I guess it's Mr. Bailey's," with a plainly sexual innuendo.[20]

Although Clark was certainly provoked by the defense, and although several of her criticisms may have been justified by the actions of defense counsel, she used hyperbole so promiscuously that it lost its impact. No defense lawyer — even the most cautious and low-key, like Gerald Uelmen — was immune from her accusations. Judge Ito admonished, sanctioned, and criticized her repeatedly for her unprofessional behavior. The defense was criticized as well for unprofessional language, but it was primarily Clark who turned the trial into a soapbox for personal attacks and hyperbole.

Finally, Judge Ito imposed several sanctions against both sides. Most of the sanctions were small fines, but he imposed one evidentiary sanction against the prosecution whose effect was to exclude evidence the lack of which some believe may have cost the prosecution the votes of at least several jurors. The FBI fiber expert, Douglas Deedrich, was prepared to testify that fibers found on the knit cap and the glove could have come only from a 1993 or 1994 Bronco. (Simpson's Bronco was a 1994 model.) This evidence, although certainly not conclusive, could have bolstered the prosecution's case. But because prosecutors violated a discovery rule by not showing the defense certain photographs of the fibers, which the defense could then have given to its experts, Judge Ito ruled that the FBI expert could not present his testimony to the jury. The jury was thus left with the impression that the fibers could have come from any Bronco, not just a 1993 or 1994 model. The prosecution's failure to disclose the photographs was either deliberate, as F. Lee Bailey argued, or negligent. In either event, it seriously wounded the prosecution's case.

By every relevant standard of professional judgment, the prosecution did worse than the defense. Most important, it lost what many observers had regarded as an open-and-shut case. Even those who "blame" the loss largely on the jury acknowledge that it was the prosecution which decided to hold the Simpson trial downtown, where a largely minority jury would be likely. Most knowledgeable commentators, even those highly critical of the defense, agreed that the defense did a far better job than did the prosecutors. Several of the jurors also agreed. One of them, who sat for the first several months of the trial, put it this way:

They just couldn't keep it sharp and simple. They fumbled and fretted, continually conferring with each other. It was like they were never sure of how to say what they needed to tell us. Sometimes they got it together, but mostly their presentation was truly pathetic; sloppy, badly organized, and rarely eloquent — even

though the evidence itself was powerful. And all too often, when the prosecution came up to bat, We the Jury
started fidgeting and getting rest-
less.[21]

Yet much of the public seems to support
Marcia Clark and her prosecutors and to
revile the defense attorneys.

There is a general reason why prosecutors are more accepted than defense attorneys, and a particular reason why this
was especially true in the Simpson case.
In general, prosecutors wear the white
hats: They stand for law and order; they
represent the victims and the people or
the state; they prosecute the guilty — at
least most of the time; they are public
servants; they are on the side of truth and
the angels. Defense attorneys, on the
other hand, generally represent guilty defendants. (And thank goodness for that.
Would anyone want to live in a country
where most defendants were innocent?
Perhaps in Iran, Iraq, or China, most
people charged with crimes are innocent.
Not so in this country, and it is the zeal-
ousness of the defense bar, among other
factors, that keeps it that way.) Defense
attorneys are outsiders; they are per-

ceived as obstructors of justice who invoke privileges, rights, and technicalities to exclude relevant evidence and to obscure the incriminating truth; if they are retained rather than appointed, they earn a profit from doing the devil's work.

Moreover, defense attorneys are supposed to be single-minded in their quest for acquittal by all legal and ethical means. They are not allowed to have any other agenda. They cannot put patriotism, good citizenship, religion, gender or racial solidarity, or commitment to any cause before the interests of their client. Nor is this a radical or modern notion. As a British barrister named Henry Brougham put it in 1820:

> An advocate, by the sacred duty which he owes his client, knows, in the discharge of that office, but one person in the world, that client and none other. To save that client by all expedient means — to protect that client at all hazards and costs to all others, and among others to himself, — is the highest and most unquestioned of his duties; and he must not regard the alarm, the suffering, the torment, the destructions which he may bring upon

any other. Nay, separating even the duties of a patriot from those of an advocate, and casting them, if need be, to the wind, he must go on reckless of the consequences, if his fate it should unhappily be, to involve his country in confusion for his client's protection.[22]

So when George Will criticized Johnnie Cochran for being a "good lawyer" but a "bad citizen," he was damning with high praise.[23] To be anything else during a criminal trial is to be guilty of serving two masters, which violates both the rules of the legal profession and the strictures of the Bible.

A good defense attorney, especially one with a civil liberties perspective, could never win elective office because he or she must occasionally represent very unpopular defendants — and sometimes even win. In Florida, public defenders must run for office. I can only imagine what the campaign must be like. One candidate says: "Vote for me as your public defender and I'll win more cases than my opponent. I'm such a good defense lawyer that the streets will be filled with murderers, rapists, and robbers." His opponent counters: "No, vote for me. I'm the world's worst lawyer. If I'm elected, no defendant will ever win. The streets will be safe with me in office."

Prosecutors, on the other hand, are supposed to be good citizens. It is no surprise, therefore, that being a prosecutor is a stepping-stone to elective office. The job of the prosecutor is to please the public. The job of the defense attorney — whether he's a private lawyer or a public defender — is to win for his client, without regard to what the public thinks. A defense attorney must represent his client zealously within the bounds of law, whether the client is guilty or innocent, popular or unpopular, rich or poor, male or female, black or white. Since most defendants are guilty, and since an even larger percentage are *assumed* to be guilty, defense attorneys will continue to disappoint most of the public most of the time. Prosecutors, on the other hand, will continue to be heroes to most of the public — whether they win or lose, whether they do a good professional job or a mediocre one, as the prosecutors in the Simpson case most assuredly did.

Recently my wife, who holds a doctorate in psychology, had a minor legal dispute, which was submitted to mediation and resolved favorably. The other side was represented by a decent lawyer who tried very hard to settle the matter amicably, which is what happened. This lawyer was unfailingly polite, soft-spoken, and low-key. As we left the mediation, settlement in hand, my wife — who is also amicable, soft-spoken, and low-key — started to tell me how she couldn't stand the opposing lawyer and thought he was a "terrible person" for representing her opponent. She realized, of course, that this is exactly how other people react to me. But even after we joked about her reaction, she quickly returned to disliking everything about the other side, especially its lawyer. She found it difficult to separate the lawyer from his client in a case in which she was so personally involved. This small incident gave me a much deeper insight into the reaction so many people have to defense attorneys, especially in cases where they *feel* — not just think — that an injustice has been done, and that the injustice was abetted by the advocacy of the defense lawyer.

So the answer to the question posed by the title of this chapter is that both prosecutors and defense attorneys are supposed to be advocates for their clients. But prosecutors are also supposed to be advocates for justice, while defense attorneys are not even permitted to try to achieve justice, if by doing so they would disserve the legitimate interests of their clients. Again, since most criminal defendants are, as a statistical matter, guilty, defense attorneys are not usually engaged in the business of serving justice — at least not in the short run. But by zealously defending their clients, guilty or innocent, they help preserve a system of justice that only rarely convicts the innocent.

IX

What If the Jury Had Convicted Simpson?

Throughout the trial, I was called by reporters inquiring about our appellate strategy. "Do you think Judge Ito's ruling on the Fuhrman tapes is a good issue for appeal?" "Do you believe Judge Ito's decision to allow Ron Shipp's testimony that Simpson dreamed about killing his former wife could reverse a conviction?" "What do you think about Judge Ito's decision to allow the jury to see the unsworn videotape of Thano Peratis without any cross-examination?"

My answer was always the same. Each of these issues was powerful, but appellate courts rarely throw out a nine-month trial on the basis of a single or even multiple issues. Appellate judges have to be convinced that the defendant suffered a palpable injustice. In theory, an appellate court is supposed to reverse any conviction tainted by a serious legal error unless that error was "harmless" — that is, unless it could not realistically have contributed to the conviction. But in practice, appellate courts have such wide discretion to determine whether an error occurred and whether it was harmless that reversals in criminal cases have become extremely rare. In some states, more than 99 percent of criminal convictions are affirmed on appeal. In others, the percentage is 95 percent. In no state is it less than 90 percent.[1*] Winning a criminal case on appeal is thus very much an uphill battle. Nonetheless, virtually every convicted criminal does appeal, and most wealthy criminal defendants begin to think about an appeal even before the trial begins. The appellate lawyer is an insurance policy in the event of a conviction.

The appeal from a criminal conviction is the least familiar, and least understood, stage in the criminal process. The general public is exposed to police investigatory and undercover operations in motion pictures and on television. Everyone knows about the *Miranda* rule; indeed, many schoolchildren can mumble the formula,

*This does not count sentencing reversals, which are higher.

"You have the right to an attorney . . ." The trial itself is a staple of drama. Even the imposition of punishment — ranging from a slap on the wrist, to imprisonment and execution — is frequently portrayed on stage and screen. But think about how many times you have seen an appeal, either actual or dramatized! Indeed, most Americans cannot even visualize what an appeal looks like.

I am often asked by nonlawyers whether there is a jury on appeal, whether there are witnesses, or whether the judges deliberate on the spot and render a verdict of guilt or innocence. There is, of course, one classic lawyer's joke involving appeals: a lawyer cables his client with the news "Justice has prevailed!" The client hastily cables back, "Appeal immediately." But even that apocryphal story relates more to the client's perception of the trial than to the appellate phase.

Despite its relative obscurity, the criminal appeal is, in many ways, the most important stage in the criminal justice process. Appeals have a profound and enduring impact on every other stage. For example, the *Miranda* formula, which is so well known, derives from an appellate decision of the United States Supreme

Court.[2] But the Supreme Court is not the only significant appellate court in the criminal justice system. Although it is the single most influential court, because its interpretations of federal law, including federal constitutional law, are binding on all other courts — it hears only a tiny fraction of criminal appeals from around the nation. The state and lower federal courts of appeal are the workhorses of the criminal justice system, deciding the vast majority of criminal appeals.

Everyone who has been convicted of a crime and sentenced to any punishment — including a suspended sentence or a fine — is entitled, as a matter of right, to one appeal. It is not entirely clear whether that right has now been constitutionalized. It is, however, plainly established under the laws of each of the fifty states as well as under federal law.

The government, on the other hand, is not allowed to appeal a jury verdict that has gone against the prosecution. The reason for this one-sided rule grows out of the double jeopardy clause of the Fifth Amendment to the Constitution (which is applicable to the states as well as to the federal government.[3]) Once a jury has acquitted a defendant, he may not be tried again for the same offense. Since he could not be retried even if the prosecution won the appeal, there would be no real point in allowing an appeal. If the defendant chooses to appeal, however, he may be retried if he wins the appeal on grounds that allow for a new trial.

If the defendant cannot afford to retain an appellate lawyer or to pay for the typing of the trial transcript or the appellate briefs, the government is obligated to pick up the tab (or, in the case of the lawyer, appoint one, thus passing the cost on to the legal profession). Once the appeal has been filed, it proceeds in roughly the following way. First, the trial transcript is typed and made available to both sides (the government and the defense). The defense lawyer, who may or may not be the same lawyer who handled the trial, reads the transcript, focusing on the trial judge's rulings of law.

This is a crucial point to understand, because an appeal is limited, at least in theory, to challenging rulings of law made by the trial judge. As the trial judge in the Claus von Bülow case put it: "The trial of Claus von Bülow is over. The trial of the trial justice is about to begin."[4] Or as a British wag pointed out, with some irony:

"The law presumes that everyone knows the law, except for Her Majesty's judges; for they have a court of appeal over them to set them right."

Points of law include rulings about evidence (both constitutional and otherwise); the judge's instructions to the jury; objections to the makeup of the jury; and, under certain circumstances, the sentence. Among the most important rulings of law a trial judge makes are those concerning the facts. And this can be quite confusing. The issue of whether there was sufficient evidence to convict the defendant — which sounds like a factual question: Was the defendant guilty? — is a question of law. It relates, of course, to the factual guilt or innocence of the defendant, but it is not the same. A defendant may be plainly innocent, yet there may be sufficient evidence for a jury to have convicted him. Let me illustrate: Imagine a case where one witness testifies that he saw the defendant deliberately kill the victim. (For the purpose of this example, assume that this is the only issue, that there is no issue of self-defense, insanity, or the like.) The testimony alone would be sufficient, if the jury believed it, for a conviction. But assume further that this sole witness was a pathological liar, intent on framing an innocent defendant. In that situation — which in real life is rarely so obvious, but sometimes does occur in more subtle ways — the appellate court could not, at least in theory, overturn the verdict. The evidence would be legally sufficient, although factually suspect.

Juries, of course, will rarely convict a defendant on the basis of a pathological liar's uncorroborated testimony. But if one did, the appellate court would have to find some means to do justice other than overturning the trial judge's ruling on the insufficiency of the evidence. And some appellate courts would go out of their way to find other grounds. When appellate judges experience real doubt about the guilt of the appellant (the convicted defendant who is bringing the appeal), many of them, although certainly not all, will figure out some way to reverse the conviction. That is what I meant when I said that appellate courts are limited *in theory* to reviewing only the rulings of law made by the trial judge. Appellate judges are, after all, human beings, who believe that guilt or innocence matters, even though it is not formally their job to second-guess a jury's verdict. Recently a prominent ap-

331

pellate judge told my criminal law students at Harvard that he and his colleagues are far more likely to find an error
if they believe the appellant may be factually innocent.

In any event, the trial transcript is the
grist of the appellate court's mill. Appellate decisions are supposed to be based on
the cold record of the trial. That's why
reviewing the transcript is the crucial
first step in an appeal. The appellate lawyer's next step is to identify what may be
erroneous rulings of law. In the often te-
dious research through often lengthy records, the appellate lawyer is aided by the
objections made during the trial by the
defendant's trial lawyer. Not all trial objections, of course, are valid or give rise
to an appealable issue. But if no objection
was made at the trial, the issue is "unpre-
served," and an appeal based on that issue
is unlikely to succeed.

Once the appellate lawyer settles on the
issues to be raised, the job of brief writing
begins. A typical appellate brief is approximately fifty printed pages long. This
page limit imposes severe burdens on the
appellate lawyer, especially when the
trial was very long. Recently some state
trials, including those of O.J. Simpson and

the Menendez brothers, have taken months. A transcript of a month-long trial will come to approximately five thousand pages (a rough rule of thumb is that one trial day will produce about 250 pages of transcript). In fact, the transcript of the Simpson trial fills approximately fifty thousand pages. Thus, compressing the issues raised during a multithousand-page transcript into fifty or so pages can present difficult choices. But choices must be made and arguments shortened or eliminated.

In addition to space limitations, there are also time limitations; generally the appellant has a month or forty-five days to file the brief. (The combination of space and time limitations often produces requests for extensions of one or both on the ground that — to paraphrase Abraham Lincoln — "if I had had more time, I would have written a shorter brief.")

A month or so after the appellant's brief is filed, the prosecution's brief is due. In its brief, the prosecution generally tries to defend the trial court's rulings. (Since it cannot appeal an acquittal, the state is rarely in the position of attacking trial court rulings in the appellate courts. Thus, the prosecutor's role as defender of the trial court creates a dangerous alliance between trial judges and prosecutors, which has implications throughout the criminal justice process.) In addition to defending the trial court's rulings, the state also seeks to demonstrate that the defendant was really guilty and that the evidence it introduced at trial was sufficient.

Unlike at trial, where the prosecutor always gets the last word in front of the jury, on appeal the defendant generally gets the last word, both written and oral. The lawyer for the appellant may file a short reply (generally twenty-five or so pages) to the state's arguments. This can be the most significant document in the appeal, because it can sharpen and crystallize the differences between the two sides, and because it gives the appellant the all-important last written word. Yet too many lazy appellate lawyers decline the opportunity to file a reply brief. Part of the reason is that they believe that some lazy judges don't bother to read the appellant's reply brief. Although that is plainly true — indeed, some judges seem not to read any of the briefs, while some appear to read only the government's brief— an appellate lawyer is rarely, if ever, justified in forgoing the filing of a reply brief.

Once all the papers have been filed, the stage is set for the only potentially dramatic confrontation in the appellate process: the oral argument. This takes place in front of a panel of judges. Most oral arguments are boring. The advocates simply read from the briefs; the judges nod off, or stare blankly ahead, or read or write other things. The tedium is interrupted by an occasional question from one of the judges. The petrified advocate tries to respond as quickly as possible and return to the prepared script.

Occasionally, one encounters a judge who seems to get a perverse sense of accomplishment from humiliating advocates or outsmarting them. Some judges seem wary of engaging counsel, lest their unpreparedness — or simple stupidity — be exposed. Others seem determined to pick a fight with counsel, or with another judge. But at its best, oral argument can be high drama and a scintillating intellectual exchange. An effective oral advocate can actually change a judge's mind before your very eyes. That doesn't happen too often, but when it does, it is something to behold.

But even at its best, an oral appellate argument is not likely to have the general audience appeal of a great trial. There is no cross-examination of witnesses, no emotional appeal to the jury, no strident objecting — and no dramatic moment when the jury renders its verdict before the trembling defendant. Thus, arguing criminal appeals is not a job for lawyers who love large audiences and dramatic moments. It is also not a job for lawyers who must always win. Almost all the criminal appellate lawyers I know lose most of their cases. That is not surprising, since only about 5 percent of criminal convictions are reversed on appeal. The task of the criminal appeals lawyer is to raise the odds for his client from 5 percent to 10 percent or maybe even 20 percent. However, it is almost impossible to make them better than even, except in the most unusual situations.

Some lawyers, of course, pick their appeals with an eye toward winning. They turn down the hard or average ones and take only cases that look like easy wins. A lawyer engaged in this kind of selection process can raise his winning percentage, but that surely doesn't make him a better lawyer. A lawyer who takes the hardest cases (say those with a 5 percent chance of winning) and wins a considerable number of them (say 20 percent) is a far better lawyer than a lawyer who takes only the easiest ones (say those with a 70 percent chance of winning) and wins most of them (say 60 percent). Like a diver, a lawyer cannot be judged without taking into account the "degree of difficulty" of the case.

I was brought into the Simpson case at the very beginning both because I have a pretty good record of victories in difficult criminal appeals and because I am a trial strategist. These two roles mesh well, since much of the trial strategy involves legal issues that may be raised at trial and then, in the event of a conviction, on appeal. My role, along with Gerald Uelmen, was to frame these legal issues with one eye on Judge Ito and the other on the appellate courts. We also wanted Judge Ito to know that we were always thinking about a possible appeal so that he might be influenced in his trial rulings by a desire not to be reversed on appeal.

My office kept a running list of possible appellate issues, which kept changing as Judge Ito made more and more rulings against us at trial. By the time the trial was over, the list was quite long. During the long night between the jury's surprise announcement that it had reached a verdict and the time the verdict was announced, I stayed up outlining what I believed would be the most powerful issues on appeal in the event of a conviction.

First in order of importance were the Fuhrman tapes. Judge Ito excluded virtually all of them, allowing the jury to hear only two relatively bland and somewhat inaudible uses of the word "nigger." He did not permit the jury to hear Fuhrman bragging about planting evidence or about improperly arresting African-American defendants, beating them up, and lying about them. Nor did he allow the jury to hear Fuhrman describe his attitude toward cops who refuse to lie and cover for each other. By admitting into evidence only two uses of the racial epithet, Judge Ito permitted jurors to infer that Fuhrman might well have forgotten that he used the word on a few occasions in so bland a manner — an inference that would not be possible if they heard how many times, and in what contexts, he really used it.

We believed, therefore, that Judge Ito had abused his discretion in so limiting our ability to prove that the officer who claimed to have found the single most important item of incriminating evidence was a self-admitted racist, liar, and evidence planter. We felt that this narrow ruling was particularly unfair in the face of Judge Ito's broad ruling regarding what the jury could hear about the defendant's alleged history of spousal discord, including the Ron Shipp "dream," the videotaped "joke," and the crude remark about his wife's crotch. We hoped that the appellate court would agree with our argument that the excluded statements by Fuhrman were as relevant to his credibility and propensity to lie and plant evidence as the joke and the alleged dream were to Simpson's propensity to kill. We were not hopeful, however, that an appellate court would reverse a conviction on the basis of these discretionary evidentiary rulings, since such rulings are considered to be judgment calls best left to the judge presiding at the trial.

We had a related issue, which we believed was stronger. It involved how Judge Ito dealt with our right to complete our cross-examination of Detective Fuhrman. After Fuhrman categorically denied that he had used the "N" word during the past ten years, and before we learned of the tapes, the defense deferred completion of his cross-examination until after we called our own witnesses, who we knew would contradict him. We wanted to keep open the possibility of confronting Fuhrman directly with the statements and evidence of these witnesses. Then, unexpectedly, we stumbled onto the Fuhrman tapes, which were far better than eyewitnesses, since Fuhrman could not deny that the jury was hearing his own voice. The tapes gave us a basis for continuing our cross-examination and asking Fuhrman questions about what he said on them. Fuhrman decided, however, to invoke his privilege against self-incrimination in response to all questions concerning the tapes. Judge Ito permitted him to invoke the Fifth Amendment outside the hearing of the jury, in response to the following questions from Gerald Uelmen:

Q: Detective Fuhrman, is the testimony that you gave at the preliminary hearing in this case completely truthful?
A: I wish to assert my 5th Amendment privilege.
Q: Have you ever falsified a police report?
A: I wish to assert my 5th Amendment privilege.

Q: Is it your intention to assert your 5th Amendment privilege with respect to all questions that I ask you?
A: Yes.
Q: I only have one other question, Your Honor.
THE COURT: What was that, Mr. Uelmen?
Q: Detective Fuhrman, did you plant or manufacture any evidence in this case?
A: I assert my 5th Amendment privilege.[5]

Since Fuhrman said he would answer no further questions, Judge Ito forbade the defense from calling him to complete his cross-examination. This left the defense in an untenable position. The jury was aware that we had not completed our cross-examination of Fuhrman. They also knew — in general — about the existence of the tapes. Yet the defense was not recalling Fuhrman to ask him any question about the tapes. We feared that this might lead the jury to speculate that we knew Fuhrman had a good explanation for the two taped snippets, and thus were unwilling to ask him further questions.

It was unfair, in our view, to leave the

Fuhrman situation hanging in the air. We wanted the jury to understand why Fuhrman was not being recalled, and to know that it was not our decision to end his cross-examination. We asked Judge Ito either to require Fuhrman to plead the Fifth Amendment in the presence of the jury or at least to have him instruct the jury that Fuhrman was not being recalled because he had invoked his privilege against self-incrimination.

There is considerable confusion about the Fifth Amendment and its relationship to *witnesses* rather than defendants. The relevant portion of the amendment reads as follows: "No person shall . . . be compelled in any criminal case to be a witness against himself." The courts have interpreted that provision to mean that a *defendant* in a *criminal* case may refuse to answer incriminating questions without the jury drawing any inference of guilt.[6] But the reality is that invoking the privilege against self-incrimination does suggest that the person has something to hide. After all, he cannot properly claim that the answers may tend to incriminate him unless they may, in fact, have that effect.

Nonetheless, when a defendant is standing trial in a criminal case, the jury is told not to draw that inference, because to do so would unfairly undercut the privilege. If a defendant could refuse to answer incriminating questions and the jury could then incriminate him on the basis of that refusal, the privilege would lose much of its protective ability. However, the courts have ruled that though a defendant in a *civil* case may refuse to answer questions that may incriminate him in a subsequent *criminal* case, the jury in the civil case may properly infer that he has something to hide. This distinction makes sense because the privilege protects only against *incrimination* — which means criminal punishment, not civil remedies or embarrassment or anything else.

A witness in a criminal case is not on trial. He is, therefore, much more like a defendant in a civil case than like a defendant in a criminal case. He could be prosecuted later in a criminal case, and if he were, the jury in that case could not draw any incriminating inferences from his invocation of the privilege. But the jury in the present case, in which he is merely a witness and not a defendant, should be free to draw negative inferences from his claim that truthful answers to the defense questions might incriminate him, since *that* jury cannot convict him. All it can do is disbelieve him.

That is essentially the argument we made to Judge Ito. He rejected it, but he did agree to "instruct the jury as follows":

> Detective Mark Fuhrman is not available for further testimony as a witness in this case. His unavailability for further testimony on cross-examination is a factor which you may consider in evaluating his credibility as a witness.[7]

However, no such instruction was ever given to the jury because the prosecution petitioned the California Court of Appeals for a writ setting aside Judge Ito's ruling and preventing him from giving the jury his proposed instruction on Fuhrman. To say the least, the filing of such petitions in the middle of trial is highly irregular; they are almost never granted. But without even giving the defense an opportunity to respond to the prosecution's appeal, the appellate court in this case granted the writ and instructed Judge Ito not to give his proposed instruction to the jury.[8] The handwriting was on the wall: We had a sign from the appellate court that we were unlikely to prevail on appeal if the jury convicted Simpson.

But we still had to prepare for any eventuality, and another issue for appeal would have been Judge Ito's decision to allow the jury to hear an unsworn and uncross-examined statement made on videotape by the nurse, Thano Peratis, who took the blood sample from Simpson. At the preliminary hearing Peratis had testified, under oath and subject to cross-examination, that he had extracted between 7.9 and 8.1 cc's of blood from Simpson. When he originally gave this testimony, neither Peratis nor the prosecution understood its significance. Only later did it become clear that the prosection could account for only 6.5 cc's of that blood, and the defense was making a strong argument that the unaccounted-for 1.5 cc's was used by Detective Vannatter to plant Simpson's blood on the socks and the back gate. It became necessary, therefore, for the prosecution to try to get Peratis to change his testimony so that no blood was unaccounted for.

After the close of the prosecution's case — during which prosecutors refused to call Peratis as their witness, since by this time they understood the devastating significance of his testimony — Peratis needed coronary bypass surgery. His doctors said he could not be called as a defense witness. The defense was permitted, therefore, to have the jury hear Peratis's sworn and cross-examined testimony at the preliminary hearing, when he recounted the removal of between 7.9 and 8.1 cc's of Simpson's blood. The prosecution was not happy with this situation, so it sent a prosecutor to Peratis's house with a videotape camera and got him to change his story; now he conveniently remembered that he had really taken only 6.5 cc's of Simpson's blood, and that his prior sworn testimony about the 7.9–8.1 cc's was mistaken. The only problem was that this videotaped recantation was not made under oath and was not subject to defense cross-examination. It was thus classic hearsay. But Judge Ito allowed the jury to hear it, on the pretext that the unsworn video was not being admitted for its own truth or falsity, but rather to contradict the earlier sworn statement from the preliminary hearing.[9] This was a sham, since juries do not make such refined distinctions. We believed we had an important issue for any appeal, since the Supreme

Court has set careful limits on the introduction of hearsay testimony not subject to cross-examination by the defense.

Our final major set of issues in any appeal would have challenged the searches and seizures conducted immediately after the discovery of the bodies. Almost no one — including, apparently, District Attorney Garcetti himself — really believed that the four police officers did not suspect O.J. Simpson of the murders but went to his home only to notify him of his former wife's death. Yet this transparent cover story was accepted by Judges Kennedy-Powell and Ito. We did not expect an appellate court to react differently. Appellate courts nearly always defer to the "findings" of the lower courts on search-and-seizure rulings. But we still had to pursue the issue. We would have argued that Judge Ito erred in refusing to reopen the search and-seizure question in light of the newly discovered Fuhrman tapes, which cast the detective's actions in a far more sinister light. Here was a police officer bragging about how he made up cover stories to conduct illegal searches. Yet Judge Ito continued to shut his eyes to the obvious violation of Simpson's Fourth Amendment right to be se-

cure against unlawful searches and seizures.

There were other appellate issues as
well, but these were the most promising.

Oliver Wendell Holmes once said that
"the prophecies of what the courts will do
in fact, and nothing more pretentious, are
what I mean by the law."[10] The job of the
appellate lawyer, then, is to prophesy accurately what the appellate courts will do
in fact. I take that job seriously. I am not
a cheerleader. In this respect, my job is
like that of a radiologist. I must read the
X ray accurately, without giving the patient false hope. I must read the record of
the trial and try my best to accurately
assess the prospects for an appeal. Bearing that in mind, I was never optimistic
about winning a reversal in the Simpson
case if the jury convicted. The issues were
strong, but appellate judges are human
beings who watch the same television,
read the same newspapers, and listen to
the same gossip as others of their background, race, social class, and gender. The
judges who would have decided this appeal come largely from the group of
Americans who believed most strongly in
Simpson's guilt.

Moreover, this was a lengthy and expensive trial that would have been even more difficult to retry. The appellate judges would almost certainly have found several of Judge Ito's rulings to have been erroneous. Several friends of mine who are appellate judges in other courts are confident of that, because some of the errors were so obvious. But I suspect that the appeals court would have found these errors "harmless." That is, they would have concluded that the prosecution's evidence was so overwhelming that any jury would have convicted Simpson even if Judge Ito had ruled correctly. This kind of speculative conclusion is common in appellate cases, and it is often wrong. But since an affirmance of the conviction denies the defendant a retrial, it is difficult to test the harmless-error assumption. If O.J. Simpson had been convicted, we would never have known which of Judge Ito's many erroneous rulings may have contributed to the conviction. Fortunately for Simpson, this is a question that will never have to be answered.

X

Was the Simpson Trial a "Great Case" That Will Make "Bad Law"?

Nearly a century ago, Justice Oliver Wendell Holmes, Jr., cautioned that

> great cases, like hard cases, make bad law. For great cases are called great, not by reason of their real importance in shaping the law of the future, but because of some accident of immediate overwhelming interest which appeals to the feelings and distorts the judgment.[1]

Holmes could have been warning about the aftermath of the Simpson trial. There is a danger that the strong public feelings about the Simpson verdict will distort the judgment of many otherwise thoughtful people and lead to changes in our criminal justice system that may disrupt the delicate balance between the powers of law enforcement and the rights of criminal defendants.

At one level the call for change is understandable. The Simpson case was the first criminal trial watched, at close range and over a long period of time, by so many people. Any complex institution observed under a microscope will display its faults. In the Simpson case, this phenomenon was exacerbated by two additional factors. First, the "good guys" lost and the "bad guys" won — at least in the view of most Americans. Second, everyone's behavior — the lawyers', the judge's, the witnesses', the police officers', the media's — was less than exemplary. To many lawyers, this was understandable in view of the pressures of a comparatively long, highly publicized, and controversial trial. But to most of the public — for whom this was the only trial they have ever followed so closely — comparisons are not compelling. What they saw, they did not like, in absolute terms.

Nor did I like everything I saw. The trial took too long. Much of the expert testimony was incomprehensible to *me* — and I have been teaching law and science for a quarter of a century. There were too many attempts, by both sides, to manipulate the jury pool. Judge Ito permitted far too much argument — and paid attention to far too little. There was far too much bickering over trivialities. Too many lawyers placed their own agendas before that of their client. Too many prospective jurors managed to avoid jury service. And the judge treated the jury in too patronizing a manner. But on balance, the trial was conducted on a somewhat higher plane than most of the trials I have observed over the past thirty years. Yet the public sees the Simpson case as proof that the system is "broke" and needs "fixing." I suspect that this perception would not be as widespread if the prosecution had won.

Already there have been calls for a change in the burden of proof so that defendants could be convicted on a standard less demanding than "beyond a reasonable doubt." There have also been demands for an end to trial by jury and the adoption of the Continental system of professional judges. Restrictions on freedom of the press and freedom of speech, such as those that govern English trials, have been proposed, as has an end to the televising of trials. Caps on legal fees for defense lawyers — akin to spending caps in elections — have also been suggested. I have even heard a proposal that defense lawyers not be allowed to defend clients they believe are in fact guilty, as well as demands that lawyers not be permitted to make political or racial appeals to jurors. Abolition of all exclusionary rules — which forbid the introduction of truthful evidence wrongfully obtained — has even been advocated as part of a movement toward turning the criminal trial into a pure quest for truth. Rescinding the privilege against self-incrimination — or at least letting the jury infer guilt from its invocation — has been advocated by some.

In addition to these fundamental changes, a large number of smaller refinements have also been floated in the aftermath of the Simpson verdict. In regard to juries alone, there has been a proposed banning of jury consultants,* the abolition of peremptory challenges to potential jurors, the acceptance of nonunanimous jury verdicts, the end of jury sequestration, and permitting jurors to ask questions of witnesses and to begin discussions with each other before the completion of testimony.

*Both the prosecution and the defense originally used consultants to help with the selection of jurors and the assessment of witnesses. The prosecution eventually stopped using its consultant.

Other observers, focusing on the length of the Simpson case, advocate fewer side-bars, greater control by the judge, less latitude to lawyers in arguing repetitively, more politeness and civility among lawyers, and a fixed time limit for each case, set on the basis of its complexity.

Most of the proposed changes are part of a law-and-order agenda that has been on the back burner since the Warren Supreme Court breathed new life into the Fourth, Fifth, and Sixth amendments in the early 1960s.* Proponents of rollbacks of defendants' rights have now used the passion generated by the Simpson case to move them to the front burner. Many of the proposals are borrowed from other countries, with different traditions of liberties, more homogeneous populations, and far less serious crime problems. Some might work in this country; others might not.

I have participated in and observed criminal cases in many parts of the world: China, Russia, Israel, Germany, Italy,

---

*The Fourth Amendment restricts searches and is enforced by an exclusionary rule; the Fifth Amendment protects against self-incrimination; and the Sixth Amendment provides the right of counsel, even to indigent defendants.

France, South Africa, Canada, Denmark, England, and Poland. I can state with confidence that there is no system in the world that strikes a more appropriate balance than ours does among the rights and interests of the prosecution, the defendant, the victim, and the public. We are exquisitely sensitive — at least by comparison with other countries — to the rights of the defendant, who may be falsely accused; to the interests of the victim, who may be improperly revictimized by defense tactics (as rape victims were before the enactment of rape shield laws, pioneered in this country); to the needs of law enforcement, which in many other countries are left unmet because of budgetary constraints; and to the rights of the public to be informed and to observe its system of justice in operation.

Justice is not only a result. It is a process. One unjust result — if you are among those who believe the Simpson verdict was unjust — does not an unjust system make. The American system of justice is not fundamentally broken. It is far from perfect, but no such system has ever been perfect. There are gross disparities between the justice accorded to the rich and that accorded to the poor, and they must be addressed by allocating more resources to the poor. There are many miscarriages of justice in the freeing of the guilty, and some in the conviction of the innocent. But there is no way of reducing the former without increasing the latter. Every time we make it easier to convict the guilty, we also make it easier to convict the innocent.

I have no doubt, for example, that recent changes in the prosecution of rape cases — the elimination of the requirement that the accuser's account be corroborated, and the introduction of rape shield laws — have resulted in the conviction of many rapists who would earlier have gone free. But at the same time, I have no doubt that these benevolent changes have also resulted in the conviction of some innocent defendants who previously would have been acquitted. The difficult question is about the ratios. I believe that the number of increased convictions of the guilty is considerably greater than the number of increased convictions of the innocent. If it is, then the trade-off was worth it. But it was a trade-off. There are no free lunches when it comes to making it easier to convict the guilty. The cost is almost always in larger numbers of convictions of the innocent, or in the increased violation of individual rights.

Such would surely be the case if we were to lower the standard of proof required for conviction. Many more innocent defendants would be convicted in close cases. If we were to abolish the rules protecting privacy and bodily integrity, there might be a few more convictions of the guilty, but there would also be considerably more violations of individual rights. We must move with extreme caution and careful consideration before we allow a single "great case," which appeals to strong feelings, to distort the judgments that have kept our system in balance for so many years.

It would be a tragedy to tamper in any fundamental way with our system of trial by jury. Like democracy itself, a jury sometimes produces a bad result. But few would call for an end to popular elections just because the electorate sometimes voted for a bad senator, governor, or president. The next election will produce a better result — maybe. And in any event, what is the alternative to popular elections? Platonic guardians? An electoral college? A panel of experts?

The alternative to the jury is judges. In this country, judges are generally either elected, and thus responsive to the demands of their electorate, or appointed for life, and thus accountable to no one. In my experience, most juries are better than most judges by every standard of evaluation. They are more honest, less influenced by outside factors, harder working, more attentive, more open-minded, less opportunistic, and often more intelligent. Most important, the powers that be cannot whisper to a jury, as they can to a judge. Everything the jury hears is a matter of public record, whereas secret, *ex parte* communication between prosecutors and judges is far too commonplace.

This is not to suggest that all juries are good and all judges bad. As an appellate lawyer, I am constantly arguing before judges against the verdicts of juries. As a professor of law, I have criticized numerous jury verdicts. Indeed, my book *The Abuse Excuse* is a compendium of complaints against juries that acquitted criminals for unacceptable reasons.[2] Moreover, some of the finest people I know, personally and professionally, are judges. There are individual judges in whose hands I would place my life or liberty, and there are individual jurors whom I would not trust in a jaywalking case. But for the most part, I would prefer to have my clients — innocent, guilty, or somewhere in between — judged by a jury than by a judge, especially in a controversial or unpopular case. The jury is an important safeguard of democracy, an insurance policy against governmental overreaching. As with all insurance policies, we may bemoan the premiums we have to pay, but they are worth it. It would be a great tragedy if the Simpson verdict, whether just or unjust, were to sour Americans on one of our most enduring and important institutions — trial by jury.

Preserving the institution of trial by jury, however, does not necessarily require us to avoid making any changes in the way it now functions. There is much to be said in favor of curtailing recent efforts to manipulate juries by the selective use of peremptory challenges, informed by polling data and other sophisticated information-gathering techniques practiced by jury consultants. So long as the playing field between the prosecution and the defense is kept level, I would have no objections to across-the-board restrictions on such aids to jury selection. The problem is, however, that without jury experts the playing field is often tilted heavily in favor of the prosecution, since prosecutors can use police and government data banks to help them pick potentially favorable jurors, whereas defendants do not have access to such state resources. If both sides had equal access — or lack thereof — to the same resources, there would be less justification for the use of jury experts.

Nonunanimous jury verdicts, on the other hand, would achieve little and cost much. Few cases today end either in hung juries or in long deliberations, and those that do tend to be at the margins of guilt or innocence. Should a defendant really be convicted if one or more jurors remains unconvinced of his guilt even after long deliberations? There is always the possibility, of course, that one or two jurors may hang a jury in a clear case for improper reasons. But there are few data to support any conclusion that this is a widespread problem today.[3] In the Simpson case, the original vote was ten to two for acquittal. Had ten votes been enough for a verdict, this jury would have deliberated even less than four hours. Moreover, as I noted earlier, one of the jurors who originally voted to convict — Anise Aschenbach — had been the lone holdout in an eleven-to-one vote for acquittal in an earlier case, but she eventually persuaded the other eleven jurors to vote for conviction. Had a nonunanimous verdict been permitted, the defendant in that case would have been acquitted.

There is one jury reform proposal that should be adopted. That is mandatory jury service for everyone, with no excuses, except for the most compelling emergencies. Today, in most states virtually anyone working in business or in a profession can worm his or her way out of serving on a jury. The result is that juries in many parts of the country consist largely of retired, unemployed, and marginally employed citizens, for whom the $5 or $10 per day is an incentive to serve. Most of those who complain about the "low" educational or occupational status of jurors have themselves evaded jury service. Whenever I speak about criminal justice, I ask for a show of hands on how many in the audience have ever served on a jury. A few hands go up. Then I ask how many have avoided service. Many hands go up. I wonder how many critics of the Simpson verdict have served on juries.

In Massachusetts, we have introduced

mandatory jury service and I have been called, as have many of my colleagues. About two years ago, a friend of mine received a jury notice. He was a very busy man with an important job, but he served on the jury. His name is Stephen Breyer, and he is currently an associate justice of the United States Supreme Court. At the time of his jury service in the state court, he was the chief judge of the U.S. Court of Appeals for the First Circuit. If Chief Judge Breyer could serve on a jury, few professionals have any excuse.

In order to make jury service more appealing to everyone, daily payments should be raised, sequestration abolished, and demeaning and unrealistic restrictions lifted. Juries should be treated like adults who have a job to do. They should be allowed to participate more fully in the judicial process throughout the trial, by asking occasional questions and by talking to each other. Trials should also be shortened by imposing realistic time limits on both sides and requiring most legal arguments to be made before or after the jury is in the box. If such changes succeed in expanding the jury pool, they will be worth the slight risk they entail.

Another major category of proposals

arising from reaction to the Simpson case relates to the imposition of severe limits on media coverage of trials and on the comments of lawyers. There has always been a strain of hypocrisy running through American attitudes toward media coverage of trials. Polls showed that Americans wanted the plug pulled on coverage of the Simpson case, while at the same time ratings showed that they watched it in unprecedented numbers. It is relatively easy for Americans to vote with their fingers; if they don't like television coverage of real trials, let them flip the channel to fictional courtroom dramas or whatever else they prefer. But as long as viewers tune in to live coverage of trials, such coverage will continue unless judges decide to pull the plug, which Judge Ito repeatedly threatened to do but never did (except for a brief few minutes during Marcia Clark's closing argument, after the camera closed in on O.J. Simpson writing notes to one of his lawyers).

Live television coverage may magnify the faults of the legal system, and show it, warts and all. But in a democracy the public has the right to see its institutions in operation, close up. Moreover, live coverage generally brings out the best, not the worst, in judges, lawyers, and other participants. If people think that what they see on televised trials is bad, I suggest they go to their local courtroom and sit quietly in the back row. They will see laziness, lack of preparation, rudeness, stupidity, posturing, and plain, ordinary nastiness — and I'm just talking about the judges! The lawyers can be even worse. The video camera helps to keep the system honest by keeping it open.

Virtually all the complaints about how the camera turned the Simpson case into a media circus are misdirected. The circus took place *outside* the courtroom and would not have been affected by exclusion of the camera from the courtroom. Some of the trials with the most circuslike atmospheres have not been televised. Remember the Chicago Seven trial, in which the lawyers and the defendants were held in contempt for their antics both inside and outside the courtroom, despite the absence of live television coverage.

This observation leads, of course, to the proposal to restrict what lawyers can say, in and out of court. If real restrictions, with teeth, were placed upon prosecutors, then defense attorneys — most of whose clients *want their names left out of* the media — would have little incentive to defend their clients in the court of public opinion. As to statements inside the courtroom, Governor Pete Wilson of California has proposed legislation barring lawyers from using "political rhetoric" in their closing arguments.[4] Although this gesture was a transparent political gimmick directed against Johnnie Cochran's closing plea to "send a message," the greatest impact of such a restriction would be on prosecutors. It is a common gambit for prosecutors to invoke political rhetoric in their closing arguments, and especially to ask jurors to "send a message" by their verdict. "Your verdict of guilty will send a clear message to abusers" — or to rapists, or to deadbeat dads, or to whoever is on trial — "that this kind of behavior is not acceptable to the good people of Los Angeles" — or Philadelphia, or Boston, or wherever the trial is being conducted.

Public trials do send messages. They are often political by nature. They are both affected by, and have effects on, the society outside the courtroom. It would be naive to pretend that jurors, even sequestered jurors, operate in a vacuum. Reasonable limitations on the excess of political rhetoric, imposed equally on *both sides,* might help to depoliticize the process slightly in some cases. But they would not remove the issues of race, gender, and police misconduct from cases in which these issues are shown to be relevant by the evidence. Juries decide cases largely on the evidence, not on the lawyers' rhetoric. In the Simpson case, if some jurors sent a message, they did so not because Johnnie Cochran asked them to, but rather because Detectives Fuhrman and Vannatter — and the prosecutors who presented these witnesses — challenged them either to accept or reject false police testimony. They rejected it.

This leads to the most important reform that should emerge from the Simpson case: a frank recognition that police perjury must be rooted out of the criminal justice system, both because it is dangerous to individual rights and because it risks acquittals even in cases where some jurors believe the defendant is guilty. New York City's police commissioner, William F. Bratton, has understood this lesson. As a consequence of the Simpson case, he has introduced a program for training police officers to give accurate testimony in court. But police will give truthful testimony only if they also conduct lawful searches and seizures. Perjured testimony typically is given in order to cover up unlawful behavior. Only time will tell whether this new resolve against police misconduct is taken seriously by cops on the beat, by prosecutors, and by judges — and whether it is emulated in other cities around the country.

While we wait for police to learn how to testify more truthfully, calls for abolition of the exclusionary rule will endure, as will arguments against the Fifth Amendment. But until we can be assured that there is some mechanism in place to assure that police do not trample on the rights of defendants, these protections should not be compromised.

As far as proposals to place a cap on the payments made to defense lawyers, this, too, is simply a knee-jerk reaction to the acquittal in the Simpson case, an acquittal that might not have occurred in the absence of a level playing field. The defense spent a lot of money because it had to — primarily to pay defense experts to reevaluate the work of prosecution experts. The fees paid to lawyers were on the low end for a case of this length, since all the lawyers agreed to caps on their fees. In the end, the prosecution spent more than the defense, as it almost always does. A reform that would serve justice would allocate more money to indigent defendants, who today cannot begin to match the resources of the prosecution, especially in capital cases.

Most of the proposals generated by the Simpson verdict have one goal in mind: to make it easier to convict those who are accused of crimes and perceived to be guilty. Any proposal that favors the prosecution and hurts the defense is certain to be popular with politicians, who always side with victims and against defendants. After all, victims vote. Criminals don't. The fact that O.J. Simpson was acquitted should not blind us to the reality that the vast majority of those charged with crimes either plead guilty or are convicted. Only a small percentage are acquitted. The balance of advantage at a criminal trial still favors the prosecution, despite the presumption of innocence and the availability of procedural safeguards. To shift that balance of advantage even further in the direction of the prosecution just because O.J. Simpson was acquitted in a highly unusual case would be to fail to heed Justice Holmes's wise admonition.

Only time will tell whether the O.J.

Simpson trial was a great case that made bad law, or merely another media event that brought fleeting fame to all who participated in it. One observation that will not be disputed is that it was a case for the 1990s, involving as it did the most controversial and divisive issues of this decade: spousal abuse, racial politics, economic inequalities, scientific innovations, criticisms of lawyers, and instant communication. It certainly was a hard case — for the families of the victims, for the defendant and his family, for the judge, for the lawyers, for the police, for the media, and for the public. The trial was of "immediate overwhelming interest" to many people around the world, and its unpopular and misunderstood verdict produced strong feelings which are likely to persist, as the verdict will continue to be debated for years to come. Because so many people saw so much of our justice system at such close range in so atypical a case, it has certainly produced some distorted judgments.

The time has come to take a step back from the glaring light and radiating heat of the most publicized and controversial criminal trial in modern history to look at the larger picture of justice in America, to reflect on its many positive attributes, and to consider carefully the changes that would improve the efficiency of the system while preserving its delicate balance between the power of the state and the rights of the individual. As a teacher of law, I had the privilege of participating in a case that has helped to educate millions of people about both the virtues and the vices of the American criminal justice system. I plan to continue to use the Simpson trial and its aftermath to teach another generation of students, both in college and in law school, about how law works — and does not work. No university course on criminal justice will find it easy to ignore a case that raises so many enduring and contemporary concerns in so dramatic a context.

Now that the criminal trial of *The People of the State of California versus Orenthal James Simpson* is over, we must all begin the hard work of understanding and implementing the lessons of that controversial and divisive case.

Epilogue:

How Would You Have Voted?

The goal of this book has been to place the Simpson verdict and its aftermath in context with respect to the law, to race, to gender, and to society. It has not been to change the minds of those readers who are certain that the evidence points unerringly to Simpson's guilt. Although I respectfully disagree, I know how futile it would be to paraphrase the argument made by Groucho Marx in *Duck Soup*: "Who are you gonna believe, me or your own eyes?"

The verdict of the jury is now in, and the verdict of history will require more time and distance. For readers who still believe that Simpson probably did it, the hardest question raised by this case will be the one that juror Lionel Cryer appears to have confronted.ᴬ I will address it directly to my readers:

How would *you* have voted as a juror in

this case, if you concluded that police had tried to "frame" a guilty man? Could *you* have voted to convict a man who you believed was guilty, if you also believed that police officers had deliberately planted evidence against him? Did those jurors who voted to acquit on the basis of these beliefs violate their oath and behave improperly?

For those readers who could not have voted to convict if they believed the police had tried to "frame" a guilty man — or even for those readers who believe that Simpson *probably* did it, but that the prosecutors failed to meet the legal standard of proof beyond a reasonable doubt — uncomfortable feelings about the law must remain. Can a historically erroneous verdict ever be a legally — and morally — just result? As a Socratic teacher of law, I leave you to ponder this uncomfortable question.

ᴬThree other jurors have recently suggested — in a book and in interviews — that they too believe that Simpson may have been involved in the killings but that the prosecution failed to prove its case beyond a reasonable doubt. Their description of the jury's decisional process corroborates much of the thesis outlined in Chapter IV of this book. They started by disbelieving the police account of the original search; this caused them to be suspicious of Vannatter's carrying around the blood vial, of Peratis's changing story of how much blood he took, of the socks, the glove, and some of the blood. See Armanda Cooley, Carrie Bess and Marcia Rubin-Jackson, *Madam Foreman* (Dove Books, 1996), pp. 100–141, 187–213.

Notes

INTRODUCTION

1. Michael Conlon, Reuters, "Simpson Verdict Stuns the Nation," October 3, 1995.
2. *USA Today*, Oct. 4, 1995, p. B1; *Los Angeles Times*, Oct. 4, 1995, p. A1.
3. *Time* magazine, 12/25/95, p. 140.
4. For a sampling of reactions to the verdict, see *USA Today*, Oct. 4, 1995, p. A1; *Los Angeles Times*, Oct. 4, 1995, p. A1; *New York Times*, Oct. 4, 1995, pp. A1, A13; *Atlanta Journal and Constitution*, Oct. 4, 1995, p. C2.
5. Quoted in Frank Rich, op. ed., *New York Times*, Oct. 4, 1995, p. A21.
6. Betsy Streisand, *U.S. News & World Report*, Oct. 9, 1995, pp. 47–51.

CHAPTER I

1. *Los Angeles Times*, June 14, 1994, p. A1. See also Testimony of Lakshmanan Sathyavagiswaran, 1995 WL 348847 at 55 (Cal.Super.Trans. June 6, 1995).
2. *Los Angeles Times*, June 30, 1994, p. A18.

3. *Los Angeles Times*, June 18, 1994, p. A1; *Los Angeles Times*, June 19, 1994, p. A1.
4. *Los Angeles Times*, June 21, 1994, p. A1.
5. *Los Angeles Times*, June 19, 1994, p. A1; *San Francisco Examiner*, June 17, 1994, p. A1.
6. *Los Angeles Times*, June 23, 1994, p. A1.
7. *Los Angeles Times*, June 24, 1994, p. F1.
8. See *San Francisco Examiner*, June 17, 1994, p. A1; Rafael Abramovitz, *Premier Story*, KCOP-TV, June 21, 1994; June 19, 1994, p. A1; *Los Angeles Times*, June 22, 1994, p. A19; *San Francisco Examiner*, June 21, 1994, p. A1. See also *Los Angeles Times*, June 24, 1994, p. F1.
9. *San Francisco Examiner*, June 17, 1994, p. A1.
10. *Los Angeles Times*, June 15, 1994, p. A1.
11. See, e.g., Cal Thomas, *Rivera Live*, July 12, 1994; Harland Braun, *Los Angeles Times*, Nov. 5, 1994, p. A1.
12. *New York Times*, February 1, 1985, p. B2.
13. Order of Recusal, in re Grand Jury Proceedings, 1994 WL 564404 at 1 (Cal.Super.Doc. June 24, 1994).
14. In determining whether the search warrant application submitted by Vannatter properly established probable cause to search the Simpson residence,

Judge Ito was required to evaluate Vannatter's affidavit to determine whether it contained misrepresentations that were made in reckless or deliberate disregard of the truth. After finding six "inaccuracies" in Vannatter's sworn affidavit, Judge Ito was compelled to conclude:

> My concern though, is that the totality of all of these causes the court more than just concern, and when I factor into that the experience of this particular detective and the number of investigations, I cannot make a finding that that is merely negligent, and I have to make a finding that it was at least reckless.

Oral Ruling of Judge Lance Ito, 1994 WL 513769 at 13 (Cal.Super.Trans. September 21, 1994).

CHAPTER II

1. Oral Argument of Marcia Clark, 1995 WL 523691 at 47 (Cal.Super.Trans. Aug. 29, 1995).
2. One popular theory of scientific knowledge does, however, portray the scientific endeavor as based on the emergence of a new paradigm, and its acceptance by the relevant scientific community after a period of adversarial conflict between propo-

nents of the old orthodoxy and proponents of the new paradigm. See Thomas Kuhn, *The Structure of Scientific Revolutions* (1969).

3. *In re Winship*, 397 U.S. 358, 372 (1970) (Harlan, J., concurring).

4. Starkie, *Evidence* 751 (1824), quoted by Justice Stevens in his opinion in *Schlup v. Delo*, 115 S. Ct. 851, 865 (1995). The sentiments are traceable back to William Blackstone's well-known maxim that under the common law "it is better that ten guilty persons escape, than that one innocent man suffer." 4 Blackstone, *Commentaries* 358.

5. *Los Angeles Times*, October 15, 1995, p. A1.

6. *In re Winship*, 397 U.S. 358, 371 (1970) (Harlan, J., concurring).

7. See *Brown v. Illinois*, 422 U.S. 590 (1975); *United States v. Havens*, 446 U.S. 620 (1980).

8. Creative lawyers on both sides have woven this motto into their closing arguments. See *United States v. Battiato*, 204 F.2d 717, 719 (7th Cir. 1953); *United States v. Eley*, 723 F.2d 1522, 1526 (11th Cir. 1984).

9. Closing Argument (Rebuttal) by Marcia Clark, 1995 WL 704342 at 24 (Cal.-

Super.Trans. September 29, 1995).

10. *Herrera v. Collins*, 113 S. Ct. 853, 856 (1993).

11. Scott Turow, "Simpson Prosecutors Pay for Their Blunders," *New York Times*, Oct. 4, 1995, p. A21.

CHAPTER III

1. Every night I received phone calls from commentators looking for input. Following Vannatter's testimony, the common private response was "Can you believe that guy tried to put that one over on the judge?" Some of the very people who were privately certain that Vannatter was clearly lying then proceeded to present a "balanced" account in their commentary. Others were clear: Barry Slotnick, a prominent New York lawyer, was quoted as saying: "I don't believe Vannatter, I think this was a big score for the defense." Jerry Froelich, an Atlanta defense lawyer, was even more blunt: "No one believed [Detective Philip] Vannatter when he said to Robert Shapiro, "O.J. was no more a suspect than you were. . . . This jury obviously sent a message to prosecutors, 'We're not going to let you lie in our justice system.' " (*Atlanta Journal and Constitution*, Oct. 4, 1995, p. 9C). In addition, John

Burris, an Oakland-based civil rights attorney, commented that "It's an integrity question. It's the extension of the Mark Furhman form of honesty. I don't think there is any doubt that Vannatter lied. The point is, can the jury trust anything else he said? If he lied about this, what else did he lie about?" (*Los Angeles Daily News*, Sept. 20, 1995, p. N1, in interview by Janet Gilmore).

2. "Simpson Prosecutors Pay for Their Blunders," *New York Times*, Oct. 4, 1995, p. A21.

3. Testimony of Philip Vannatter, 1995 WL 11189, at 4 (Cal.Super.Trans. March 16, 1995).

4. This is because the police may conduct a search of a person's home without a warrant if "exigent circumstances" are present that can justify the search. In general, courts have limited the doctrine of "exigent circumstances" to situations where the police honestly and reasonably believe that someone inside the home is in imminent danger of death or serious physical injury. Thus, in this case, had the detectives testified that they suspected Simpson and had they also honestly and reasonably believed that someone's life was in danger inside Simpson's home, a

udge could have upheld the warrantless entry, as well as the searches of certain items that were in "plain view." Alternatively, the judge could have admitted some of the evidence obtained during the search on the basis of a doctrine known as "inevitable discovery." The rationale for this exception is that if the government can demonstrate that the information or evidence in question ultimately or inevitably would have been discovered by lawful means, had the police not already done so by unlawful ones, there is little value in excluding the evidence in an effort to deter future police misconduct. Thus, if the prosecution in this case would have shown that some of the evidence at O.J. Simpson's home inevitably would have been discovered by the police, a judge may very well have concluded that this evidence could be used against the defendant at trial even though the officer's search of his home was illegal.

5. *People v. McMurty*, 64 Misc. 2d 63; 314 N.Y.S.2d 194 (Crim. Ct. N.Y. County. 1970).

6. Ibid. See also Irving Younger, "The Perjury Routine," *The Nation*, May 8, 1967, p. 596.

7. Ibid.

8. Stuart Taylor, Jr., "For the Record," *American Lawyer*, Oct. 1995, p. 72.

9. See Morgan Cloud, "The Dirty Little Secret," 43 *Emory L. J.* 1311 (1994).

10. Commission to Investigate Allegations of Police Corruption and the Anti-Corruption Practices of the Police Department, Milton Mollen, Chair; July 7, 1994, at 36.

11. Ibid., 38.

12. Ibid., 41.

13. Ibid., 42.

14. See Report of the Independent Commission on the Los Angeles Police Department, "The Christopher Commission," Warren Christopher, Chair, 1991.

15. See, e.g., Cloud, op. cit.; Stanley Z. Fisher, " 'Just the Facts, Ma'am': Lying and the Omission of Exculpatory Evidence in Police Reports," 28 *New England Law Review* 1 (1993), and references cited therein.

16. *New York Times*, Feb. 14, 1995, p. B5; Jan. 4, 1996, p. B5.

17. *New York Times*, Nov. 1, 1995, p. B3.

18. Hearing on 1538.5 Motion, 1994 WL 513769, p. 6 (Cal.Super.Trans. September 20, 1994).

19. Alan M. Dershowitz, *The Best Defense* (1982), pp. xxi–xxii.

20. Alan M. Dershowitz, "Accomplices to

Perjury," *New York Times*, May 2, 1994, p. A17.

21. *Today* (NBC), Nov. 9, 1995.

22. *Good Morning America* (ABC), March 15, 1995.

23. Dershowitz, *The Best Defense*, p. 377.

24. *Larry King Live* (CNN), March 17, 1995.

25. *Newsweek*, June 5, 1995, p. 7.

26. *Boston Globe*, Nov. 15, 1995, p. 1.

27. *New York Times*, Nov. 15, 1995, p. B3.

28. *Newsweek*, April 10, 1995, p. 6, and interview with reporter.

29. *Boston Globe*, March 20, 1995, p. 1.

30. *Time*, March 27, 1995, p. 65.

31. *Washington Post*, March 17, 1995, p. B1.

32. *Los Angeles Times*, March 17, 1995, p. A22.

33. "Simpson Prosecutors Pay for Their Blunders," *New York Times*, Oct. 4, 1995, p. A21.

34. *The MacNeil/Lehrer NewsHour* (PBS), Oct. 4, 1995.

35. Ibid.

36. *New York Times*, Nov. 15, 1995, p. B3.

CHAPTER IV

1. For polling data, see *Dallas Morning News*, Oct. 8, 1995, p. 30A; *USA Today*, Oct. 4, 1995, p. 2A; *Los Angeles Times*,

Oct. 8, 1995, p. A2.

2. *Holland v. United States*, 348 U.S. 121, 140 (1954).

3. Jon Newman, "Beyond Reasonable Doubt," 68 *N.Y.U.L. Rev.* 979, 984 (1993).

4. *Jacobellis v. Ohio*, 378 U.S. 184, 197 (1964) (Stewart, J., concurring).

5. This was the instruction given in the second trial of Claus von Bülow, which ended in an acquittal. See Alan Dershowitz, *Reversal of Fortune* (1986), pp. 224–25.

6. Newman, op. cit., p. 985.

7. Jury Instructions, Westlaw, Unofficial Transcripts, September 22, 1995 (A.M.), p. 39.

8. *Chicago Tribune*, Oct. 5, 1995, p. 1.

9. Interview of Anise Aschenbach, *Prime Time Live* (ABC), Oct. 4, 1995.

10. Interview of Yolanda Crawford, *Dateline NBC*, Oct. 10, 1995, 1995 WL 6296539.

11. Interview of Lionel Cryer, *Today* (NBC), Oct. 7, 1995, 1995 WL 9759767.

12. Interview of Brenda Moran, *Dateline NBC*, Oct. 6, 1995, 1995 WL 6296526.

13. John Larson, *Dateline NBC*, Oct. 6, 1995, 1995 WL 6296526.

14. LAPD Inventory Sheet, June 29, 1994. See also Testimony of Gregory Matheson, 1995 WL 254414, at 9 (Cal.-

Super. Trans. May 2, 1995).

15. Oral Argument on Motion in Limine by Deputy D.A. Rockne Harmon, 1995 WL 42098 at 7 (Cal.Super.Trans. Feb. 3, 1995).

16. Ibid.

17. In addition to testing the bloodstained portions of one sock, the FBI lab also used "negative controls," running portions of the sock known to have no blood on it through the same procedures that were used to test the bloodstained portions of the sock. These results came back negative, strongly suggesting than no other substances on the sock (such as laundry detergent) could account for the positive EDTA result. See Testimony of Frederic Rieders, 1995 WL 462293 at 29–30 (Cal.Super.Trans. July 24, 1995).

18. See Testimony of Roger Martz, 1995 WL 465136 at 6–10 (Cal.Super.Trans. July 26, 1995).

19. Testimony of Frederic Rieders, 1995 WL 462294 at 13 (Cal.Super.Trans. July 24, 1995).

20. Testimony of Herbert MacDonnell, 1995 WL 465788 at 7–8 (Cal.Super.Trans. July 31, 1995).

21. Testimony of Henry Lee, 1995 WL 521228 at 47 (Cal.Super.Trans. August 28, 1995).

22. *Chicago Sun Times*, Oct. 15, 1995, p. 39.

23. Interview of Lionel Cryer, *Dateline NBC*, Oct. 6, 1995.

24. Indeed, throughout their closing argument the prosecutors repeatedly urged the jurors to reject many of these "coincidences." Here are two examples:

So now we have the defendant getting his hand cut on the night of his wife's stabbing, cut on his left hand, which just happens to be the hand that the murderer cut that same night. That's an alarming coincidence. And there's more.

We know that on June the 15th, the defendant went to see Dr. Huizenga, not his own doctor. No, this was not even a doctor he had ever seen before. This is the partner of a doctor that treats his lawyer. And he's not an arthritis specialist. He's an internist.

And this doctor describes four cuts, four cuts and seven abrasions on the defendant's left hand and on the right hand, a little paper cut on the pinkie, four cuts and seven abrasions, and the murderer was cut on the left hand when he lost the left glove.

You know, I can see getting one cut, maybe two on your hand. But four cuts

385

and seven abrasions? And we're supposed to believe that that's unrelated to a murder in which the killer's left hand was cut and bleeding as he left the crime scene.

But there's more. When the defendant got the call in Chicago from Detective Phillips, he tells him of Nicole's murder, he realized he had to come up with an explanation for the cut on the middle finger, and that's why we got to hear from the Chicago Detective, Berris. He recovered the broken glass in the sink.

Closing Argument by Marcia Clark, 1995 WL 672671 at 9–10 (Cal.Super.Trans. September 26, 1995).

So what we have, about two minutes after the thumping, the defendant was walking up — was walking into his house from the driveway and Kato out in the side yard.

In other words, we have the thumping, and Kato walking out and the defendant walking around at the same time and the thumping happened very shortly, what is it, within half an hour of the murders.

And the defense would have you believe, ladies and gentlemen, that the defendant's appearance on the driveway just two minutes after the thumping on Kato's wall is a coincidence and the defense would have you believe that the thumping and the appearance of that glove, the defendant's glove, were unrelated events.

Closing Argument by Marcia Clark, 1995 WL 672670 at 40–41 (Cal.Super.Trans. September 26, 1995).

25. Closing Argument by Marcia Clark, 1995 WL 672671 at 36, 39 (Cal.Super.Trans. September 26, 1995).

26. Instructions to Jury, Westlaw, Unofficial Transcripts, September 22, 1995 (A.M.), p. 28.

27. Interview of Anise Aschenbach, *Today* (NBC), Oct. 12, 1995.

28. Interview of Anise Aschenbach, *This Morning* (CBS), Oct. 12, 1995; interview of Anise Aschenbach, *Prime Time Live* (ABC), Oct. 4, 1995.

29. Interview of Sheila Woods, *Today* (NBC), Oct. 9, 1995, 95 WL 9128705.

30. Testimony of Henry Lee, 1995 WL 510285, at 26–27 (Cal.Super.Trans. August 23, 1995).

31. Jack B. Weinstein, "Considering Jury 'Nullification': When May and Should a Jury Reject the Law to Do Justice?" 30

Am. Crim. L. Rev. 239, 339 n. 1 (1993).

32. *Sparf and Hansen v. United States*, 156 U.S. 51 (1895).

33. See Weinstein, op. cit., p. 242.

34. See *Beckwith v. State*, 615 So.2d 1134 (Mississippi Sup.Ct. 1992).

35. Weinstein, op. cit., p. 247.

36. See *Los Angeles Times*, Jan. 22, 1994, A1.

37. For a discussion of some of these doctrines, see Yale Kamisar, "Comparative Reprehensibility and the Fourth Amendment Exclusionary Rule," 86 *Mich. L. Rev.* 1 (1987).

38. See *Napue v. Illinois*, 360 U.S. 264 (1959); *Alcorta v. Texas*, 355 U.S. 28 (1957).

39. Interview of Lynn Abraham, *Dateline* (NBC), Oct. 20, 1995.

40. Comments of Judge Lance Ito Responding to Marcia Clark's Objections to Defense Closing Argument, 1995 WL 704342 at 24 (Cal.Super.Trans. Sept. 29, 1995).

41. *Newsweek*, Oct. 30, 1995, p. 84.

CHAPTER V

1. *New York Times*, Oct. 8, 1995, Sec. 4, p. 1.

2. Ibid.

3. *Wilmington News Journal*, Oct. 5, 1995.
4. *Los Angeles Times*, Feb. 8, 1995, and *Larry King Live* (CNN), Sept. 16, 1995.
5. *Newsday*, Nov. 5, 1994, p. A6.
6. *New York Times*, Nov. 4, 1994, p. A18. Of the ten peremptory strikes exercised by the defense, only one was to exclude a black juror.
7. See Defendant's Motion and Amended Motion for an Evidentiary Hearing to Determine Whether the Investigation and Selective Disqualification of Jurors and Alternates Have Been Engineered by the Prosecution in Order to Obtain an Unfair Tactical Advantage and Requesting That This Court Take Urgent Action to Prevent a Mistrial.
8. Interview of Prosecutor Scott Gordon, *CNN and Company*, Oct. 13, 1995.
9. Ibid.
10. Lenore E. Walker, *Battered Woman Syndrome* (1984).
11. *Los Angeles Times*, Jan. 8, 1995, p. B1. Strictly speaking, domestic abuse itself would not *be* a motive for murder, but it might suggest the presence of some motive. The prosecution also claimed to establish "intent" through evidence of threats by Simpson, but this is irrelevant. The physical evidence left no doubt that

the murders were deliberate.

12. *Larry King Live* (CNN), June 14, 1994.

13. Abraham P. Ordower, "Balancing the Presumption of Guilt and Innocence: Rules 404(b), 608(b) and 609(a)," 38 *Emory L. J.* 135 (1989).

14. *Boston Globe*, Jan. 19, 1995, p. 1.

15. *CNN News*, Oct. 17, 1995.

16. *Los Angeles Times*, Oct. 9, 1995, p. S9.

17. *Rudolph v. Alabama*, 375 U.S. 889 (1963).

18. *Nightline* (ABC), Oct. 18, 1986.

19. Ibid.

20. *Los Angeles Times*, Oct. 9, 1995, p. S9.

21. Nancy J. King, "Postconviction Review of Jury Discrimination: Measuring the Effects of Juror Race on Jury Decisions," 92 *Mich. L. Rev.* 63, 77 (1993).

22. Ibid. On the other hand, King (op. cit.) described a number of studies finding race *not* a significant predictor of verdicts:

> Several researchers who have studied the correlations between verdicts and various characteristics of defendants, victims, jurors, and cases have concluded that juror race was not significant in predicting the verdict or sentence outcomes of the actual or mock juries they studied. *See* Reid

Hastie et al., *Inside the Jury* 128–29 (1983) (little if any correlation between race and predeliberation verdict preferences of 828 jurors); [Saul M. Kassin & Lawrence S. Wrightsman, *The American Jury on Trial: Psychological Perspectives* 29–31 (1988)] (collecting studies finding juror characteristics unrelated to verdicts in any consistent manner); Rita J. Simon, *The Jury: Its Role in American Society* 45–46 (1980) (finding "only slight and not consistent differences in the verdicts of jurors with different class, ethnic, and sexual characteristics"); John R. Hepburn, *The Objective Reality of Evidence and the Utility of Systematic Jury Selection*: Ethical and Empirical, 17 Jurimetrics J. 3, 16 (1976) (study of 480 jurors showed that the four best predictor variables, including demographics and attitudinal variables, accounted for less than 13% of verdict variance).

23. Marina Miller and Jay Hewitt, "Conviction of a Defendant as a Function of Juror-Victim Racial Similarity," 105 *J. Soc. Psychol.* 159, 160 (1978).

24. Sheri Lynn Johnson, "Black Inno-

cence and the White Jury," 83 *Mich. L. Rev.* 1611, 1625–26 (1985). See also J. L. Bernard, "Interaction Between the Race of the Defendant and That of Jurors in Determining Verdicts," 5 *L. & Psychol. Rev.* 103 (1979); Denis C. E. Ugwuebgu, "Racial and Evidential Factors in Juror Attribution of Legal Responsibility," 15 *J. Experimental Soc. Psychol.* 133 (1979); Linda A. Foley and Minor H. Chamblin, "The Effect of Race and Personality on Mock Jurors' Decisions," 112 *J. Psychol.* 47 (1982).

25. Carol J. Mills and Wayne E. Bohannon, "Juror Characteristics: To What Extent Are They Related to Jury Verdicts?," 64 *Judicature* 22 (1980) ("The findings were not what we expected: black females reported the highest percentage of guilty verdicts").

26. Nancy J. King, op. cit., p. 84.

27. Darryl K. Brown, "The Role of Race in Jury Impartiality and Venue Transfers," 53 *Md. L. Rev.* 107, 121 (1994).

28. Ibid., p. 123.

29. Ibid., p. 129, n. 125.

30. Nancy J. King, op. cit., p. 78.

31. John R. Hepburn, "The Objective Reality of Evidence and the Utility of Systematic Jury Selection," 4 *Law & Human*

Behavior 89, 98 (1980).

32. Tanya E. Coke, Note: "Lady Justice May Be Blind, but Is She a Soul Sister? Race Neutrality and the Ideal of Representative Juries," 69 *N.Y.U.L. Rev.* 327, 354–55 (1994).

33. Ibid.

34. Ibid., p. 355; *Wilmington News Journal*, Oct. 5, 1995.

35. *New York Times*, Oct. 29, 1995, sect. 4, p. 12.

36. *Norfolk Virginian-Pilot*, Oct. 4, 1995, p. A12.

37. *Atlanta Constitution*, Oct. 4, 1995, p. 6C.

38. See *New York Times*, Oct. 8, 1995, p. 1; *San Francisco Examiner*, Oct. 4, 1995, p. A1.

39. *New York Times*, Oct. 8, 1995, p. 1.

40. Ibid.

41. *San Francisco Examiner*, Oct. 4, 1995, p. A1.

42. *Los Angeles Times*, Oct. 9, 1995, p. S9.

43. Ibid.

44. Ibid.

45. Ibid.

46. *CNN News*, Sept. 28, 1995.

47. Ibid.

48. Alan M. Dershowitz, "In Defense of Cochran," *The Jewish Forward*, Oct. 13, 1995, p. 71.

49. Interview of Anise Aschenbach, *Today* (NBC), Oct. 13, 1995.

50. Interview of David Aldana, *Larry King Live* (CNN), Oct. 12, 1995.

51. *USA Today*, Oct. 4, 1995, p. 1A.

52. *St. Louis Post-Dispatch*, Oct. 8, 1995, p. 2B; *Providence Journal-Bulletin*, Oct. 10, 1995, p. 4B; *Chicago Sun-Times*, Oct. 5, 1995, p. 41.

53. *Both Sides With Jesse Jackson* (CNN), Oct. 8, 1995; *Los Angeles Times*, Oct. 25, 1995, p. A1.

54. In a famous corporate case of the 1980s involving the Texaco and Pennzoil oil companies, the failure of extremely well-respected New York counsel to connect with Texas juries was a contributing factor in one of history's largest civil damage awards. *Los Angeles Times*, Jan. 19, 1986, Bus., Part 4, p. 1.

55. The exception to this rule is slow-talking Wyoming lawyer Gerry Spence, familiar to many Americans as a TV commentator throughout the Simpson trial. In 1990 Spence successfully defended former Philippine first lady Imelda Marcos from racketeering charges brought in New York. But even Spence had his problems adapting to the New York style of trying cases — his folksy

opening statement was apparently not well received. *Manhattan Lawyer*, May 1990, p. 1. But his closing argument was excellent.

56. Interview of Anise Aschenbach, *Prime Time* (ABC), Oct. 4, 1995.

57. *Los Angeles Times*, Oct. 9, 1995, p. S7.

58. Ibid.

59. *Los Angeles Times* poll, Oct. 10, 1995, S2.

60. *Los Angeles Times*, Oct. 9, 1995, p. S9.

61. Ibid.

62. *Idaho Statesman*, Oct. 16, 1995, p. 7A; *Arkansas Democrat-Gazette*, Oct. 13, 1995, p. 9 (characterizing the Simpson jury as "dominated and controlled by highly emotional, racist blacks"); *Cleveland Plain Dealer*, Oct. 9, 1995, p. 11B; *Newsday*, Oct. 10, 1995, p. A30.

63. *San Francisco Examiner*, Oct. 29, 1995, p. B2.

CHAPTER VI

1. *The Montgomery Advertiser*, Oct. 4, 1995, p. 16A.

2. Interview of Linda Deutsch, *Today* (NBC), Nov. 27, 1995.

3. *Denver Post*, June 16, 1995, p. 1.

4. *New York Times*, June 16, 1995, p. 16.

5. *Denver Post*, June 16, 1995, p. 1.

6. Testimony of Herbert Leon MacDonnell, 1995 WL 619212 at 15–23 (Cal.Super.-Trans. Sept. 18, 1995).

7. See Testimony of Richard Rubin, 1995 WL 366155 at 23–24 (Cal.Super.Trans. June 16, 1995).

8. *The Montgomery Advertiser*, Oct. 4, 1995, p. 16A.

9. Ibid.

10. *Washington Post*, April 30, 1987, p. A19.

11. *Des Moines Register*, May 31, 1995, p. 1.

12. *St. Petersburg Times*, Oct. 4, 1995, p. 1A.

13. *Atlanta Constitution*, Aug. 17, 1995, p. A16.

14. Kenneth Noble, *New York Times*, May 11, 1995, p. 1. "Wide-ranging" was used in the *New York Times* news service.

15. See, e.g., *Washington Post*, Dec. 3, 1993, p. A1 (after being acquitted in BCCI case, Clark Clifford and Robert Altman criticized Morgenthau for extensive leaks to media); *Washington Post*, Jan. 15, 1988, p. A4 (noting that Judge Duffy of the Southern District of New York criticized Giuliani in the Bess Myerson case for "leaks" that "at first blush . . . can be attributed only to the government"); *Newsday*, Sept. 20, 1993, p. 6 (noting that

Giuliani was frequently criticized for his "frequent news conferences" and his "fortuitously timed news leaks").

16. *Los Angeles Times*, Oct. 9, 1995, p. A1.

17. Ibid.

18. 501 U.S. 1030, 1043 (1991).

19. See Briefs for Appellant and Petition for Certiorari in *Tyson v. State*, 626 N.E.2d 482 (Ct. App. Ind. 2d Dist., 1993), cert. denied, 114 S. Ct. 1216 (1994).

CHAPTER VII

1. See Alan M. Dershowitz, *The Best Defense* (1982), Chapter 9.

2. See *New York Times*, Dec. 2, 1995, p. A1.

3. *Time*, Oct. 16, 1995, p. 48.

4. James P. Levine, *Juries and Politics* (1992), p. 66.

5. Levine, op. cit., p. 63.

6. *Providence Journal*, August 20, 1995, p. A20.

CHAPTER VIII

1. *Washington Times*, Oct. 10, 1995, p. A1, corrected Oct. 20, 1995, p. A3 ("It's ironic that Johnnie Cochran, who was such a clear voice for justice, yet trivialized the Holocaust, will stand next to a man who not only trivialized the Holocaust, but says it didn't happen").

2. *Los Angeles Times*, Sept. 30, 1995, p. A1.
3. See Text of Vice President Al Gore's Remarks at Days of Remembrance Ceremony at U.S. Capitol, U.S. Newswire, April 7, 1994.
4. Henry Louis Gates, *New Yorker*, October 23, 1995, p. 59.
5. Ibid.
6. Testimony of Mark Fuhrman, 1995 WL 97332 at 35–39 (Cal.Super.Trans. March 9, 1995); 1995 WL 97333 at 1–2 (Cal.Super.Trans. March 9, 1995).
7. Defendant's Motion That the Defense Be Permitted to Cross-examine Det. Fuhrman About His 1981–1983 Lawsuit in Which He Admitted to an Uncontrollable and Disabling Rage and Bigotry Against Criminal Suspects and African-Americans; see also *Fuhrman v. City of Los Angeles*, Findings, at 1; *Memorandum of Points and Authorities in Support of [Fuhrman's] Petition for Writ of Mandate*, Sup. Ct., Dkt. Nos. C465544 (Los Angeles County, August 23, 1983), at 5–6 (urging that Fuhrman be found "clearly disabled from his position as a police officer" on the ground that his "return to any police-related activities would present a threat to petitioner himself, the Police department [sic] and to the public at large").

8. Defendant's Motion That the Defense Be Permitted to Cross-examine Det. Fuhrman about His 1981–1983 Lawsuit in Which He Admitted to an Uncontrollable and Disabling Rage and Bigotry Against Criminal Suspects and African-Americans, at 6–8; see also *Fuhrman v. City of Los Angeles*, Findings, at 2–3 (dismissing the action on the ground that Fuhrman "was not truthful to the doctors when he described his allegedly violent behavior").

9. Letter from Kathleen Bell, 1994 WL 774010 at 1 (Cal.Super.Trans. July 19, 1994).

10. Declaration of Lucienne Coleman, 1995 WL 536134 at 6–9 (Cal.Super.Docs. Sept. 11, 1995).

11. 1995 WL 366155 at 56 (Cal.Super. Trans. June 16, 1995).

12. Ibid., at 8.

13. 1995 WL 77473 at 7 (Cal.Super.Trans. Feb. 27, 1995); 1995 WL 79805 at 4 (Cal.Super.Trans. Feb. 28, 1995); 1995 WL 84694 at 38 (Cal.Super.Trans. March 1, 1995).

14. 1995 WL 540596 at 48, 50 (Cal.Super.Trans. Sept. 5, 1995).

15. 1994 WL 510858 at 11 (Cal.Super.-Trans. Aug. 17, 1994).

16. Exchange between Marcia Clark and

Johnnie Cochran, 1995 WL 322833 at 26 (Cal.Super.Trans. May 24, 1995).

17. 1995 WL 324771 at 19–20 (Cal.Super.-Trans. May 30, 1995).

18. 1995 WL 462222 at 4, 8 (Cal.Super.Trans. July 20, 1995); 1995 WL 462224 at 2 (Cal.Super.Trans. July 20, 1995).

19. 1995 WL 465788 at 53–54 (Cal.Super.Trans. July 31, 1995); 1995 WL 508727 at 7 (Cal.Super.Trans. Aug. 22, 1995).

20. Legal Argument of Marcia Clark, 1995 WL 109035 at 13 (Cal.Super.Trans. March 15, 1995).

21. Michael Knox, *The Private Diary of an O.J. Juror* (1995), pp. 262–63.

22. Quoted in Alan M. Dershowitz, *The Best Defense* (1982), pp. xv–xvi.

23. *Chicago Sun-Times*, Oct. 5, 1995, p. 41.

CHAPTER IX

1. According to a 1993 study, approximately 94 percent of criminal convictions in California were affirmed on appeal. J. Clark Kelso, "A Report on the California Appellate System," 45 *Hastings L. J.* 433, 445 n. 43 (1993).

2. 384 U.S. 436 (1966).

3. See United States Constitution,

Amendment V ("nor shall any person be subject for the same offence to be twice put in jeopardy of life or limb").

4. Alan M. Dershowitz, *Reversal of Fortune*, (1986), p. 63.

5. 1995 WL 550493 at 29 (Cal.Super.-Trans. Sept. 6, 1995).

6. See *Griffin v. California*, 380 U.S. 609, 615 (1965); *Baxter v. Palmigiano*, 425 U.S. 308, 318 (1976).

7. 1995 WL 550495 at 4 (Cal.Super.Trans. Sept. 7, 1995).

8. Alternative Writ of Mandate and Stay Order Concerning Giving of Proposed Jury Instruction, 1995 WL 536142, at 1 (Cal.App.Doc. Sept. 8, 1995).

9. 1995 WL 564555 at 41 (Cal.Super.Trans. Sept. 12, 1995).

10. Oliver Wendell Holmes, "The Path of the Law," in *Collected Legal Papers* (1920), p. 173.

CHAPTER X

1. *Northern Securities Co. v. United States*, 193 U.S. 197, 400 (1904).

2. Alan M. Dershowitz, *The Abuse Excuse — and Other Cop-Outs, Sob Stories and Evasions of Responsibility* (1994).

3. See Edward Schwartz and Warren Schwartz, "Decisionmaking by Juries un-

der Unanimity and Supermajority Voting Rules," 80 *Geo. L. J.* 775 (1992).

4. *Time*, Oct. 16, 1995, p. 62.

Acknowledgments

This book could not have been finished so quickly without much midnight oil being burned by my research assistants, associates, and staff. Special thanks — as usual — to Maura Kelley for producing the numerous drafts of the manuscript; to Gayle Muello for running the office — and me — without ever losing her smile; and to Lisa Green for her assistance. Michael Schneider, my associate, organized the research, which was brilliantly executed by student assistants Zachary McGee, Elizabeth Brown, August Horvath, Dan Libenson, Anthony Tu, Aya Gruber, Andy Walter, John Turner, Elizabeth Pontefract and Yan Senouf. The wonderful folks at Simon & Schuster — Fred Hills, Burton Beals, and Hilary Black — were remarkable in their efficiency, encouraging words, and editorial judgment, as was my agent, Helen Rees.

My loving appreciation to my family, especially Carolyn and Ella, who endured the difficulties of the case, ranging from

403

strangers cursing to phones ringing, television sets blaring, and unexpected trips to L.A.

Special thanks also to Section IVa of Criminal Law (fall '95) for serving as a sounding board, both in class and over our many lunches, for some of the ideas contained in the book. There is no doubt — reasonable or otherwise — that you are all destined to be great lawyers. And speaking of great lawyers, my deep appreciation to Victoria Eiger, Amy Adelson, and Michael Schneider for their innovative ideas and brilliant legal work during the Simpson case.

About the Author

Alan M. Dershowitz is the bestselling author of *Chutzpah*, *Reversal of Fortune*, *The Best Defense*, and many other books. He was first in his class at Yale Law School, and was editor in chief of the *Yale Law Journal*. After clerking for Judge David Bazelon and Justice Arthur Goldberg, he was appointed to the Harvard law faculty, where he became a full professor at age twenty-eight, the youngest in the school's history. *Newsweek* has described him as "the nation's most peripatetic civil liberties lawyer and one of its most distinguished defenders of individual rights." Professor Dershowitz has served on the national board of directors of the American Civil Liberties Union and as consultant for various foundations and presidential commissions. His clients have included Claus von Bülow, Patricia Hearst, Mike Tyson, Senators Alan Cranston and Mike Gravel, Harry Reems, Anatoly Scharansky, F. Lee Bailey, William Kunstler, and several death row inmates.

His articles and syndicated columns appear regularly in newspapers and magazines, and he comments frequently on national television. He lives in Cambridge, Massachusetts.

The employees of Thorndike Press hope you have enjoyed this Large Print book. All our Large Print titles are designed for easy reading, and all our books are made to last. Other Thorndike Large Print books are available at your library, through selected bookstores, or directly from us.

For information about titles, please call:

(800) 223-2336

To share your comments, please write:

Publisher
Thorndike Press
P.O. Box 159
Thorndike, Maine 04986